HEADING
SOUTH

First published 2021 by
FREMANTLE PRESS

Fremantle Press Inc. trading as Fremantle Press
PO Box 158, North Fremantle,
Western Australia, 6159
www.fremantlepress.com.au

Cover images: All images used are from www.shutterstock.com:
YurkaImmortal; Neale Cousland; YUKI ISHII; NTL studio; Ensure.
Cover design by Carolyn Brown, tendeersigh.com.au.
Printed by McPherson's Printing, Victoria, Australia.

A catalogue record for this book is available from the National Library of Australia

ISBN 9781760990015 (paperback)
ISBN 9781760990022 (ebook)

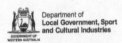

Department of
Local Government, Sport
and Cultural Industries

Fremantle Press is supported by the State Government through the Department of Local Government, Sport and Cultural Industries.

MIX
Paper from
responsible sources
FSC® C001695

HEADING SOUTH

FAR NORTH QUEENSLAND TO WESTERN AUSTRALIA BY RAIL

TIM RICHARDS

 FREMANTLE PRESS

To Narrelle for standing by me

To George Stephenson for his marvellous invention

and

To the colonial engineers who provided Australia with a dizzying array of rail gauges and gave me something to talk about

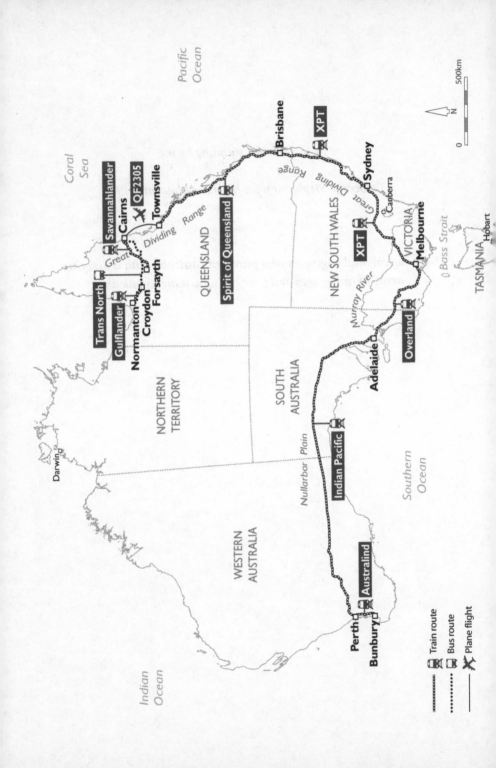

Contents

Introduction

This journey came about because of a map, and a crisis.

Many countries have a national rail company that handles long-distance train journeys. For such countries, from such companies, there will be a full network map upon which one's mind can luxuriate: the eye darting here and there, up and down lines, across country, imagining possible rail treks and the destinations along the way. Such fantasies of planning, for trips that might never eventuate, are some of the greatest pleasures of travel, without all the fuss and bother of actually going anywhere. Although I am no armchair traveller, I've often shared Samuel Johnson's sentiment on beholding the Giant's Causeway in Ireland: 'Worth seeing, but not worth going to see.' I particularly enjoy long-distance rail travel, something I've indulged in on five continents. As I've written more than once, to me, trains are vastly superior to planes, cars and buses, especially over distance. In a train you're *in* the landscape, but not *of* the landscape – observing everything as you pass through, unimpeded, along the rails.

In Australia, passenger rail travel is largely the province of state governments, so the network maps are limited in scope. But one day I was gazing upon a non-official map created by Australian Rail Maps, on its website at railmaps.com.au. It laid out all the long-distance rail services across the continent, and was tantalising in its possibilities. There were the various inland trains of Queensland, peeling away from the Cairns–Brisbane spine. There were the spiders' legs of lines radiating out from Sydney and Melbourne, touching at Albury-Wodonga. There were the famous transcontinental trains that linked Adelaide, Perth and Darwin to the east-coast networks.

I puzzled over the routes, fancifully devising lengthy rail trips via the possible connections, and a thought came to me: 'What would be the longest rail journey you could take in Australia, without backtracking?' My eye was drawn to the north-east and south-west extremes of the map, from the privately run *Savannahlander* train in Far North Queensland to the state-run *Australind* train in south-west Western Australia. As the crow flies, their respective termini of Forsayth and Bunbury are over 3,200 kilometres apart. By rail, they would be seven trains and 7,725 kilometres apart, equivalent to about a fifth of the circumference of the planet ... It would be the long way round, via a variety of terrains and climates: sparsely treed savannah, tropical rainforest, the sandy Pacific coast, sheep-farming plains, wine country, wheatfields and treeless desert. The route would also include all five mainland state capitals, as well as big regional cities such as Cairns and Bunbury, and tiny settlements between them. And while in Far North Queensland, one could tack on the separate *Gulflander* train, the oddest experience of the lot. I yearned to take this journey, to see Australia's diversity from a train window, to meet people along the way, and to break up my journey with excursions to overlooked places related to the railways or my pet interests.

As for the crisis, it was a slow-motion one. I'd been working as a freelance travel writer for almost fifteen years, and it felt as though my job was slowly collapsing. The internet was doing a number on the business models of print publications, which provided the bulk of my income, and in the past two years my income had started to decline. This situation had undermined my confidence and motivation. I needed to try something new, and researching this book was it. I sensed it was a journey I'd have to do alone; though I often travelled with my wife, Narrelle Harris, this trip was going to be introspective and filled with note-taking – not the ideal jaunt for a couple. I would, however, see her again when I reached Melbourne, at roughly the midpoint of the trek. For I had decided to do it: book the trains and travel from the tropical north to the temperate south-west by rail. With a few days at Normanton, my starting point, plus breaks in the big cities and a stay with my family in Western Australia, the entire trek would take six weeks.

This is my account of that epic train trip, and of the places I went and the people I fleetingly met while undertaking it. It was the latter that most surprised me. I'd been focusing on the locations, but it was inevitably the men and women in them that lent meaning and joy to the journey, and solace when things went wrong. Writing the account of my journey cheered me up about the apparent decline of travel writing, and made me feel there was still a place for my kind of work. How could a popular online resource like Tripadvisor relate the experiences I'd had in my progress around the continent? Travel wasn't an atomised selection of individual attractions, as such sites would have you believe, but a continuity of thoughts, feelings and encounters. A narrative. And here it is.

It didn't turn out to be Australia's longest train journey, by the way. When I researched track distances, it turned out a route from Mount Isa to Darwin would have been marginally longer than the one I followed. But that would have meant skipping the Cairns-connected trains, and all of Western Australia. And there seemed a neat symmetry in travelling from the far north-east to the far south-west – the diagonal extremes of the continent. Even then, I didn't manage to travel the entire route as I'd intended.

I'd envisaged the journey as a kind of triumphant progress: gazing upon my conquered lands as they slid past, metaphorically waving at my subjects, the smooth motion of each train bearing me onward. This was hubris, plain and simple, and the experience of the nineteenth-century explorers Burke and Wills – whose path I would cross more than once on my expedition – should have prepared me for what happened next. It did not go entirely to plan.

But then, travel never does.

Normanton

If a crocodile the size of Krys attacked, I'd be doomed.

I was sitting in the shelter next to the Norman River boat ramp on a quiet Sunday afternoon, taking notes, when my eye was caught by a sign near the water featuring 'ACHTUNG' in black lettering. The German word was more noticeable than the red 'WARNING' in English above it. The rest of the sign stated casually that a saltwater crocodile had been sighted here recently and people should keep away from the water's edge. Well crikey, as Steve Irwin would have said. I relocated to the picnic area several metres further back, and scoped out a place to climb higher should a crocodile attack.

This line of thought was becoming a habit in Normanton, a remote town of 1,200 people near the Gulf of Carpentaria in Far North Queensland, ten hours drive west of Cairns. I was marking time there until the weekly run of the *Gulflander* train, and had been growled at by a lot of dogs as I walked around the township (eccentrically, as everyone else drove). Just the day before I'd been sitting in the empty Normanton railway station when I'd heard, rising in volume, the barking of many angry dogs. They were domesticated animals, I'd assumed, and maybe safely behind a fence somewhere nearby – but I didn't fancy taking my chances. I'd looked around casually for a place to escape from an enraged pack, and had sighted an old carriage once used to transport maintenance crews. I could be up the metal rungs of its ladder before any dogs could reach me, then fend them off with my large black boots. Sorted.

Bouts of animal-based peril should seem surprising at the start of a series of journeys by train, a mode of transport not usually associated with danger. But it was clearly hard to fully tame the Australian outback, and that lingering wildness was appealing to a big-city boy like me.

Not that I wanted to meet the now-here, now-not crocodile. Next to the shire office in the centre of town was a life-sized model of Krys, at 8.63 metres in length the biggest recorded crocodile ever shot in the region. If anything like that showed up, that would be the end of my round-Australia rail journey before it had started. But if the croc was of smaller dimensions, I could possibly scramble to the top of the inclined exercise bench behind me. There was also an old crane set in concrete by the wharf. Though further away, it would be easy to climb.

Tension, though likely to be unfulfilled. Travel is like this, full of 'what might have been' moments that mean nothing in the end, but add grotesque savour.

'What if I'd been in New York City on 9/11?'

'I was in Christchurch a few months before the big earthquake.'

'We passed a burnt-out car that had been bombed in Cairo.'

'I once snorkelled in the same spot Steve Irwin died.'

'That woman was bitten by a snake exactly where I'd been walking the day before.'

Travellers probably used to spout self-dramatising hypotheticals about visiting Honolulu on 7 December 1941, or taking a stroll through Sarajevo on 28 June 1914.

The crocodile never turned up, as it happened, though small black flies crawled annoyingly over my face when they felt they could get away with it, and at one point a kite flew under the canopy of the picnic area, hunting for small mammals. Mostly I was alone, sitting near what had once had been a busy rail wharf transferring goods from boats onto waiting trains. It was a soothing experience, despite the heat and my little insect friends.

Jake, a barman at the Albion, the pub where I was staying, had given me a card for Gulf Getabout. It promised to be 'Like a taxi, but *better*!' I rang and asked them to pick me up from the river. It beat walking back into town, and there was another local creature I wanted to meet before I left: a fish on a stick. Mel the driver chauffeured me through the late wet-season heat to the Big Barra, Normanton's entry in Australia's fabled pantheon of Big Things (Krys didn't count, being life-sized). It was a huge replica of a barramundi, standing upright on its tail, outside a motel. Barramundi fishing was a popular pursuit around here.

On the way back into town, Mel swung onto the other side of the road to let me photograph the town's welcome sign:

> Welcome to Normanton
> Population small
> We love them all
> Drive carefully

What was I doing here, I wondered, in a moment of doubt. Because I'd decided to embark on this rail trek in the first week of March, I'd arrived in Normanton at the tail end of the tropical north's wet season. So far, the season had been a less-than-damp squib, but in the past few days the rains had kicked in and threatened the running of the *Gulflander* train from Normanton to Croydon. As the Gulf Savannah region was so flat, heavy rainfall to the south took its time to meander north to the Gulf of Carpentaria, making for unpredictable rises in the various rivers that intersected rails and roads. On the way out from Cairns to Normanton by bus, I'd almost been stranded on the wrong side of the rising Gilbert River. If the rains continued, the tracks could be covered to an extent that the train's weekly run would be cancelled. If the roads were also flooded, I could fly out of Normanton to Cairns – but that would mean skipping my first two trains (the *Gulflander* and the *Savannahlander*), thus falling at the first hurdle. Would I really be on that train out of town on Wednesday? I hoped so. There was something curiously attractive about small, remote places such as Normanton, far from city life and the stresses of the twenty-four-hour media cycle. Every day I spent in the place, I could feel the horizons of my universe contracting. Leave it long enough and I'd get used to being here, buy a cheap old shack and spend my days propping up the bar of the Purple Pub in the middle of town, cursing the flies and the humidity and the barking dogs. And what's more, I'd probably like it. (Pushing Akubra hat up onto the back of my head, sipping beer, muttering under my breath about the heat.)

####

'Business is down a bit since the kitchen caught fire,' Frog had said ruefully on Friday when I'd arrived in Normanton, 'But we're cooking stuff on the barbecue and it's going all right.'

After dropping my backpack in my room I'd soon ended up at the bar with Frog, the publican of the Albion Hotel, and his part-kelpie, Toots. He had earlier shown me the blackened, unusable rear section of the old building.

I shook my head in sympathy, hoping its disordered state wasn't a metaphor for my onward itinerary, and ordered another beer.

The Albion was a hotel that had once been a blacksmith's shop. It was a classic country pub and Frog a big, genial bloke in a rugby shirt.

We were surrounded by men in battered Akubra hats and rugby tops. Some looked like they'd just come from work, others were older retired blokes. It all felt very familiar – part of the Aussie cultural canon from 'Waltzing Matilda' to *Crocodile Dundee* – but I also felt like an alien. I wasn't familiar with the Queensland beer brands or the state's glass sizes, and I hardly ever paid cash for anything in Melbourne, so I fumbled around trying to order. Beer in hand at last, I discovered Frog and I had both lived in Perth around the same time, when he had been a member of the SAS. Its headquarters on the Indian Ocean coast was famously adjacent to a nudist beach beyond the adjoining dunes, on federal land rather than state. The Western Australian capital was on my route, as it happened, nearly 8,000 kilometres and several weeks away: a reminder of how big this country was, and yet Frog's story, and mine, illustrated how casually people relocated within it.

In my room, I reflected that the Albion wouldn't be an unbearable place to while away a few days until the *Gulflander's* next scheduled run. Though it had an old-fashioned motel look of lurid coverlets and painted concrete walls, my room was well maintained and large, with a double bed and two singles. I'd be there five days in total, only because of my overdeveloped sense of caution. The bus I'd used to travel from Cairns ran roughly every second day, and I hadn't wanted to risk missing the train's weekly departure if a later bus had been cancelled. I also fancied the idea of hanging around somewhere quiet for a change; most of my travel-writing trips were a blur of appointments and note-taking, so quiet time in a nearly-off-the-grid place like Normanton had its appeal.

When I returned to the pub's outdoor deck a few hours later for dinner, it was transformed. The Friday-night Albion had become a community hub, with kids playing on the pub's lawn while their parents had a beer and a meal under madly whirring ceiling fans. The regulars still propped up the bar, but the big back deck was filled with younger people including neatly dressed families. Some of the girls were wearing fairy costumes. I ordered a pizza from a Spanish bartender (one of many working holiday visa holders filling service jobs in the outback) and chose a table near the edge of the deck. Then a nearby group of diners warned me that bees had been swarming around that corner a few minutes before. This random threat lifted my spirits. The caress of humidity by night, the energetic conversation all around, the daggy music on the sound system and random, swarming bees: the outback had not entirely been tamed, after all.

The only fly in the ointment was the rain. If only it would ease just enough for my journey to actually begin. When I asked one of the bar staff to write the pub's wi-fi password on the pizza box I was carrying, Frog came over and said he'd earlier asked Ken, the *Gulflander* driver, about Wednesday's service.

'He reckons the train will run,' he said.

When I finally met Ken a few days later, I asked him what he thought were the chances of the *Gulflander* running as scheduled on Wednesday.

'Fifty-fifty,' he replied.

On Tuesday, that long-hovering coin came down on the right side. Ken's crew checked the entire route that day, and gave it the all clear.

I was on my way.

Normanton to Croydon
Gulflander

Train travel is all about leaving things behind.

Today it was the Albion Hotel, and I hauled myself bodily over a timber railing to escape its grounds. It was a simple technique: I dumped my backpack on the other side, then dragged myself up and over. It was good to know I was still agile enough to do that, and lucky that I only ever travelled with a single backpack. Though I'd been in town a few days by now, I had never figured out how to leave the Albion's grounds gracefully in the early morning, when the car park was locked and the bar closed. Hence the climb onto the front verandah, to descend to the street from there. Once I was out, I walked to Normanton's railway station to catch the *Gulflander*.

For the present, the rain had stopped. The empty streets had a damp grassy smell as I passed the life-sized fibreglass model of Krys the croc I'd been thinking about at the river. There were doubts as to whether Krys had really been 8.63 metres long, but it made for a scary model. The original Krys had been downed in 1957 by Krystyna Pawlowski, a Polish immigrant. She later regretted that fatal shot and became a conservationist in partnership with her husband, Ron, and together they helped prompt the federal government to ban the hunting of crocodiles in the 1970s. Whatever the truth of its size, its effigy was huge –

monstrous – and even in fibreglass form it made for a disturbing start to my journey.

But I was on the move, heading out of town aboard the first of the eight trains which were to bear me to Cairns and then around the edge of the continent, out of hot, wet, humid crocodile country all the way to the distant south-west corner of Western Australia. I knew it would be pleasant in that part of Western Australia, as I'd grown up there, among green, temperate and pretty countryside. Much tamer than this strange tropical savannah town with its thwarted ambitions to be a thriving northern metropolis. Though it was hard to believe of its sleepy streets at this time of the day, Nevil Shute had had Normanton in mind when writing his novel about how a remote settlement could be developed to resemble 'a town like Alice'. I passed the vividly painted Purple Pub on the main drag, then the old town well, whose explanatory signage was guarded by even more bad-tempered dogs in the adjacent front yard, and turned down a side street so I could approach the station from its front. A kid was playing on the broad roadway ahead of me, while his mum yelled at him to come in because she was running late. Galahs flew high above the boy as I neared him. In the soft early light, the sight suggested a scene from an award-winning arthouse film. I wanted to dwell on it a moment, to fantasise about what might happen next in the screenplay, but I had a town to leave behind and a train to catch. Sorry, small kid in the street, I never would find out whether you listened to your mum.

At the station the *Gulflander*, sometimes called the 'Tin Hare' after the zippy mechanical rabbit lures used in greyhound racing, was waiting beneath its corrugated canopy, engine running and frame vibrating as its crew readied it for departure. Although the railway had been in operation since 1889, the *Gulflander* name dated only to 1953, when it was unofficially adopted to mimic the '-lander' suffix used by Queensland's other long-distance trains. Ken, who was the stationmaster as well as the driver, passed by in his uniform, a pale khaki shirt over black trousers, and said hello.

After a lot of stress and uncertainty over wet weather, my first outback Queensland train was actually about to run.

At a bench near the rear of the two-carriage train I met my three fellow passengers: Shane, Alison and their teenage daughter Ashley. Shane was both a rail man and a rail fan from Sydney, who worked on the New South Wales railways. I sensed that this most remote of Australia's state-run rail journeys – dubbed 'the train from nowhere to nowhere' – was a magnet for rail enthusiasts. (I'd call them nerdy rail fanboys, except I suspect I have a form of the condition myself.) Shane wasn't chatty, preferring to talk shop with his fellow professionals on the *Gulflander* team. His wife was less keen on trains ('I'm more of a cruise person'), but was evidently fond of these family outings to distant rail highlights.

We boarded, Ken confidently manipulated the various sticks before him, and we pulled out past his stationmaster's house with its dog, cat, sheep and chickens.

'Simon's with us as guard today, and my name's Kenneth,' said Ken into a hand-held microphone. Kenneth! Posh. 'We'll be taking it slowly as the rails are wet today.'

Ken and I had been playing cat and mouse since I'd narrowly missed meeting him at the Albion on the evening I'd arrived.

'Keep an eye out for him,' I'd been advised by Frog. 'He drives an old red Land Cruiser.'

I sighted that battered vehicle all over town in the next few days: driving away from the Albion as I arrived for a drink, passing me as I sat at the empty railway station on an early visit, Ken waving at me from it as I walked along carrying groceries. I'd finally met him and ridden in the Land Cruiser, which had borne Ken to remote Normanton at the end of a round-Australia trip, to fall into the job of his life as head honcho of this obscure line at the end of the world. He'd given me a lift back to the Albion after we'd discussed the train's weekly run to even tinier Croydon.

Now, slowly, we were leaving Normanton together, and I breathed a sigh of relief. Crossing the main street, we passed light industrial buildings, then a compound of huge cattle trucks. On our right, workers were doing maintenance to the fence around the airport. They waved. We waved. It's a universal law of tourist trains: you have to wave as they go by. And this one went by only twice a week – once out and once back – so you were fortunate if you happened to spot it in motion at all.

As we bumped along the rails, Ken inserted commentary via his microphone. 'You're lucky to be here this time of year,' he said. 'The countryside is very green. Later in the year it's brown – still beautiful, but not as green.'

It was indeed verdant and lovely on that Wednesday morning as we entered the savannah dotted with slender trees with dark trunks. The rain I had been cursing had left everything soft and fresh as we headed out, under a big sky of light-grey cloud that seemed luminous as the sunlight tried to break through.

Normanton was about to have its 150th anniversary, and the railway itself was 126 years old. It was curious that such an odd, remote line should have been operating all this time, trundling between two obscure towns that had a population of 1,500 people between them.

The line had originally been intended to reach Cloncurry to the south, but was diverted to Croydon after the town's 1885 gold rush began. A later plan to extend it east to Georgetown and eventually link it to Cairns had come to nothing. Had it ever been connected to the rest of Queensland's rail network, it might well have closed by now, along with many other branch lines. But this wasn't a branch line at all. It was separate and unique, a curious and sentimental survivor from a distant world of nineteenth-century bush ingenuity.

The track and sleepers were clearly visible from my position, seated to Ken's left. They had an unconventional appearance, the sleepers deeply embedded in the soil, some almost concealed. These 'hollow' (actually arched) steel sleepers of the *Gulflander* were its most famous feature, and a key factor in keeping the railway operating so long. An innovation of engineer George Phillips, who'd immigrated to Australia at the age of eight from

Burslem, Staffordshire, these unique sleepers had allowed the rails to sink into the ground, anchoring the track against wet-season floods. They'd also confounded the region's many termites, which were always happy to chew up timber. A drawback was the slight unevenness of the track as over time the sleepers had shifted and settled.

'The maximum speed we can go is twenty-five miles per hour,' Ken said, 'and we're currently doing fourteen. We still use miles here, as the line's still marked that way.' Each stretch of track was 26 feet long and bolted together, rather than spiked.

The peculiar trees we were passing had distinctive black trunks and small, serried leaves. They were eerie in the soft morning light, as if they were photo negatives of a saintlier plant. Ken identified these as gutta-percha trees, a name I recognised. Because they oozed a latex sap, they'd been used in the early days of the telegraph as an insulator to coat undersea communications cables. The name had a Malay origin, derived from *getah* for gum, and *percha*, the tree itself. Knowing that, I'd assumed they only grew in Asia, and was surprised to see them here.

A big black-necked stork took flight in front of us, its broad wings paralleling the track before it veered away. Further on, a group of brolgas stood by the rails as if contemplating their plans for the day. They took off just in time as we rumbled toward them. I was pleased we were seeing so many species, and suggested to Ken (well, yelled, over the noise of the engine) that they should officially restructure the supplied fauna list as a bingo card.

The four passengers were spread out with a seat each in the front carriage, myself on the left and the others on the right. Each bench-style seat was covered in what appeared to be reddish-brown vinyl, next to sliding windows framed by maroon curtains. There was a distinct vibe of 1950s school bus about the interior, especially with Ken in the cabin with us, up front on the right.

His amplified voice competed with the engine noise. 'Gold is long gone, but the train survived because it could still get through floods – it was useful.'

This was a unique selling point of the railway. Because of its sunken tracks, it could operate in 6 inches or so of floodwater, giving it an advantage over other modes of land transport. In the early days, the railway company kept passengers and freight in motion even when floodwaters covered the tracks so deeply that the train couldn't ford them. On more than one occasion in the 1890s, passengers were conveyed by boat over flooded sections to connect with trains at either end, which showed a commitment to service that could be usefully adopted today by Metro Trains in Melbourne, whose suburban Sandringham line floods at the drop of an open water bottle. Floods did cause problems for inland Croydon in particular, reliant as it was on freight carried by rail from the Gulf of Carpentaria. The fickle tropical rains were always hard to predict. After frequent water-related delays in 1920, food supplies in the town were rationed. According to J.W. Knowles's comprehensive account of the Normanton–Croydon railway, *Lonely Rails in the Gulf Country*, there were then no railway delays at all due to flooding from 1925 to 1936; but the 1950s saw frequent delays, including a two-month cessation of service in early 1951.

The line's busiest days were in the gold rush era of the 1890s, when its trains hauled large amounts of freight. It's hard to imagine now, in this era of all-weather roads, how essential a train was to such a remote community. By lowering the cost of transport in the region, the Normanton–Croydon line lowered the cost of all the goods hauled along it, so life on the Croydon goldfields became more affordable, and leads with lower gold yields could be worked.

Steam trains left the line in 1929, having been progressively replaced by railmotors: carriages with their own integrated engines. The first of these was a striking 1918 vehicle based on a truck made by the French firm Panhard et Levassor (taken out of service in 1938, it's now on exhibition at the Workshops Rail Museum in Ipswich, west of Brisbane). Behind the driver it could carry just ten passengers, which indicates how far passenger traffic fell with the waning of the gold.

By 1934 the railway had settled on a timetable of just one scheduled service each way per week, leaving Normanton at 8 am on Wednesday, taking five and a half hours to Croydon and returning the next day. That's precisely the timetable it keeps today. This scheduling allowed passengers, mail and goods to travel from Normanton to Cairns over four days via the *Gulflander* to Croydon on the first day, then by truck to Forsayth, connecting with the train now called the *Savannahlander* to the Pacific coast.

There were fifty-five staff on the railway in 1892. By the 1930s just nine *Gulflander* employees remained. Now there were eight, including the track gang I'd already met. They looked after endless maintenance tasks, including the spraying of the native grass that Ken pointed out by the track. If left to itself, it grew up between the rails, causing a fire hazard.

'By hook or by crook, the railway's been kept running all these years, and may hopefully continue,' he said.

I liked the sentiment, but it was a minor miracle that the *Gulflander* had survived once the region had gained all-weather roads. Heritage railways were often revived as tourist operations from systems that had already closed. This train had surprisingly managed the transition with little interruption, beyond a suspension due to a major flood in 1974. Normanton had that year become an island in a temporary sea as the waters surrounded the town and washed away its wharf. On a single day near the end of January, over 500 Normanton residents were airlifted to Cairns and Mount Isa by emergency services, as the floodwater crept to only a metre below the airstrip. With both the Norman and Gilbert rivers in flood, almost the entire railway line lay underwater.

It's remarkable that the line didn't close at that point. It was already endangered because the 1967 completion of a sealed road from Julia Creek to Normanton meant freight could be conveyed by rail and road from Townsville. Though the Normanton–Croydon trains started running again in April 1974 after three months of closure, government engineers recommended further track and bridge repairs, the expense of which could have shut down this odd orphaned railway. Ironically, politics – often the cause of railway closures elsewhere – saved the day. The Queensland premier, Joh Bjelke-Petersen, was a divisive, reactionary figure then involved in a war of attrition with the federal government of Labor prime minister Gough Whitlam. Whitlam was a proponent of federal control of Australia's state-owned railways, so it's possible that Bjelke-Petersen decided to revive the Normanton–Croydon railway as a gesture of defiance toward Canberra; otherwise it may have been a gift to a rural constituency of his own country-focused National Party. Whatever the reason, the cloud of closure briefly hovered then lifted, and the line was fully repaired over the next few years.

Beyond its ability to withstand floods, the longevity of the *Gulflander* owed something to the vision of Normanton as a north-coast powerhouse. As *A Town Called Alice* outlined, there had been a big postwar push to populate Australia's empty northern quarters. The then recent Japanese bombings of Queensland, the Northern Territory and Western Australia had supercharged a long-held fear of invasion from the populous north. The word 'development' was key. Even now, the road paralleling the *Gulflander* is called the Gulf Developmental Road, while the one heading south to Cloncurry is the Burke Developmental Road. The d-word might have justified any expense on infrastructure, even ageing infrastructure such as this train. There had, after all, been a rise in goods traffic on the line during World War II, and postwar development projects further boosted its use.

Development mania goes back a long way in the Gulf Country. It was famously one of the drivers of the nineteenth-century Burke and Wills expedition from Melbourne to Australia's north coast, the final campsite of which, Camp 119, lies 42 kilometres south-west of Normanton. In 1861 that spot had provided a miserable stopover for the four men remaining on the expedition, especially the two who stayed on in camp while their leaders covered the last leg to the Gulf. As an excellent book recounting the expedition, *The Dig Tree*, relates:

> Up at Camp 119 there was mud everywhere. When it rained, which was often, the glutinous slime clung to their boots, blankets, camel harnesses and cooking pots. When the sun came out, it set like concrete. The monsoon turned the camp into a quagmire reminiscent of those on the journey towards Menindee.

In the present day, that combination of rain and unsealed roads had put paid to my plan to visit the campsite from Normanton. It was simply inaccessible in the muddy conditions. The elements still overruled human desires up here, and it was hard to imagine people believing those postwar mega-city dreams as we chugged through an empty, sandy area, part of the Norman River's broad flood plain. That river had its own link to Burke and Wills, having been named (as was Normanton) after Commander William Norman of the Victorian Naval Forces, the navy of my home state (then a colony). When news had reached Melbourne that the explorers were missing and possibly in danger near the Gulf of Carpentaria, he was commissioned to sail the steam-powered naval sloop HMVS *Victoria* to the Gulf to land a rescue mission. This mission, along with others by land launched by Victoria, South Australia and Queensland, had opened up the north. The would-be rescuers had found prime grazing land and other exploitable treasures along their paths. Within a few years the difficult territory that had defeated Burke and Wills on their return leg was being 'tamed', though at great cost to the Kurtijar, Gkuthaarn and Kukatj peoples of the Normanton area who were attacked, murdered and dispersed by the new settlers and the associated Native Police, an arm of the state that conducted

26

numerous attacks on Indigenous people as pastoralists laid claim to the region. It was sobering to imagine how many similar stories lay on or near the lines of rails that would take me around the continent.

My reverie of lost explorers and ruthless settlement was interrupted by a group of plains turkeys (another fauna bingo card cross), which scattered as we approached. It seemed our fate this day to startle large birds into flight.

Clarina was the first signposted location we passed, at the 11-mile mark. As it had a fresh water source, in the early days it supplied water for the locomotives and was home to Chinese market gardens, which provided Normanton with fresh produce. Clarina's reclamation by nature and its picturesque waterhole made it the perfect destination for one of the *Gulflander*'s shorter tours in the dry season, a three-hour return trip with billy tea, damper and scones. Such picnic excursions had always been a feature of the line, even in the nineteenth century. A few times each year from the 1890s, Croydon's churches or other groups would charter a train for a picnic along the line, accommodating large numbers who rode in wagons temporarily fitted with seating. In this way up to 750 people could attend, well exceeding the 200 or so seats then available in the regular carriages. Even in the twenty-first century the *Gulflander* is still commissioned for special events, such as weddings.

An agile wallaby ('agile' being both its breed and description) tore across the front of the train without mishap, adding another cross to my notional bingo card.

I was happy. The air was fresh and not too humid, the scenery was moist but stunning, and around to the north a band of pale blue sky had broken through the grey. Being on the move felt energising and good-cheer-making. The rain had not flooded the line as threatened, and I was finally on my way to Western Australia, albeit the long way round. As if reading my mind, Ken mentioned that in 1974 the bridge we'd just crossed had lain beneath 12 metres of water. 'But not today, Ken,' I thought. 'Not today.'

The streak of open sky soon stretched around to the south-east, and we were heading straight for it. I hadn't seen much of the sky on the bus out to Normanton from Cairns. Now it was revealed as a dramatic component of the landscape, its vast dome accentuating the flat savannah.

This big sky made me think of Morning Glory, a local meteorological phenomenon, which can be spotted from Burketown to Normanton between September and November. This rare occurrence consists of a series of long cylindrical clouds in parallel ('roll clouds'), a spectacular sight. Though it's not entirely understood, Morning Glory is associated with high humidity and strong breezes. It's also unreliable, with no guarantee as to which day it'll appear. A report in the *North Queensland Register* from the previous year cited a roll cloud that had been fortuitously spotted just in time for the Morning Glory Festival in Burketown (to the west of Normanton and with a population of 238). Involving rodeo, music, market stalls and tours, the festival was a canny way of drawing people to the highly speculative activity of cloud spotting, while offering alternative entertainment if no Morning Glory eventuated.

We next passed Critters Camp, named by a railway construction crew in honour of its plentiful mosquitoes, scorpions and snakes. Near here was a wye, a spur of two curved rails meeting at a short, straight dead end, so that when needed the *Gulflander* could execute a three-point turn to head the other way. As for running the train backwards, Ken said that was never a good idea. It was a straightforward engine under the thrumming box on his left, he said – basically the rail equivalent of a truck engine with a gearbox.

Whether the weather had significantly changed, or it was a product of being on the move, this was the first day of the trip I hadn't felt overly hot and sweaty. The humidity seemed balmy – that pleasantly enveloping moisture one felt when, say, dining outside a Brisbane restaurant on an evening after a warm day.

A hymn that my favourite author, P.G. Wodehouse, was fond of quoting to comic effect, ends with the lines:

What though the spicy breezes
Blow soft o'er Ceylon's isle;
Though every prospect pleases,
And only man is vile

I thought of it now in relation to the serene, unpeopled landscape we were moving through, via the noisiest train I had ever ridden in: the intrusion of man-made chaos into the peaceful wilderness. There was the constant low growl of the engine beneath us, and a loud scissoring sound of vibrating metal which seemed focused just above us. Add to this the nonstop rattling of the railmotor as it passed above the slightly uneven sleepers, and it was far too noisy to talk to my fellow passengers. So apart from shouting the odd question to Ken, who had the advantage of wielding a microphone in reply, I sat back on my padded vinyl bench and took in the view.

I was pleased I'd removed the social media apps from my phone for the duration of this trip. My concentration span had improved in the few days I'd been without them. My generation had a unique place in the history of information technology, I thought: old enough to have lived a good chunk of our adult lives without computers, but young enough to be able to get a lot of use out of them. Which meant I could cope without social media for the six weeks of the trip, at least.

There was something meditative in this ride, despite the noise, as with all train journeys. The process of heading down a defined track at a steady pace, being in the landscape but not entirely of it, prompted contemplation. Especially if you could see ahead. With nothing to view but nature from my forward vantage point, I felt as though I could watch it all day. Occasionally a fragment of the twenty-first century would rudely impose itself on our nineteenth-century simulacrum. We'd been roughly following the main road between Normanton and Croydon, and for a period we ran right beside it. At 32 miles from Normanton the train stopped at a large, train-shaped mailbox for Haydon Station, one of the bigger cattle stations in the area, and one of the train crew hopped down to deliver letters and a parcel containing a satellite TV set-top box. I liked seeing the train still being used for a practical purpose it would have fulfilled throughout its history.

I'd spotted a few cattle by the line, mostly Brahman. These creatures were well suited for the unpredictable local climate, as their loose skin and dark pigmentation helped keep them cool. They also had a slight hump composed of fatty tissue, to draw on in hard times.

It was getting warmer but not yet uncomfortable, and we still had the window of sky beckoning us to Croydon. Somewhere on the stretch to Blackbull, I nodded off – an unlikely thing to happen, given the jolting, but somehow caused by the rocking movement of the train.

#####

'Lefty loosey, righty tighty.'

At the Blackbull stop I asked Ken about the lever he operated by rotation when driving, and he explained it was the handbrake. His quoted mnemonic was an old one (though new to me) that helped you remember which direction to rotate a nut to tighten or loosen it. Apparently it applied to the brake lever too.

We'd stopped for morning tea break, something the *Gulflander* had done at this spot since the nineteenth century. Blackbull had had a refreshment room from the earliest days of the railway, and was also the site of a former camp for fettlers (rail maintenance workers). Its prominent shed was the first railway building I'd seen since leaving Normanton. Not that it was an original.

'In 1943 the station building was destroyed by a storm, and its remains were used to build this shed,' said Ken.

Across the track was a block of roadside toilets. On its side I saw a poster seeking information about a motorcycle ridden by a mysterious missing person named Hayden. I'd heard about Hayden on the bus out from Cairns, when he was mentioned by Pat, a roadhouse owner heading back to her business at Mount Surprise. The man had disappeared three months before, after apparently riding a black motorbike to the foot of a remote communications tower in the Newcastle Range. The only trace he'd left behind was some items of clothing. His family had hired a helicopter to search for him, but thus far his location remained unknown. It was a reminder of how big and relatively empty the Gulf Country was.

As Shane was involved in deeply technical talk with the train crew, I chatted to Alison about her travels while we sipped tea and ate blueberry muffins. She'd been to Hawaii recently, just before a false alarm had been issued about an incoming North Korean missile. That was the sort of thing that would freak you out when travelling, but made an excellent anecdote afterwards. As long as you survived it, it was a good story.

They were planning to take the *Rocky Mountaineer* luxury train in Canada next, coupled with an Alaska cruise. Since they were serial rail travellers, I told them about the time I'd ridden the extravagant *Eastern & Oriental Express* from Bangkok to Singapore. As it had been necessary to dress for dinner aboard that train, I'd had to carefully fold my suit jacket and a couple of neckties within my backpack. The formal gear hadn't stopped me making a fool of myself with dreadful singing to tunes played by the onboard pianist, but in any case it was a far cry from the anything-goes dress code aboard the *Gulflander*.

Back on board and moving again, Ken had a story of his own. In 1907 a train guard had acted strangely on the journey out, then shot himself dead at Blackbull Station. 'Maybe Blackbull's got a bit of a curse on it,' he added laconically, giving the tale a showman-like spin. 'We try not to stop there too long.'

As a follow-up, he told us about the night he'd been driving the train through the area after dark, in order to return it from a special event. Though people weren't supposed to camp at the Blackbull site, they sometimes did because of the handy toilet block. As the train had come through Blackbull that night, he had looked up to see surprised, half-awoken campers looming out of the darkness, like a latter-day knock-off of Michael Jackson's 'Thriller' video clip. 'It was a bit scary, actually.'

As we progressed toward Croydon, we heard more about the modern technology that had been subtly inserted into the *Gulflander*. For example, its classic maroon and gold colours were applied with a modern paint that hid wear and tear well. But not everything was new.

'The engine in this is about seventy-five years old,' said Ken. 'It can be crank-started if we get into trouble. There's also a GPS.'

We were now passing paperbark trees, in blossom from the recent rains. Ken also pointed out the bloodwood tree, the tallest in the region. The train slowed at this point to traverse a particularly bumpy section. Then, the sky having gradually grown grey and heavy, it finally started to rain.

I was surprised to note we were less than an hour from Croydon.

Over the past few years I'd become increasingly perturbed by an apparent speeding up of time. An overseas trip would be months away, then upon me, then months ago in what seemed no time at all. On a trip, time stretched out as it does when encountering new experiences, but once home, that journey zoomed into the past. And what are memories but the lasting impression of what is occurring now? It was mildly disturbing.

The rain – which I increasingly regarded as a foe – was soon falling heavily. I yearned for a time in my future when I wouldn't have to worry about rising rivers and their effect on train schedules. It was all very well to want to live in the present and take in the world in a leisurely style from a train window, but it was hard to shake off the travel writer's instinct to meet schedules. In the lead-up to the *Gulflander*'s run, I'd already had to learn far too much about the Gulf catchment area and its various tributaries. The sooner I left it behind, the less likely it was that my journey would be derailed due to weather.

Passing a location once known as Ellavale, I wondered about the settlements that had once been served by this train, and had since vanished from the map. Each small town would have had its own histories, traditions and families. In towns that endured, these lived on, subtly influencing each generation, but in ghost towns they were snuffed out. Such places had literally become deceased. This was a familiar concept when travelling overseas, visiting such places as the former port of Ostia Antica outside Rome, abandoned once its river access silted up. Applied to a town less than a century old it seemed an unsettling thought, an intimation of mortality.

I knew first-hand the melancholy that hung over the remains of a once working town. I'd grown up in such a place: Argyle in the south-west corner of Western Australia (no relation to Lake Argyle in the state's north). When I was a boy there was little left of the original townsite: only a post office in eerie isolation near a grove of trees that ringed a demolished school. The only other items of infrastructure that marked Argyle's existence were a large former packing shed on the highway, which my dad leased to sell fruit to passing travellers, and a small shed on the railway, from which cases of fruit could be sent as freight. I could faintly remember the steam trains that still hauled freight along the line when I was very young, and the railway turntable that had existed in the town of Donnybrook, where I went to school. I hadn't considered this until recently, but I imagine those steam trains of the late 1960s – almost ethereal now in my boyhood memory – might have sparked my love of rail travel. I was never much of a country boy, and those rails alongside our orchard were ever-present reminders that there was a wider world at their far end. As the widespread availability of private cars had undermined the viability of rail, so had it undermined the need for small towns. So Argyle's post office was demolished after the last postmistress retired, removing from us kids the adventure of walking the few kilometres there to collect the mail, breathing in the strange but heady atmosphere of old post-office ink and mouldering paper. The railway shed was also demolished. Argyle eventually became a general locality rather than a signposted town. Even its postcode was retired from use, but I remembered it: 6238.

We were almost at Croydon now, passing another abandoned townsite, Golden Gate. In its goldmining heyday this was a town of 1,500 people. It survived until 1929 when the gold ran out. Because it was only five miles and a twenty-minute ride from Croydon, the *Gulflander* had run additional services between the two places for a decade or so from 1902. There were two trains each way on Saturday nights, allowing Golden Gate residents to party in Croydon then return home. Thus Croydon had its own improbable suburban train service for a time. Beyond Golden Gate, whose station saw its last passengers in 1923, was a scattering of abandoned mining machinery from the glory days. It had a gloomy aspect: a ghostly junkyard with large rusting objects scattered among the trees, a monument to boom and bust. Ken mentioned that they'd had to re-lay some of the sleepers in this stretch, as a result of fool's gold (iron pyrite) which had turned to acid in the soil. It seemed a fitting analogy for what happened to the real gold: here one day, gone the next, leaving decay in its wake.

Near the end of our journey we ascended True Blue Hill, named after a former mining company and the steepest point on the route, after pausing to let a couple of Brahman cows cross. The termite mounds clustered more thickly here, as if marking the end of the line. Then Ken eased the *Gulflander* into Croydon's station, a simple metal structure built in 2005 after termites had fatally undermined its predecessor.

The railway had reached Croydon in 1891, over three years after the first track had been laid at Normanton's railway wharf in 1888. To celebrate, a banquet was held in the mining town in honour of George Phillips and his remarkable steel sleepers. There must have been some present who doubted the railway's ability to withstand floods, but they would be proven wrong.

The gold that had prompted the line's construction had quickly run out. In 1891, bustling gold-rich Croydon had multiple hotels, banks and newspapers, and a school. It was the social hub of the region, with dance halls and other entertainments. But from 1905 the gold became harder to extract, and the population declined sharply. Businesses disappeared from its streets, and its empty houses were dismantled for their galvanised iron. By 1933 Croydon had only 226 residents, not counting its Aboriginal residents, who were excluded from census counts until the late 1960s. The total isn't much different today – the 2016 census counted 258 inhabitants. If not for its utility as a service centre for the cattle industry, Croydon might now be as deserted as Golden Gate.

Big sister Normanton didn't fare much better as the years passed. As the railway line from Townsville headed ever west from the Pacific coast toward Mount Isa, Normanton's importance as a port for the Gulf Country faded. Its port was problematic in any case, with an immovable mud bar at the Norman River's mouth forcing the offloading of cargo from steamers onto smaller boats, which would carry it along the long winding waterway to the town's railway wharf. As the steamers only arrived every third week in the early days, this led to an eccentric train timetable that varied depending on whether it was 'steamer week'. Normanton's population had dropped from a gold rush era high of 1,251 down to 338 residents by 1933, though by 2016 it had recovered to 1,210. With these challenges at both ends of the *Gulflander*'s route, it's not surprising its closure was first mooted by the authorities in 1910. But it trundled on, somehow, though becoming ever more marginal.

In the 1970s there dawned a recognition of the Normanton–Croydon railway's historic significance, so Normanton Station and its artefacts were registered by the National Trust. But beyond the government's decision to repair the line after the 1974 flood, the working railway's salvation was cemented by that much-maligned group: tourists. Ironically, the improved roads which had done so much to undermine the *Gulflander*'s economic viability now delivered paying customers wanting to ride it. In the late 1970s, without much prompting, groups of travellers began arriving at Normanton Station to catch the scheduled weekly service. This precipitated the addition of more passenger carriages to the train and the running of shorter trips to intermediate points such as Critters Camp. In 1988 the *Gulflander*'s fares were increased to levels above the normal per-kilometre rates elsewhere in Queensland, marking, perhaps, the moment this neglected workhorse line became a tourist railway. It's now in the best shape it has ever been, with stations and rolling stock kept in good order rather than patched up sporadically as they were for most of the line's history.

So much I'd seen on this journey had emphasised the endurance of nature compared with the designs of humans. But the *Gulflander* was an exception to that, a strange little train that had survived when logic suggested it should not have. I was glad it had.

####

I would have liked to look around Croydon; old gold-rush towns are always worth a glance for their architecture. I had a room booked at the town's Club Hotel, as I'd originally planned to take the next day's bus from there to Georgetown, and thence south to meet my second train, the *Savannahlander*, in Forsayth. But there was bad news. The *Savannahlander*'s run out of Cairns had been shortened due to flooding, and the Gulf Country's rivers were still rising unpredictably. That would potentially make it difficult to meet the train at its temporary new terminus, Mount Surprise.

To be on the safe side, I caught that afternoon's incoming Trans North bus back to Normanton so I'd be on the right side of the rising Norman River if I had to catch a plane to Cairns from the town's airport. At the Purple Pub, I asked a local what he thought about the coming weather. After a moment, he cocked his head and said, 'Might be a cyclone forming in the Gulf. Drag all of this away.'

I hoped he meant the rainfall, not the town.

The next day would see me on either a bus to Mount Surprise or a plane back to Cairns. Whether I made it to the train was up to the weather.

Normanton to Cairns
Trans North bus

I took the bus, and the outback reversed itself as we headed east. The pointy termite mounds thinned out, then became rounded in form, then disappeared. The trees became less sparse, the roadhouses more substantial. At Mount Surprise we stopped for lunch at the BP roadhouse and I found another poster about the vanished Hayden taped to the counter.

Across the road, I wandered through the town's railway station. I wouldn't be catching the *Savannahlander* here after all, as its run had been cut back even further, to distant Almaden. That was a disappointing bit of news. Still, it was heartening to know this atmospheric set of old timber buildings was still in use for the weekly train when the weather wasn't throwing its weight around.

Inside the station was a series of exhibits about the line. One board detailed the top-secret radar station that had been established in the town in 1943, as Far North Queensland became a hub of military activity in the war against Japan. The Atherton Tablelands east of Mount Surprise had hosted thousands of soldiers training in jungle settings before their deployment to the Pacific Theatre, and a bomber base had been built at Mareeba. As a result the railway from Cairns had become vital for the movement of troops, and civilians were banned from travelling along its eastern section as wartime activity reached its peak.

In an amusing footnote to this frantic era, a caption in the Mount Surprise station stated that due to wartime rationing the local pub had received by rail a single 9-gallon (34-litre) keg of beer per week, which was then generally consumed within two hours.

The *Savannahlander* train took its name from the flat, lightly wooded savannah country at its western end, but the most dramatic section of its route was anything but flat. From Cairns, it threaded through the Macalister Range, sharing the rails with the Kuranda Scenic Railway, before passing this station on its way to the former mining town of Forsayth.

On the bus I'd started reading *Conquest of the Ranges*, by the late local historian Glenville Pike, which detailed the building of the railway from Cairns through the mountains to Kuranda and beyond. Pike loved to imagine dialogue for historic figures in his non-fiction books to add dramatic flair. In the first chapter, three men in a pub discussed the tension between coastal towns as they vied to be the starting point of a railway through the ranges:

> Lannoy shrugged. 'Ah, that is the vital question. If there is a railway built at all, there is no guarantee Port Douglas will get it. I think Cairns has a good chance.'
> 'Cairns! That vaporous pest hole! Nothing but a fever ridden swamp! An ideal place for Dr Koch to dispense his fever mixture, but no use for much else!' The doctor was vehement, and leaned forward in his chair as he spoke.

Flowery dialogue aside, it was an interesting read. I'd had no idea such uncertainty had attended the railway's route, and how much had depended on the expertise of Christie Palmerston, an experienced but brutal bushman who had a habit of abusing non-white people who got in his way, including Chinese goldminers and Indigenous people. He was hired to find a practical path for the rails to follow. It was a difficult task; Palmerston and his Aboriginal offsider, Pompo, struggled with heavy rain, bouts of fever and an attack by Indigenous locals.

Palmerston eventually decided against the suitability of a railway up the slopes of Barron Gorge, as Pike reimagines:

> There would be miles of cuttings,
> sidings, and tunnels, he thought. He
> added in his diary that 'it would cost a
> mint of money and be dangerous, for
> the mountains are so precipitous there
> would be landslips continually.'

However, that daunting route was the one chosen in 1884 by the state's chief engineer, largely because of the superiority of Cairns' harbour over those of its rivals. It was no easy option, however, requiring fifteen tunnels and dozens of bridges to carry the railway. Ironically, the difficulty of the terrain has kept it in operation all these years for both the *Savannahlander* and the shorter runs of the Kuranda Scenic Railway, as the rugged route is spectacularly scenic. The KSR had started as a tourist service in 1936, an early example of the adaptation of pioneer railways for the amusement of travellers.

Nowadays the *Savannahlander* is also, like the *Gulflander*, a tourist train – though operated by a private company rather than Queensland Rail. It runs along the Tablelands line extending from Cairns through the ranges west to Almaden, then on to Forsayth via the former Etheridge Railway, which once conveyed copper ore for the Chillagoe Railway and Mining Company. The line was completed in 1908 and, being built on the cheap, it had numerous steep grades.

As the Normanton–Croydon line had never been extended to the east, so the Cairns–Forsayth line never fulfilled the plans mooted for its extension further west. The *Savannahlander* eventually replaced regular passenger services on the line in 1995, its name another nod to the long-distance '-lander' services operated by Queensland Rail elsewhere in the state.

Though it has a private operator, the *Savannahlander* maintains its delicate historic minuet with the timetable of the *Gulflander*, to the benefit of travellers. During the height of the tourist season, from March to October, the company sells packages that combine the two train rides with a bus transfer between. As in the past, it takes several days to progress from Normanton to Cairns via this tour, with optional side-trips to attractions such as the picturesque Cobbold Gorge near Forsayth, the Chillagoe Caves, and the Undara Lava Tubes near Mount Surprise.

The *Savannahlander* is pulled by railmotors, though they possess a sleeker appearance than that of the snub-nosed *Gulflander*. Its three railmotor units date from the 1960s and early 1970s, their interiors having timber elements and vinyl seats beneath steel roofs with distinctive longitudinal corrugations. The mix of past and modernity in the train's materials suggests the spaceships pictured in postwar science fiction magazines: sleek, shiny, streamlined, and a symbol of the future.

But it was not for me to experience today, sadly, thanks to the whims of what Edna Everage would call Dame Nature. Back on the bus, heading east, our driver, Ron, received a message that there was flooding in Ravenshoe and we'd have to detour around it.

When we started descending through the ranges past Kuranda, it was raining heavily and I had the impression of moving through a mysterious misty world that only existed at the level of the roadway, bounded by heavy foliage and fast-flowing waterfalls. Just below us was a soft grey void, as if we were floating in the air. It was eerily similar to the view from the window of a plane flying just above cloud, though in this case there was no blue sky above. It wasn't yet 5 pm, but the saturated clouds had so dimmed the daylight that everyone on the road was driving with their headlights on, carefully and slowly forming a convoy down the mountain.

So I would have to cross my second train, the *Savannahlander*, off my list and with heavy rains on the Pacific coast it was a toss-up as to whether I might have problems with my next train, the *Spirit of Queensland* to Brisbane. It was discouraging, but the bulk of my itinerary and many thousands of kilometres of rail still lay ahead of me. One day, soon, I would leave this tropical climate behind. That was a cheery thought worth clinging to.

####

I mooched about in Cairns for three days, praying for the rain to ease so the disrupted trains to Brisbane could resume and allow me to head south. To while away the time I took a side-trip to Port Douglas, where I rode on the converted sugar cane train of the Bally Hooley Railway, and back in town I met an interesting duo at the Cairns Central YHA whose job involved sleeping for days in cramped quarters at sea, in order to cull crown-of-thorns starfish. But nothing took my mind off the rain for long.

On the Sunday I rang Narrelle from my next accommodation, the Cairns Novotel, to pour out my rain-related problems, so early in the epic journey which I'd imagined would reset my career. She was sympathetic, but so far away in Melbourne, and who could give advice in order to second-guess unpredictable Nature?

'You could always go back and do the missing train later,' she suggested, but that offended my sense of order and progression. I was concerned this mighty trek would soon turn into a confused muddle. And there was more than one train that was in trouble. I rang off, feeling down and alone, and as if my careful travel plans were about to completely unravel. Obviously itineraries are always in danger of being derailed due to unforeseen circumstances, and normally there's enough wriggle room to reschedule. But my remaining six trains and booked accommodation were lined up like ducks in a row, and would be a nightmare to reschedule. I wanted to avoid that problem at any cost.

Later that evening I sat in the hotel bar, as a lounge singer sang hits from a decade before she was born. She was talented, but to my ear such performers conveyed a melancholy air, as if their listeners were in a waiting room anticipating the dismal end. After she sang 'Time After Time', there was a smattering of applause and she asked, 'Who doesn't love the 80s?'

And I thought, 'It's time to go.'

I left Cairns the next morning. But not, sadly, by train.

Cairns to Townsville
Qantas flight 2305

'I first went to Ubud in 1985. It's changed a lot since then, especially since that bloody *Eat Pray Love*. Loads of lonely women around, looking for ...'

'... their soulmates?' I suggested.

I glanced away from my flying companion through the window of the aircraft. The Coral Sea was rippling gently below the Dash 8's propellers as we flew south to Townsville, sunlight glinting on the wave crests. I thought I saw low, dark islands among them, but then realised they were the reflections of scattered clouds.

The Bruce Highway south of Cairns was flooded, and had been for days. At first Queensland Rail had scheduled buses to replace the Brisbane-bound *Spirit of Queensland* train between Cairns and Townsville, then cancelled them when it became clear the highway was going to stay blocked indefinitely.

If I missed that train, my onward schedule would fall apart. So I'd bought a ticket on the 8.35 am flight to Townsville, where I could board the *Spirit of Queensland* in the afternoon. Which is how I came to be sitting next to Linda, an Australian with a flowing red scarf who ran a dog refuge in Bali. I was starting to see that a highlight of this epic journey would be the strangers I met along the way, the random acquaintances who brightened my day by sharing something of their lives – sometimes, as now, while I scrambled for a notebook and pen as I told them I was writing a book.

'I thought I'd set it up and hand it over to someone else after a year,' said Linda, as I jotted. 'Twelve years later and I'm still there. But I'm trying to get out of it now – tired of people taking it for granted, dumping dogs out front.'

When I'd heard where she worked, I'd asked Linda not to show me any photos of animal cruelty – I could never bear to see it – but she'd pulled out her phone anyway and flicked through some before-and-after photos of gaunt, starving dogs and their happier later selves.

As Linda was also an artist, she showed me images of her work. The big colourful paintings featured people, dogs and other animals, the fluid figures rendered in vivid colours.

Linda was flying to Townsville for the funeral of an aged aunt. 'I'm not looking forward to it,' she said.

It was only a fifty-five-minute flight. As we descended, I looked out past the spinning propellers at the water's surface. The sunlight on the shifting currents now made it look as though there was a mysterious map traced on the surface of the water, a maze of pathways.

####

Townsville's former railway station between Flinders Street and Ross Creek was grand, but also mildly depressing. Trains hadn't stopped there since 2003, when a new station had been opened further west to accommodate the introduction of faster 'tilt trains', and I could see where the remnant rails had been cut off where new apartment buildings now stood.

The line almost hadn't come this way at all. When the Queensland government had started building the first railway from Townsville to the goldmines at inland Charters Towers in 1878, it had commenced near the barracks to the south of Ross

Creek. Railway workers ('navvies') were slaving away laying track when the business community of Townsville, on the north bank of the waterway below the imposing monolith of Castle Hill, raised an outcry and insisted the terminus be built next to the main commercial thoroughfare, Flinders Street. After a petition to the authorities in Brisbane and a visit by a government surveyor, they got their wish.

That original station had been replaced by this substantial pile. Opened in 1913 as the terminus of the Great Northern Railway to Mount Isa, it was a graceful if neglected structure eccentrically blending Edwardian Gothic and Art Nouveau styles. Inside the rail booking office that still inhabited the building, I suggested to a clerk that the old station should be repurposed for something grand, perhaps a hotel.

'That's what I keep saying!' he replied.

High in the adjacent lofty old ticket hall with its tiled surfaces and green ceiling was an honour board of railwaymen who had died in World War I. It hung above dusty floors that hardly felt a footfall nowadays. Ten columns picked out over 400 names in gold lettering, with the title above: 'Railway patriots of the Northern Division, who volunteered to fight for the Empire'. The past was a different country, as L.P. Hartley wrote, and in that country 'the Empire' clearly meant something more than moustachioed people in linen sipping gin and tonic on a verandah at sundown. It was a pity the board was stuck in this lonely place, rather than in a museum or war memorial. The woodwork was skilfully detailed and the tribute heartfelt, and both deserved to be noticed.

Returning to the visitor centre where I'd left my backpack, I walked along Ogden Street, which ran behind Flinders Street as a gritty service lane. Flinders' name pops up around the nation: Flinders Street is also a major street in Melbourne. But when I glanced at Google Maps, I noticed the following Townsville street names: Flinders, Sturt, Stanley, Gregory, Wills, Mitchell, Eyre, Ogden, Stokes. They were all explorers, of Australia or some other part of the British Empire. On the basis of Wills Street, I searched for and found a Burke Street, intersecting with Mitchell and Eyre. Someone in Townsville had been an explorer fanboy. It didn't take much scratching of the surface to find fragments of Empire here. It struck me that this was another aspect of Victorian-era Australia that had lingered on well into the twentieth century, into my schooldays: the desire to anchor the developing nation in a mythos of explorers 'discovering' and pioneers 'settling' a continent that had been well and truly discovered millennia before by its Indigenous people. It suggested a certain level of denial by the new occupiers, if not outright insecurity.

There was spectacular street art on Ogden Street, including a towering lizard covering a high brick wall. Looking for coffee I found The Quarters, a tiny, hip space, the polar opposite of the sun-drenched streets outside. Its interior was painted completely black, and it was furnished with mismatched pieces of dark retro furniture. The walls were covered in chalk illustrations accompanied by coffee-related text: 'There is too much blood in my coffee stream'; 'Coffee: starter fluid for the morning impaired'; 'Vengeance is sweet when served ... roasted'.

I felt like I wanted to coin another, based on Samuel Johnson's comment about patriotism, and scratch it onto the wall: 'Cutesy coffee aphorisms are the first refuge of the scoundrel'.

'I want to move somewhere else,' said the young barista, Kris, after serving me a long black. 'Byron Bay, or Melbourne.'

'They're very different climates,' I said.

'I hate the heat,' he replied. Kris said he was part Torres Strait Islander, part white Aussie and part Scottish.

It was a quiet day, so we talked about coffee etiquette, including those infuriating people who ordered coffee while talking on their phones. I also wondered why all the cafes in Cairns and Townsville seemed to close at 2 pm.

'It's too hot here to drink coffee in the afternoon,' said another customer, who'd been listening in. Actually, that made sense.

As I left to catch my train, I reflected on the drift of young people to big cities, but also on how regional centres like

Townsville were countering that shift by adopting the trappings of their bigger rivals, good coffee and street art among them.

####

Townsville's current railway station was a kilometre west of its predecessor. It wasn't as ugly as Cairns Station, the latter being a concrete platform attached to a shopping-centre car park. But that was a low bar to clear. This was a bland concrete and steel structure, with a single customer service officer seated behind a glass window. On the other hand, the blue highlights throughout the building matched the sunny sky, trees stood beyond the tracks, and it was pleasant to sit on a platform bench and catch the light breeze.

A yellow-and-black sign on a wall read, 'WARNING: PLASTIC SNAKES ON STATION TO DETER BIRDS'.

It struck me that they might also deter humans, so I asked a passing crew member where they were. She said, 'That's a little puzzle we like to set our passengers.' Then, relenting, 'Near the entrance.'

I looked all around, but I couldn't find them.

What was more important was the actual train waiting for me at the platform. It was now 12 March – ten days since I'd arrived in Normanton, five days since I'd caught the *Gulflander*. I'd seen some beautiful places, but the stress caused by second-guessing rain delays had not been pleasant at the start of such a long trip. However, I hadn't become stranded in Normanton as I'd feared, and I'd made it out of the tropics. Now I was leaving North Queensland behind altogether, by rail. Cheerfully, ironically, determinedly heading south.

Townsville to Brisbane
Spirit of Queensland

We pulled out on schedule at 3.24 pm and passed swiftly out of Townsville, over Ross Creek and past the city's light industry. We soon passed cows in grassy fields as we ran to the east of the ranges. It was uncomplicated countryside, low and green with stretches of wetlands where I could see waterbirds fishing. On this sunny day, the water glowed blue with reflected sky, and the hills had a hazy aura.

Placed in the RailBed section, my seat was unlike any I'd previously experienced on a train. Similar to that found in business class on a plane, it was contained within its own shell, and could be transformed into a flat bed. I say 'be transformed', because the passengers couldn't do this at will. The seats, we were told, would be changed into beds by the staff between 8 pm and 10 pm. Why there were RailBeds at all, and not the traditional sleeper compartments with berths, was a complicated story. As the previous Brisbane–Cairns train, the *Sunlander*, had drawn to the end of its useful life, the state government of the day had commissioned a replacement with modernised sleeper compartments. That government fell from power and the new administration tore up its plans, to start again with the RailBed concept. The government had changed again since then, but the RailBed had won through. As a lover of compartments I was curious to see whether it was a reasonable substitute. The RailBeds were set up in a two-one configuration, and I was in a single seat to the right of the aisle. Each seat was relatively wide and the leg room was undeniably great, with 2 metres or so between seat backs. There was carpet underfoot and a large airline-style storage bin above. What did seem odd was the dimensions of the seat cushion. It was very short, only reaching halfway along my thigh. Attached to it was a padded section which could be separately swivelled up, but I was puzzled as to its purpose. Later I was told it was a footrest, though it sat directly behind my knees. The seat had clearly been designed for people far more petite than myself.

The scenery remained idyllic through the afternoon, though I was surprised to see a feature of my outback adventures reappear: termite mounds. These ones looked grey, as if composed of concrete.

This was sugar country. Plantations slid by, with their sheds looming up beyond the fields. I spotted the narrow-gauge tracks of sugar-cane trains cross our own on one occasion. Sugar had driven railway development in the region. The northernmost section of the line from Cairns to Townsville had once been a humble tramway connecting Cairns' port to a sugar mill at Gordonvale. Opened in 1897, it had eventually reached as far as Babinda, 58 kilometres south of Cairns, and included a passenger service. Another isolated sugar-carrying line had been built from Innisfail, 84 kilometres south of Cairns, further south through El Arish to Feluga. They were eventually incorporated into the North Coast line through to Brisbane in 1924. That was the cue for a ramp-up in passenger services along this coastal route, with a peak in traveller numbers in the war year of 1944.

Though the *Spirit of Queensland* ran along rails that were more widely spaced than those of the dinky sugar-cane trains, they were still regarded as narrow-gauge. They lay just 1,067 millimetres (3' 6") apart, compared to the 1,435 millimetres (4' 8½") of standard gauge. Not that this narrower gauge limited velocity: with a maximum speed of 160 km/h, this train was as fast as any I would take on my journey.

Despite that potential velocity, it took what seemed minutes to cross the Burdekin River, a broad expanse of blue-brown water. Because we were meeting rivers on the coast, we were seeing them near the ends of their journeys when they had become impressively wide. It was a nice change to encounter waterways without worrying about them breaking their banks.

The RailBeds came with a seat-back entertainment system, with large screens on the back of each unit. The movies were an inoffensive selection of classics (e.g. *Sleepless in Seattle*) and what I called 'arthouse-lite', represented here by *Victoria and Abdul*. They were the sort of movies I'd watch on long flights, if I was tired and didn't have anything better on my iPad. The TV shows were a lightweight collection of lifestyle programs and sitcoms, though thankfully there was no *Big Bang Theory*, a painful sitcom unaccountably found on every plane. There were music albums too, equally harmless, and someone had had me in mind with their generous selection of 80s artists including the Eurythmics and Cyndi Lauper. It was all very middle-of-the-road. When I then discovered that the supplied headphones were actually earbuds, my mind flitted to the Medium Place, the compromise afterlife in the Netflix series *The Good Place*. The Medium Place is designed for just one person, a character who did many bad deeds in life but thought up one extremely positive idea before her death that ended up helping many. As she was unable to be placed in either Heaven or Hell, the compromise was the Medium Place: where the video entertainment was *Cannonball Run II* on VHS cassettes and the beer was good but never cold. This train was the railway version of the Medium Place, with everything – food, entertainment, comfort – neither brilliant nor awful. It was all just okay.

About twenty minutes from Bowen I imagined I saw the ruins of a square white castle, overgrown with vegetation, guarding an approach to the hills. In reality it was a lone outcrop of rock, a blocky protrusion. I was reminded of a vision I'd had on my initial bus trip to Normanton, of an Eden without people. So much of travel between cities in Australia involved moving through apparently near-empty landscapes, beautiful but eerily without human presence. Perhaps beautiful *because* of the lack of human presence. This coast was actually well-populated, I knew, but it didn't seem like that from a fast-moving train.

I bought a snack from the Club Car in the next carriage, a fairly Medium cheese, avocado and tomato sandwich. Then I walked further back to the Premium Economy section to see what the seats were like there. I sat in an empty spot and found it comfortable, though narrower than the RailBed. These seats also had access to the entertainment system, though on a smaller screen. Crucially, the seat cushion seemed more supportive. If I was taking a daytime-only trip, I'd sit here.

Back in the RailBed section, one of the disadvantages of travelling in an open carriage rather than a compartment became evident. A family with a small child had boarded with me at Townsville, and the child was emitting loud cries at regular intervals. I discreetly asked an attendant where the family was disembarking and was relieved to hear it was Mackay. That meant hours more of noise, but not overnight. They'd be alighting about two hours after Bowen, where I saw mango trees and palms, and a small flock of sheep cropping grass. The vivid green was a reminder of how fertile the rain could make this region at the right time of year.

Dinner had to be negotiated. While the train had been stuck in Townsville, awaiting the clearing of the floods, there'd been a power loss and the crew had had to go grocery shopping. The resulting approximation of the usual menu – a pumpkin and spinach filo pastry, Greek salad, custard tart and a glass of shiraz – was on the good side of Medium. I decided to succumb to the seemingly unavoidable Medium Place vibe, and watched *Victoria and Abdul* with my dinner. It was as heavy-handed as arthouse-lite gets. This sub-genre of my own invention referred to films that were easy to digest but were designed to make the viewer think they'd watched something intelligent. If the movie in question featured a British monarch, or Churchill, or the colourful days of the Raj, so much the better. As I consumed an after-dinner mint with a weak coffee, Abdul kissed Victoria's feet, and the sun set over Proserpine State Forest out the window to my right. Despite the bland entertainment, it was good to be sitting on a train after dark, watching a movie while I headed south from the tropics. This would be my first night on a train on this trip. I was finally making progress.

At about 8 pm I asked the attendant to set up my bed. It seemed sensible to do so before we reached Mackay, where there would be a bustle of people boarding and disembarking. On traditional sleeper trains, the attendant physically pulls down a bunk bed from a cavity in the wall, or folds down the seatback of a lounge. This process was subtler. The attendant plugged a controller unit into a socket on the seat. The seat back then folded forward (rather than backward as on a plane), to reveal a mattress. The attendant then laid a sheet and duvet atop it, folding the duvet corner into a triangle as a final flourish.

After my evening ablutions, I had a brief moment of panic when I couldn't find my phone. I searched the overhead locker, took out my backpack and searched that, then told a nearby attendant I might have mislaid it.

'I hope it hasn't gone down the gap next to the seat,' she said. 'We can't get anything out of there.'

Finally I got down on hands and knees – and saw the phone where I'd left it, plugged in and charging while propped against the wall. I stowed it firmly in the overhead locker.

As a bed, the RailBed was no narrower than the traditional sleeper berth. If I lay on my side it felt comfortable, and the mattress was softer than most business-class seats laid flat. I had an odd impression that the upper section of the bed leant too far back, though maybe that was down to me – I'd felt the same sensation in business class on flights, and usually tilted the surface up a bit.

I couldn't do that here, but piling up two pillows helped. The lack of privacy in this set-up was a negative compared with the classic sleeper, but there was one clear advantage – not needing to climb into an upper berth. I disliked upper berths intensely. One of my earliest memories was of falling out of an upper bunk as a child, when my family had been living in a caravan temporarily while our house was being built.

I read for a while. In *Affection*, a novel I'd picked up in Townsville that was set in that city in 1900, the mayor was waxing lyrical on an apt topic:

> 'And you have to build train lines; the
> modern businessman can't run a show
> without them. The North especially
> needs the railways now. One day soon,
> Row, you and I could catch a train
> from the station in town here and
> travel all the way to Brisbane. What do
> you think of that?'

It was a reminder that it had taken a long time for Queensland's long coastal railway to be built. On a map it seemed the spine of the state's network, with four lines peeling off west to termini at Charleville (via the *Westlander*), Longreach (the *Spirit of the Outback*), Mount Isa (the *Inlander*) and Forsayth (the *Savannahlander*). But all these branch lines had been built first, to convey produce and minerals from inland areas to the coast. The North Coast line, which had finally linked them all together, was only constructed between 1911 and 1924.

I was growing tired, so, worrying that the seat gap might devour it should I fall asleep and lose it down the side, I stowed my Kindle away.

By night the train was a rocket flying through a void. The minimal light outside was overpowered by the reflection of the train's interior, creating a faint mirror image beyond the windows. As I made notes, a spectral version of myself did the same, hovering in the night, vibrating as if out of tune with our plane of existence.

The train staff turned the lights out at 10 pm, a surprising reminder of my years at boarding school. It took a while for everyone to drift off. I heard some grumbling directed at a raucous snorer a few seats ahead. Then a voice said distinctly in the darkness, 'Someone stinks!' I hoped it wasn't me.

I never expect to fall asleep on a sleeper train, but always do, and am always surprised after the fact. I woke occasionally in the night. The train seemed to be moving faster, enhancing its impression of a rocket. Only three years old, it was much speedier than its retired predecessor. The *Sunlander* had taken thirty-one hours to cover the 1,681 kilometres of the Cairns–Brisbane route, while the *Spirit of Queensland* took twenty-five hours to make the same distance. It would take eighteen hours to convey me the 1,341 kilometres from Townsville to Brisbane.

Its maximum speed of 160 km/h was good for an Australian train, though eclipsed by the fastest I'd ever been on: the maglev train from Shanghai Pudong International Airport to Longyang Road Station, which reached 431 km/h. If you could run a train at that speed over distance, you could cover the Cairns–Brisbane route in under four hours.

About 4.30 am I awoke and heard someone mention a forthcoming stop, so I unclipped the velcro curtain over the window. We were on the outskirts of a town, and the train seemed for a moment to be trundling along the middle of a suburban street, the front yards of houses a few metres away. Then we traversed another large body of water, and passed through Bundaberg.

####

'My family's always been in the railways,' said the woman from Sarina, a town near Mackay. 'One of them is the troubleshooter for the whole South Island of New Zealand. If something goes wrong, a derailment or whatever, he has to go out. Now his daughter wants to be a ticket collector.'

It was 5.30 am and I was in the Club Car, talking to other passengers as we approached Maryborough. The seating here encouraged interaction, as its nooks with their narrow tables faced each other across the aisle.

There was a glimmer of light in the east, with trees and powerlines silhouetted against it. That's a minor miracle of sleeper trains: the prospect of an eighteen-hour journey stretches in front of you, then suddenly you've eaten food, watched a bland movie about a dead monarch, slept for a bit, and there are only a few hours to go.

In addition to the couple from Sarina, I talked to Barry, a friendly white-haired bloke from Airlie Beach. Having recently moved there, he was heading back to his former home in Maryborough to pick up some items.

'I haven't been on the train for years,' he said, adding, incredulously, 'There's a shower!'

It was charming to meet someone who wasn't jaded by long-distance rail travel. If only we could all be so uplifted by a shower in motion.

'Do people always talk so much on trains?' asked Barry. 'Or is that just a Queensland thing?'

I said I'd noticed the phenomenon on all sorts of trains, as long as there was a space onboard in which to socialise. My theory was that a long-distance train was like a small town in motion. For the duration of the journey we were townsfolk, and the chat in the cafe or bar car was our meeting at the agora.

After Barry disembarked at Maryborough, I showered. My second law of long-distance train travel is to get up early enough to use the shower before anyone else does, so you encounter it while it's pristine. (The first is never to buy coffee at a train station.) 'Showers on trains are impressive, Barry,' I thought.

It was getting light quickly. The sun didn't dawdle at dawn and dusk in Queensland, it came up and went down with rapidity, and I could see we were now in a classic Australian setting of grassy paddocks and gum trees. If McCubbin or another of the gang from the Heidelberg School had been present, I would've encouraged him to paint it.

When I got back to my RailBed an attendant had stripped its bedding and was turning it back into a seat. I hadn't slept too badly, I reflected, and that pointed to another advantage of the RailBeds – they faced the direction of travel. On most sleeper trains, berths were perpendicular to that direction, which meant you experienced a lot of rocking, especially if the tracks were poorly maintained.

North of Gympie I spotted a former rail carriage in the yard of a house, fitted out as living quarters, or maybe as a shed. I liked the look of that. There was a romance to living in a former carriage or, even better, a former railway station, as if the glamour of travel had soaked into its timbers. As a kid I had watched the TV series *Catweazle*, in which an eleventh-century wizard accidentally arrives in the twentieth century. In the second season he lives in an abandoned railway station, Duck Halt, and I'd thought that was the coolest thing ever. Probably another seed for my later love of railways, come to think of it. It was broadcast in 1971, directly after the extensive British railway closures prompted by a report from British Railways chairman Dr Richard Beeching, and thus would have tapped directly into the dismay felt by many at the loss of their local stations.

Shortly there was a very long announcement which amounted to two things: that we were running thirty minutes late, and that it would be possible to step out briefly on the platform at Gympie North for a breath of fresh air. For some reason announcements on the train took ages, often full of redundant or unnecessary information. As the speakers relayed them at a high, piercing volume, they were hard work to endure. I suspect they became rambling through a kind of misplaced friendly folksiness on the part of the announcers, especially when having to deliver bad news about delays. I would have been happy with the gist. Anyway, I decided to pass on the opportunity to experience the pleasures of Gympie North Station, it being about 6.30 am.

Near Pomona I saw a remarkable rock formation to the west, a craggy mini mountain that protruded from the ground, lightly covered with trees. This was Mount Cooroora in Tuchekoi National Park. A 439-metre-high volcanic plug, it played host each year to the King of the Mountain festival, which involved a footrace to the summit. It had started in 1958 after a local railway porter, Bruce Samuels, had been disbelieved at a pub when he stated he'd run up it in under an hour. After he'd proved the feat to witnesses, it had evolved into a competition drawing competitors from around the world. The record to the top now stood at a little under twenty-three minutes. Rather them than me, I thought, though I had to admire the runners' prowess.

We were now passing through the Sunshine Coast region, and I caught a glimpse of another mountain, a familiar one. The previous year I'd attended a conference for travel writers at Twin Waters, and had joined a side-trip to the Sunshine Coast Hinterland with Narrelle and a group of my colleagues. One of the activities we undertook was painting the Glass House Mountains in watercolours, seated at the lookout at Mary Cairncross Scenic Reserve. We hadn't done a bad job as beginners, or so we flattered ourselves, when coached by a local expert. I still had the painting pinned above my desk.

I could now see Mount Ngungun to my right. Though the collective name for the mountains was bestowed upon them by then Lieutenant James Cook in 1770, the names for the individual peaks were Aboriginal and many thousands of years old, being located in the lands of the Jinibara and Gubbi Gubbi people.

Long train journeys often finish too abruptly for me. I suppose they act as a stress reliever, suspending one's troubles until arrival. As a result I felt a slight unease as we relentlessly bore down on the state capital. After Caboolture there was hardly anyone left in the RailBed carriage. We pulled into Brisbane's Roma Street Station just before 10 am, and everyone dispersed. I felt unexpectedly shell-shocked as I walked into the Brisbane CBD along George Street, startled by the tall buildings, the traffic and the plentiful people in suits. I'd only been in the tropics a short time, but I'd absorbed something of its slower pace of life. I'd relaxed, and had begun thinking more clearly – and now it was back to big-city pace. No wonder there was a disconnect between Queenslanders in the north and those in Brisbane. They lived in different worlds.

On my way to the Ibis Styles hotel I stopped at a bagel place, mostly to take a breath and adjust to the speed and anonymity of my new surroundings. I ordered a feta and beetroot bagel, and considered my reactions. After taking a few breaths, I discovered I was mildly elated. It was only now, upon arrival in Brisbane, that I truly realised I'd left behind the mess of bad weather and train cancellations that had bedevilled me in the north. The big journey really was going ahead.

Brisbane to Grandchester (via Rosewood)
Ipswich/Rosewood line and 539 bus

On the train to Ipswich, a recorded message before every stop said, 'If this is your station, prepare to disembark.' It was an automated echo of the longwinded announcements on the *Spirit of Queensland*. Did people really need to be advised to leave the train when it reached their stop? (Though I honoured the writer of the message for using the word 'disembark' rather than the hideous 'detrain'.)

I was heading west from Brisbane, riding the city's suburban trains. As I had a few days before my long-distance service onward to Sydney, I wanted to explore the state's rail heritage, and I had somewhere in mind for a daytrip.

As we left the CBD we passed Milton, with the XXXX Brewery standing next to the station. I'd written a story about it during my first Brisbane visit a decade before, taking the brewery tour as part of the research. I hadn't been on many brewery tours since: there came a time when you'd learned all you ever needed to know about tuns and mashes. We then passed Toowong, where I'd joined a ghost tour of the cemetery on that same trip. After that point I was heading into terra incognita.

I spotted Oxley Station, which reminded me that Pauline Hanson had originally been elected as the federal member for Oxley in this very area. Now, over twenty years later, she was back in Parliament and selling repackaged versions of the same snake oil. Her original fish and chip shop wasn't far away either, in Silkstone.

That reminded me again of the political and cultural gaps between Brisbane and regional Queensland, and, as if following this line of thought, the train stations became more 'countrified' after we passed Wacol ('Home of the RSPCA', said a sign), where there were tall stands of trees on one side of the line. A lot of cars were parked at stations, a sure sign of commuter country.

Periodically a message blasted over the train speakers: 'The Games are coming! So get prepared!' The Commonwealth Games were being held on the Gold Coast, Brisbane's neighbour, and the message flagged big temporary changes to the public transport system, ending with the advice: '... or walk, for shorter journeys.' Someone up top was clearly concerned about how well the system would cope.

The spelling caught my eye at Ebbw Vale Station. That name had to be Welsh, given that 'w' was a vowel in that language. I looked it up online and, sure enough, a local coal mine was named after an industrial town in Wales. It underlined the importance of mining in Queensland, and its links with the Industrial Revolution in the UK. Rails for the Stockton and Darlington Railway, the first steam-powered passenger railway in the world, had been created in the Welsh Ebbw Vale in 1829, and decades later, I was amused to note, so was steel for the Sydney Harbour Bridge.

I changed at Ipswich for the twenty-minute run to Rosewood. There were rail history attractions out this way: the Workshops Rail Museum in Ipswich, and the Rosewood Railway, a heritage line. From this point I was travelling along the oldest railway in all of Queensland: the line from Ipswich to Grandchester had opened in 1865, though nowadays passenger trains only ran as far as Rosewood. It was curious that the colony's first railway had not started or ended in Brisbane, the capital. But since the colony of Queensland had separated from New South Wales in 1859, large numbers of sheep and cattle farms had been established west of Ipswich, and those pastoralists had lobbied for the line. Rail would cut down the time it took to ship goods to and from Brisbane's port, to which Ipswich was connected via the Bremer and Brisbane Rivers. The laying of the first section of the line was a big deal, attended by a party of toffs including Governor Bowen. His wife, Lady Diamantina, did the honours by tapping a symbolic silver spike into the first sleeper. She then delighted the boy tasked with holding it steady, thirteen-year-old Bill Morrow, by gifting him the spike along with a sovereign. The boy's story is taken up in *The Puffing Pioneers and Queensland's Railway Builders*, a history of Queensland's railways by Viv Daddow. Morrow, then a helper with the construction gang, went on to have a long career in the colony's railways, heading ever north to lay new track. By retirement age he was a maintenance inspector on the Etheridge line, by which I'd paused earlier in Mount Surprise, now used by the *Savannahlander*. He lost a leg there, amputated after a shunting accident, but survived the injury and eventually passed away at eighty-three, having forged a career in an industry that hadn't existed in Queensland when he was born.

As always with Australian cities, the further out from the centre you went, the more Aboriginal place names showed up. My theory was that early European settlers were obsessed with remaking their new home in the image of what they'd left behind but, as time passed, more recent newcomers felt more 'local' and at ease with the ancient Indigenous names for their expanding suburbs and towns. After my train passed Ipswich, there were only four stations before Rosewood, whose names were recorded thus in the Queensland Government's online names database: Wulkuraka, Indigenous dialect unrecorded, 'Either red flowering gum tree, or plenty of kookaburras'; Karrabin, from the Ngaraangbal dialect of the Bundjalung language, 'Red gum'; Walloon, 'Possibly after the French speaking area of southern Belgium'; and Thagoona, 'No details available'.

The biggest surprise for me was the 'possibly' registered against Walloon. In an area colonised by Europeans less than 200 years ago, you'd think there'd be a record of why places had received such specific names.

I was out in the countryside now. It was properly rural, the railway line running between paddocks of sheep and cattle, with gum trees between.

Outside Rosewood Station, a big New Zealander was having a poetic argument with someone on his phone about money. 'How am I going to *luv* for today, where is the *spurut*?' he asked plaintively. As with the kid on the street in Normanton, and with almost everyone I spoke to on this journey, this was a scene doomed to have no conclusion.

Rosewood was an attractive town of old buildings, including a pub with a pleasant-looking upstairs verandah, and a heritage-listed courthouse. Some shops had timber walls and corrugated iron awnings. Almo's Family Shoes had colourful women's party shoes down the front, and a line of gumboots up the back. Harry's Place, a cafe, was in a low brick building with steel fences around its outdoor area. It looked more like a place you'd pick up garden supplies than coffee. The post office, however, was a keeper: a great weatherboard building with a pitched roof. As I admired it from across the road, a huge truck bearing recently felled timber rumbled past.

Signs on shop windows always hinted at a town's character. I saw one advertising 'lantana cleaner', and in block letters in the window of the Rosewood Bakery appeared this:

HAVE COFFEE WITH US
IT WON'T BE A FUSS
WITH A SLICE – IT'S A MUST

The Uniting Church had a splendid belltower, a pioneer-era job consisting of a tapering wooden frame supporting a bell and a canopy. A plaque read, 'This bell is the gift of Mrs J.E. Evers, in memory of her late husband, 24th May 1925.' It was interesting how such memorials endured without fulfilling their purpose. I could discover the existence of J.E. Evers via the plaque, but who was he really? The name lived on, but not the memory.

At the end of the shopping strip was a full-sized Cobb & Co. coach inside a glass box. The fabled stagecoach company had been founded in 1853 to serve the Victorian goldfields, then expanded northward over the following decades. It was doomed to be eclipsed by the railways as they expanded, though the company lingered into the 1920s in Queensland. It was hard to tell if this coach was a replica, but it looked convincing. Two years before, I'd ridden a coach along the old Cobb & Co. track outside Longreach, and could imagine how juddering a ride this would produce. No wonder people had so warmly welcomed the coming of the railways. An adjacent screen played a history of the town: 'Rosewood took its name from the rosewood trees that grew in the area, prior to widespread felling.' You could divine a lot about Queensland from that one sentence. From minerals to trees, the state's history was one of digging things up or chopping things down.

On the bus to Grandchester, there was talk between the driver and a passenger about a cyclone. 'It's supposed to hit the Gold Coast this afternoon, isn't it?'

I groaned inwardly. Spare me more extreme weather.

The driver dropped me off at the Grandchester bus stop, outside the Grandchester Hotel. 'Going to the pub, mate?' he asked.

Not yet, as it happened. I walked along a gravel road toward my goal: the Grandchester railway station. The original terminus of Queensland's first railway line, this was the oldest station still standing in the state, and included rare features such as the stationmaster's living quarters.

The station had been standing since 1865, when the rails had first reached the town. Grandchester was then known as Bigge's Camp; urban legend has it the town's name was eventually changed to avoid people calling it 'Big Scamp'. Once the track was completed, excursion trains ran on Sundays to test out the line, carrying members of the public. These Sunday outings were condemned by some churches, which was no doubt excellent publicity for the new form of transport. As Wodehouse says in his novel *Cocktail Time*:

> Just as all American publishers hope
> that if they are good and lead upright
> lives, their books will be banned in
> Boston, so do all English publishers
> pray that theirs will be denounced
> from the pulpit by a bishop.

I imagine railway ministers and engineers felt the same.

On 31 July 1865, a colony-wide holiday was declared and the Governor and Lady Bowen turned out again to declare the line open at Bigge's Camp Station. Chief Engineer Abram Fitzgibbon made a speech in which he declared himself vindicated for backing the controversial choice of a 3' 6" narrow gauge (the fool! But more on that later) and thus Queensland's railway era officially began – very close to where I was now standing, in fact.

Nowadays Grandchester Station was only open on certain Sundays, but I assumed I could walk up to the exterior and have a look. I assumed wrongly. A gate was firmly locked on my side of the railway line, with the station standing on the other. As I discovered this, a long freight train sounded its horn and rumbled past.

What to do? I took out my phone and looked at the satellite view via Google Maps. I might have been avoiding social media on this trip, but you couldn't beat a good mapping app as a useful travel tool. *Aha*. If I walked along the sealed road to the nearest level crossing, I'd be able to approach the station via an unsealed roadway. This time I got closer to the station building. There was another locked gate, though it was only 25 metres or so from the building, so I could make out its details. It was disappointing not to get closer. I'd known the building wasn't open to the public that day, but I'd assumed I could walk right up to the exterior to photograph it. I took a photo from the gate anyway, then started on the long walk back to the pub.

A car passed me, then parked near the gate, and a woman got out. I turned around, walked back and asked if she had a key, as I thought she might be a maintenance worker. She wasn't. She was Melissa, a local who had heard about this historic building, and at that very hour had decided to drive down and take a photo. She had a camera in her hand, and was also disappointed the station wasn't accessible.

I started walking down the long unsealed road again. Melissa was busy trying to take her own shot from the gate, and it felt presumptuous to ask her for a lift back to town. Her mother had no doubt sensibly warned her about offering lifts to strange men in Akubras who drooled over vintage railway infrastructure.

This time a small truck came along. I waved the driver down, and discovered he was a Queensland Rail worker.

'Any chance of having a look at the old station building?' I asked.

'No worries,' he said, and unlocked the place to let both me and Melissa in for a few minutes. He was there to do some work anyway, and we promised to be quick.

It was a lovely building, beautifully maintained. We couldn't enter, but could walk along the platform and through the ticketing area. It had broad eaves and a timber plank platform, and felt like a small colonial house, which in some ways it had been. I could happily live there as a modern-day Catweazle.

It was always stimulating to see the earliest examples of an architectural form. When architects had designed the first railway station, they were creating something new and had to consider all sorts of factors, from practicality to comfort. From nation to nation the resulting designs differed, due to climatic considerations. Grandchester Station had originally been built with 2.5-metre-wide verandahs on three sides, resembling a house of that era with plentiful space to sit in the shade on a hot day. This little station looked perfect for its purpose, and all three of us expressed regret that it was no longer used by passengers. The twice-weekly *Westlander* train to Charleville passed through here, but it didn't stop.

As we walked out of the gate, Melissa asked me where I was from.

'Melbourne,' I said.

'Ah. I was wondering about your accent.'

This was getting annoying. People in Queensland kept mentioning my 'accent', and asking if I was British. I assumed this was because I pronounced most of my consonants. I'd had some trouble understanding the nasal drawl of the bus driver to Grandchester, and he me. All I could think of in response to this was: 'When I visit Britain, no-one thinks I'm British.'

Lunch was at the Grandchester Hotel, one of Queensland's endless supply of atmospheric old pubs. I ordered the flathead with chips and salad, and a beer, then got talking with my baseball-cap-wearing neighbour at the bar.

'What kind of farming do people do around here?' I asked. 'Cattle?'

'A bit,' he said. 'But a lot of people around here are into rodeo. Horses and bulls.'

Two years before I'd seen a man riding a bullock at the Stockman's Hall of Fame in Longreach. He'd played a guitar while doing so. That had been entertaining, but I hadn't expected to find that sort of activity here, where it was so much greener and so much less outback.

'The dairy farming around here is mostly finished,' he continued. 'Can't make money from their quotas.'

Was it too far for commuters?

'Not really,' he said. 'Some people go back and forth, use this area as a break from the city.'

I said they were lucky to still have a good pub in town, given there were hardly any other businesses.

'Yeah, it's great,' he said, brightening. 'This is a good community: everyone knows each other, people barter back and forth.'

I asked about the local sawmill, which I'd heard was still steam-powered. He nodded, and mentioned a late owner who'd once sawn his thumb off.

'Hazards of the job,' I suggested.

'Yep,' he said, and held up a finger that was missing a joint.

I had thought about visiting the sawmill, but I was horribly behind on my notes and needed time in the city to catch up. I was also tolerably full of beer, and a return bus was due in a few minutes.

I headed back to Brisbane, to the sound of another freight train passing the ghost station of Grandchester.

####

The next day I visited the MacArthur Museum, an overlooked fragment of Brisbane history, but one that dovetailed with what I'd learned at Mount Surprise. Its remote railways had been made busy by the movements of troops and materiel in World War II, and on the eighth floor of this 1934 office building was the wartime headquarters of General Douglas MacArthur.

The foyer of the museum was decorated with a portrait of the US general, who was Supreme Commander for the Allied Forces in the Southwest Pacific. Next to this was a large photograph of MacArthur inspecting Australian troops, superimposed on a glass wall. It was an excellent shot, capturing both MacArthur's trademark sunglasses and swagger, and the small T-shaped badges on the sleeves of soldiers who'd served at Tobruk. Accompanying MacArthur's biography was a photograph of him from his graduation ceremony at West Point military academy in 1903. This caused me to do a double-take. It was so clearly from an earlier era than World War II, and my mental image of the general was so tied up with that conflict, that it seemed at first glance that he was displaced in time. He had graduated well before the key tools of twentieth-century warfare – planes, tanks, aircraft carriers – were established. I was delighted to see there was a railway element in MacArthur's famous 1942 escape from the Philippines, besieged by Japanese forces. After he had been flown to Alice Springs, he'd caught the *Ghan* train to Adelaide. Pausing at the small town of Terowie in South Australia, he'd given a speech in which he first made his famous promise, 'I shall return.' He did return, in October 1944. To the Philippines, that is. As far as I could judge, he never got back to Terowie.

The remainder of the museum focused on Brisbane's role in the war. I'd had no idea of the scope of wartime intrusion into everyday life, and the details were fascinating. When MacArthur had relocated his headquarters from Melbourne to Brisbane, he was entering a city of a mere 350,000 people. It quickly became a garrison town with 100,000 American troops stationed in the area. This presence was largely welcomed. It's difficult now to understand the fear of invasion that swept Australia, but it was a reasonable reaction at the time. Singapore had fallen to Japan in early 1942, and the Japanese then launched bombing raids on Darwin and locations in Western Australia and Queensland, with Townsville bombed in July of that year. The Townsville attacks caused little damage, but they focused minds in Brisbane. The city council erected bomb shelters, and residents turned out to cheer arriving American soldiers and sailors. 'The significance of these American emissaries of goodwill is not lost on the Bananalanders,' intoned the soundtrack to a historical newsreel playing on the museum's big screen. The level of wartime control over everyday lives was remarkable. Everyone in Brisbane was issued with identity cards, travel became restricted, and censorship was enforced. Pubs had their hours cut back, and groceries were rationed. A display about children's experiences of the war was disturbing. A kit had been issued to kids, containing a wooden clothes peg to bite on when bombs exploded nearby. Another sign explained that 'Children are called on to make sacrifices, going without toys, new clothes, Vegemite ...' Crikey, what privations.

There were positive aspects to this hothouse atmosphere. Women took on work previously denied to them, for example, and a special order allowed entertainments to be staged on Sundays for the first time. 'Jitterbugging attracted a lot of disapproval,' read a caption. There was also an intriguing photo of the Gumleaf Band from Cherbourg, an Aboriginal group continuing an ancient tradition by playing gum leaves held between their lips as musical entertainment.

I'd never heard of the 'Battle of Brisbane' in November 1942, in which a riot erupted between Australian troops and American military police. One Australian was shot dead, eight wounded, and many more injured. Anxious to limit the impact of the news, the *Courier-Mail* newspaper published a cartoon celebrating Thanksgiving the next day.

I was fascinated by the feverish atmosphere of wartime Brisbane. Beyond the hustle there must have been a great sense of solidarity and purpose. With troops in town from Asia and Europe as well as North America, it had made the city more cosmopolitan. It was a foretaste of the influx of migrants lying just ahead in the postwar era, though I learned later that not everyone was treated equally in this brave new world. An earlier brawl in March 1942 had involved white American troops attacking their black comrades-in-arms, incensed by the relative freedom that African-Americans had to socialise in unsegregated Brisbane. As a result, black American troops were moved by their superiors to the south side of the Brisbane River, and re-crossed it at their peril.

The finale of the museum's exhibits was MacArthur's original office, fitted out with replicas of its furniture. It was solid, sensible 1940s gear: a desk with pen holders and wooden in-trays, beneath a portrait of George Washington.

'It's said he had that there because President Roosevelt was a Democrat,' said the museum's executive officer John Wright, who was stationed in the room. 'And we had this desk made to order. We know it's a precise replica because it's modelled on the original in the MacArthur Memorial in Norfolk, Virginia.'

And with that Wright pointed out the ink stains and cigar burn on the surface of the desk, which had been reproduced exactly.

I liked this office. It felt uncluttered, organised, a good place to sit and think. The decisions that were made here had involved matters of life and death.

Why had MacArthur felt it necessary to base himself in Brisbane, I asked. Was it because it was closer to the war?

'MacArthur had a big ego and he liked to be in control,' said Wright. 'The further south he went, the more he had to listen to politicians. So he liked it here in Brisbane.'

I wondered if this folk memory of MacArthur as virtual dictator of Brisbane partly explained later enthusiasm for the premiership of Johannes 'Joh' Bjelke-Petersen. Joh had run Queensland as a virtual police state, aided by gerrymandering and corruption. He had liked being in control too.

####

I spent my last afternoon in Brisbane on the river, catching a CityCat ferry from South Bank to Regatta Terminal at Toowong. As it headed upriver, a forest of glass and steel commercial buildings lay on my right, and low, boxy cultural centres on my left. Brisbane wasn't a subtle city, its contending characteristics laid out with geographical precision.

Three storeys high, with river views and iron lace on its balconies, the Regatta Hotel was about to prove an apt place to end the Queensland portion of my journey. On an interior wall were black-and-white photos of key points in the hotel's history, from its establishment in 1874 (with the current grand edifice dating from 1886). A constant thread was the impact of floods.

The hotel had been invaded by the rising Brisbane River in 1887, 1890, 1893, 1974 and 2011. As I knew from the Gulf Savannah country, that was another thing Queensland did well: floods. I was leaving them behind too.

Brisbane to Sydney
XPT

I walked through the dark, empty, humid streets of Brisbane at 3.45 am on 16 March, southward-bound toward climates where autumn would have more meaning. Despite the earliness of the hour, or perhaps because of it, I was alert with anticipation. I'd often felt this way upon heading to a railway station for an early train. Narrelle and I used to have weekend getaways in Alexandria in the two years we'd lived in Egypt teaching English, back in the 1990s. Those trains had left early too, and the busy, exotic atmosphere of Cairo's main station in the early morning couldn't be beaten. Brisbane wasn't as glamorous as Cairo, yet that keenness existed. I was about catch the XPT train operated by NSW TrainLink all the way to Sydney, a fourteen-hour daytime trip that started in the dark.

Only one daily train ran each way between the two cities. During New South Wales' daylight-saving months the sleeper train arrived in Brisbane at 4 am, then turned around and left for Sydney at 4.55 am. Why this was so was a mystery. The key factor in making a successful sleeper train is to time it to arrive when the terminus city has awoken for the day, so passengers can get a reasonable sleep then continue their journey by local public transport. Arrival at 4 am meant passengers were stranded in central Brisbane until its first trains and buses ran. I'd heard a rumour the Queensland railway authorities had forbidden the New South Wales train from arriving later in morning, citing congestion on the city's railways in peak hour. Another source suggested that the New South Wales government didn't care about running a convenient train service for Queenslanders. Whatever the answer, stubborn old state rivalries were probably at the heart of it. For a reminder of what happened when they got in the way, I had only to look down at the track laid next to Platform 2: it was dual gauge, with standard-gauge rails outside a narrow-gauge inset.

Where Queensland trains ran on narrow-gauge rails 1,067 millimetres apart, New South Wales trains operated on standard-gauge track with a width of 1,435 millimetres. To add to the confusion, Victoria's trains mostly ran on a broad gauge of 1,600 millimetres. Western Australia's suburban trains and my final train to Bunbury would be on the same narrow-gauge track as Queensland's. It was the sort of madness only rival colonies could summon up. This was a problem that had arisen in the early days of railway building in Australia. The standard gauge had been written into law in the UK in 1846, after its own 'rail gauge war' in which the famed engineer Isambard Brunel had once favoured an enormously broad gauge of 2,140 millimetres (7' ½"). Unfortunately in practice the Australian colonies often ignored London's guidelines in favour of economy, or the hobbyhorses of particular engineers.

In Queensland, there was a bit of both. Debate over the correct gauge for its railways had been heated in the years immediately after the colony's separation from New South Wales in 1859. That argument had been won by Abram Fitzgibbon, a newly arrived engineer with railway-building experience and a penchant for spotted bow ties. Fitzgibbon had pushed for a 3' 6" (1,067-millimetre) gauge as it would be cheaper and quicker to build than the standard-gauge lines already under construction in New South Wales, the smaller gauge catering for narrower cuttings and tighter curves. He also claimed it would be safer, partly because it would be slower due to the usual ratio between wheel diameter and gauge; presumably this was an age when the need for speed was not paramount. Fitzgibbon had a meteoric rise, becoming chief railway engineer and then Queensland's first railway commissioner by the time he was thirty years old. What was his legacy, however? At the time, he must have seemed a dynamic young man in a hurry (though not aboard his relatively slow trains). With a focus on connecting Queensland's inland to its ports, there wasn't much attention on the problems that would be caused when the colonies' rail networks started to intersect. When that finally happened in the 1880s, it caused headaches that recur to this day.

When the XPT pulled in on time at 4 am, there weren't many of us waiting for it, and some of my fellow passengers looked the worse for wear, as if they'd been sleeping rough just before buying a ticket. But goodwill was present on the fluoro-lit platform. A woman who'd just disembarked was looking for change for a trolley, so a waiting passenger gave her the dollar coin she needed and told her to keep it.

As we waited for the train to be cleaned, I found my carriage and peered through the window at my seat. It would be facing forward on the way to Sydney. Excellent.

Everything about the XPT seemed subtly dated. The streamlined steel exterior of the carriages, the sky-blue exterior, the power car with its distinctively angled nose. Designed in the 1980s, the train had been modelled on the InterCity 125, a British train which was the backbone of long-distance services there in the 1970s.

We boarded, and at 4.55 am precisely were on our way to Sydney. Roma Street Station slid away in that blissful moment of not moving / moving that signals the start of a long train journey, and we started our long haul south. Brisbane appeared depopulated as we passed through it, as if an apocalyptic event had removed the people without harming the structures. South Brisbane Station was pristine but completely empty as we passed, its automated advertisements scrolling up and down robotically within their frames.

I had a sleeper compartment all to myself. Confusingly, the XPT had two fare classes but three seating types. Economy was economy, but the first-class seats divided into two types: the usual two-across seats with more leg room than economy, and those situated within the sleeper compartments, known as Daysitters during the day. It's always worth ringing in advance and asking for a Daysitter seat. There are three of these per compartment and they're wider than those in the regular first-class section. There's plenty of leg room and if, like me on this occasion, you score a window seat, there's a broad ledge to lean on. At night there were only two passengers in each compartment, each with a berth. I'd be trying out that configuration on my Melbourne train the following week. Between each compartment was a small bathroom, within which the toilet pan and a steel sink folded out from cavities within the wall. There was a shower head too, though that could only be used on the night trains.

On our way out of Brisbane we passed stations for places I'd never heard of: Moorooka, Rocklea, Salisbury. The moon hung in the sky as a thin crescent, a reminder of the earliness of the hour.

An attendant came to check my ticket, and I commented on the generous space of my compartment.

'I remember way back when these were new,' he said. 'The new trains should be good, too.' The XPT, almost forty years old, was slated to be replaced by a new design in the near future. I wondered if they'd have sleeper compartments.

'I think they'll go for the open-plan seating,' he said, which sounded like something along the lines of the *Spirit of Queensland*'s RailBeds or, worse, sit-up seating all the way. A pity. I was very comfortable here in my little room in motion. It would not be the same in an open space. Sadly the trend in Australia was toward the removal of sleeping accommodation on trains, seen as an archaic leftover from the era before mass air travel: sleeper carriages had been removed from the *Overland* train between Melbourne and Adelaide in 2007, and from Queensland's *Inlander* and *Westlander* trains in 2014. Now it looked as though the train services from

Brisbane to Sydney through to Melbourne might follow suit. Frustratingly, this was the opposite of what was occurring in Europe, where long-distance sleeper services were undergoing a renaissance due to concerns over climate change and aviation emissions. There was no reason why Australia couldn't successfully run modern high-speed sleeper trains, but that possibility seemed beyond the capability of governments to envision or fund.

After the attendant left, I idly contemplated the carpeting and seat moquette, which was blue, inset with splotches of three other colours. It looked like the carpet of a cinema chain.

Half an hour into the trip, the eastern horizon was lit with an orange glow, silhouetting palm trees and eucalypts. Then we were suddenly surrounded by trees as we left the city behind. Then something wonderful happened. As it became light, the farming country we entered was wreathed in mist as the sunlight warmed up the humid air. For a while the world outside was a semi-concealed place where trees and cattle could be only vaguely glimpsed, soft around the edges. And at one point I saw a hot-air balloon in the distance, rising against the golden dawn.

At 6.15 am I awoke from a short nap. I'd set the alarm on my phone because I wanted to be awake when we crossed the border from Queensland to New South Wales. What I hadn't reckoned on was the Border Ranges National Park, and I was surprised and delighted to see the world had changed while I dozed. Its mountains had multiple hilly ridges that made it seem as if they'd been folded by a giant. The sun lit the grass on their slopes, accentuating their crumpled curves. I was enchanted by this countryside as it was struck by the soft early light. It was magical, a pastoral idyll spread across rugged hills, with an occasional farmhouse providing contrast. It was a mixture of wild and tamed, of big and small, the illumination magnifying its emotional impact. Whatever hidden, possibly sadistic motives had led to our 4.55 am departure, it had also delivered the most stunning views I'd seen on this trip. I'd never heard of Border Ranges National Park before, but assumed it was part of the same ancient volcanic caldera that stretched through to Queensland's Lamington National Park, which I'd visited years before. It was now part of the Gondwana Rainforests of Australia World Heritage Area, the world's most extensive area of subtropical rainforest.

The scope of my rail trek, covering thousands of kilometres in just six weeks, was having an impact on my perception of nature. As I kept moving, I was repeatedly presented with new vistas. I'd moved from savannah to tropical to subtropical environments, and was being reminded by degrees that I was traversing a continent. Glancing down, I noticed the time on my phone didn't match that on my watch, as we'd changed to a new time zone: Australian Eastern Daylight Time. There'd be three more of these changes before I reached Perth, one of them to a contrived 'train time' aboard the *Indian Pacific*.

We went through several tunnels as we progressed. The most impressive were part of the Cougal Spiral, which contained three tunnels stretching 1,600 metres in length. At this point the mountains were so steep it had been necessary to lay the rails in a long loop that curved around above itself, to allow trains to rise 30 metres higher in order to crest the slopes before descending. The daunting topography helped explain why this North Coast line had been built so belatedly. When it had opened in 1930, it replaced the earlier inland line which connected the two states at a break-of-gauge station at Wallangarra, further to the west. Passengers had been forced to change there, between Queensland's narrow-gauge trains and New South Wales' standard-gauge ones. It was lucky that the North Coast line had been completed at all, given the political and economic headwinds it had endured in the early twentieth century. The outbreak of World War I in 1914 had cut off the loans from the London money market which were financing the line's construction, throwing large numbers of construction workers off the job. Then, after it had resumed inching northward from Maitland to the Queensland border in the 1920s, the Great Depression had commenced in 1929, reducing government revenues as the economy contracted.

Luckily, the railway was almost complete by the advent of that decade of worldwide economic misery. On 26 September 1930 a special train inaugurated the line, leaving Sydney in order to progress along the final section from Kyogle to the border with Queensland (from where it ran onwards to Brisbane). That was the section I was traversing now, though headed the other way.

As the XPT headed south into New South Wales, I spotted a sign on the side of a tiny station, Glenapp, which we breezed past without pause. It read, 'Thanks for the memories.' I later discovered that this outpost, actually just a remnant signal box, was being maintained by Rob and Dennis Sibson, brothers who had grown up in the area when their dad was a water pumper for steam trains. The original station building had been moved to the nearby town of Rathdowney to serve as a visitor centre, but the brothers had renovated the signal box and kept the surrounding grass cut and weeded. At Christmas they hung out fairy lights. Clearly I wasn't the only one with an emotional connection to the railways.

Further south at Wiangaree, the mist returned and became so heavy that the sun appeared only as a pale white disc. Suddenly the effect was less magical, and more capricious and inimical, as if it were deliberately hiding the landscape.

Outside Kyogle, a golf course had a glinting sheen of dew that made it appear as if the grass had been woven. Then we entered cattle country, filled not with exotic Brahman cows but the mundane beasts I was used to. The paddocks here looked like parks, uniformly grassed with the odd remnant tree.

With no-one else in my compartment, and no-one expected, I'd had a nap by pushing all the armrests up and stretching out along the seats. There were still over eleven hours to go to Sydney, so I pulled off my boots.

Casino was the first sizeable town we stopped at in New South Wales. For the first time since leaving Brisbane there were signs of life: people boarding, having caught buses from towns to the east, such as Byron Bay and Lismore.

Food – reheated – was available from a cafe a few carriages along. It was simple fare, but cheap. I had a scrambled egg wrap, which was fine, but I was unimpressed with the coffee: a cup of hot water with a coffee bag. That was $3.50 for a cup of hot water, and to do the rest myself. That seemed like taking the piss. Oh, for the glory days of dining cars serving cups of tea in crockery! It was a pity the XPT trains had no such dedicated area at which to eat. In the absence of tables it would be impossible to strike up conversations with strangers, as I had aboard the *Spirit of Queensland*. This was a step down from the catering experience of the 1920s, when the New South Wales railways had operated their first dining cars. The very first such carriage, delivered in 1926, was used on the train to Broken Hill. The train initially ran overnight from Parkes to the remote outback mining town to improve passenger comfort in summer, and its twenty-five-hour travel time meant an onboard dining option was essential. More trains were fitted with dining and buffet cars in the following decades, which helped speed up timetables through the elimination of meal stops at stations. This transition led to the slow death of refreshment rooms at stations, which became unprofitable from the 1950s.

On the way back from the cafe I tried out one of the regular first-class seats. As far as I could judge, it wasn't any wider than an economy seat. Given that a new train was in the works, I drew up a basic wish list of what I'd like to see on it:

- sleeper berths, including singles
- power points
- wi-fi
- food prepared onboard; in fact, a dining car would be nice
- somewhere to chat to fellow passengers, perhaps casual seating near the café
- wider first-class seats.

Australia's state-run railways were bad at creating premium seats that people would want to pay a premium for. In Victoria, the state rail company V/Line's first-class seats on its longer routes were similarly unimpressive. Making long-distance trains popular again in part required a product that would appeal to those happy to pay more for comfort. I was dubious that open-plan sleeper carriages would achieve that. One of the most appealing aspects of rail travel compared to air travel was the relative freedom of movement and wider seating in the former. Rail companies should double down on that advantage, I thought.

Grafton at 10 am had the rough-edged look of a busy, practical service town, as we passed its shopping streets and its houses with their corrugated roofs. We crossed the Clarence River via the lower deck of the bascule bridge which was once raised for shipping. It had been opened in 1932. Before the completion of the bridge, rail passengers had had to be ferried across the river; the special train that had opened the North Coast line in 1930 had crossed aboard the train ferry *Swallow*. The bridge's upper deck carried cars, a curious feature of which was the sudden bend at each end as vehicles left the bridge, requiring a scary and surprising manoeuvre for out-of-town drivers. Presumably the bends were necessary for the road to avoid the railway line, but local legend had it that a publican had insisted the road be diverted in order to take drivers past his establishment. In any case, the bridge was soon to have a partner – I could see construction taking place on the river to the east of a new bridge scheduled to open the following year.

A long announcement after Grafton detailed the consequences of lingering too long on station platforms for a cigarette, then went on to announce the train company's alcohol service policy, which was 'two items per passenger per hour'. One of the dispiriting things about riding on government-run trains was that I sometimes felt I was back at boarding school, with housemasters monitoring one's behaviour. But for the main part the staff of the New South Wales train were less fond of issuing directions than their Queensland counterparts. Possibly having passengers scattered through separate compartments made them feel less need for crowd control.

South of Grafton was a world of trees, as we passed through wooded country interrupted only by the odd paddock. I was enjoying the splendid isolation of my compartment, my solitude enhancing the observational aspect of train travel. I spotted lusher foliage as we neared Coffs Harbour, including banana plants growing beside the line. Finally I was back near the coast – like stout Cortez, I could glimpse the Pacific – and Coffs Harbour Station was parallel to the beach. Somewhere near here was the Big Banana, one of the earliest of Australia's Big Things. Constructed in 1964, it was the same age as me. While we had mobile reception I searched for information on Coffs' banana industry. Its farmers had faced tough times recently, with unusually dry conditions in recent years affecting production. The big picture was grim too – three decades ago there were more than a thousand banana growers in the area. Now there were fewer than thirty. The reason for this decline lay behind me on my journey, in the Atherton Tablelands I'd passed through west of Cairns. When tobacco was finally phased out in that region in the early 2000s, bananas and other crops expanded to fill the gap. With its superior climate for banana growing, tropical Queensland had inevitably eclipsed Coffs. It wasn't all bad news though – in a deft shift, Coffs now produced 80% of Australia's blueberries.

After Coffs, our station stops increased dramatically. At the start of the journey we'd only been stopping every hour or two. Now our halts were more frequent, sometimes just a quarter of an hour apart (from Coffs to Sawtell was eleven minutes). We were still nine hours from Sydney, but it felt as if the XPT had transformed into a regular country train rather than a long-distance one.

The bush was thick near the coast, comprised of gum trees with white trunks above tree ferns on the forest floor. We crossed broad rivers more frequently now, first the Bellinger past Repton, then the Kalang before Urunga. South of Urunga I was surprised by the sudden glimpse of a sandy white beach at a river mouth, only 200 metres or so from the train – the Dalhousie Creek emptying into the Pacific at Hungry Head (for whose name no-one had a clear explanation). The trees had been so thick with foliage and tangled branches, I'd had no idea we were close to the water again. An indication we were nearing the New South Wales heartlands was the prosperous appearance of the railway stations. Rather than basic platforms and shelters, these were solid civic buildings, often painted brick-red and well maintained. The stations at Nambucca Heads and Macksville both contained potted plants and waving staff.

It struck me that my rail journey down the east coast presented an idyllic view of the fecundity of Australian nature, mostly traversing the greener, wetter areas east of the Great Dividing Range. Nowhere on this particular route was I likely to glimpse the effects of prolonged drought or desert conditions, though no place was safe from bushfire.

At Kempsey I could see two solid religious buildings to my right, the larger of which was the Macleay Valley Parish Catholic Church. I was reminded of growing up near Donnybrook in Western Australia, in an era when there was still a lingering suspicion between Catholics and Protestants. One of my great-grandfathers on my father's side had once marched regularly in parades of Orangemen, in his small town in Western Australia. It would take mass postwar migration to put that sectarian rivalry to bed, when all Anglo-Celtic Australians suddenly became part of a bigger, more complex picture.

On the other side of the line was a scattering of the smaller, older houses you usually saw near train stations in country towns, with their corrugated iron roofs and front verandahs. I liked the idea of living so near a station that you could walk there. The noise of train movements wouldn't bother me, no doubt taking on a soothing background hum. I knew as much from living in an apartment in the Melbourne CBD, above a busy tram line; passing revellers spilling out of late-night bars were far more of a nuisance than the occasional soft 'ding' of a tram's bell. I occasionally toyed with the idea of moving back to a country town, but it would have to be one with a train to the city. This thought had already occurred to thousands of commuters, however, and as a result property prices in towns within an hour or so of Melbourne had headed sharply upward.

As we travelled I dipped into *Affection*, whose plot had been slow to build. With the arrival of a disease expert from Brisbane, things were heating up. A shipload of passengers had been held in quarantine on Magnetic Island, one of them suspected of having contracted the plague. Among them was a local politician involved with the coming of the railways, so there was tension in the air. Looking up from the text, I saw random animals near the line south of Kempsey. A lone chicken walked slowly across a grassy field, lifting its legs high to clear the blades. A cow on a side road waited for the train to cross.

After Wauchope, near Port Macquarie, we swung further inland, well away from the coast. A lonely house had the sort of half-organised, half-messy garden I remember from my Nanna's old house in Western Australia. Two bushes framed the front gate, sculpted into spheres. A tree with bright purple flowers stood near them, half its blooms dropped to the ground.

At Taree we halted at the station for an unusually long time. The train's air conditioning was becoming oppressively cold, so I leant out of an open door to gain some warmth from the afternoon sun. Taree Station was impressive, a statement of civic pride in brick. It had opened in 1913, in the early days of the very gradual construction of the North Coast line to Brisbane, and had been the terminus for two years before it inched on to Wauchope.

Eventually we started moving again. I overheard a staff member saying some luggage had been incorrectly offloaded earlier at Wauchope, and had had to be retrieved via taxi before the train could continue.

Standing in the corridor, I mentioned the freezing air conditioning to a passing staff member. A voice behind me said, 'It's arctic on these trains, mate, you have to rug up.'

This was Jacob, the occupant of the compartment next to mine. He was wearing a Los Angeles Lakers hoodie above two or three other layers. I had a feeling he'd been on this train before.

'Yeah, I'm going down to visit my dad,' he said, 'But trains aren't what they should be in Australia. The road transport companies have it all sewn up.'

Jacob lived east of Casino, and mourned the defunct Murwillumbah rail line, which had once snaked up from Casino via Byron Bay. I'd seen remnants of a branch line in that area on a previous trip when I'd passed through Bangalow and stopped to look at its old station. That would have been a scenic route.

Jacob was a support officer for Aboriginal and Torres Strait Islander students at a university campus.

'It's casual work; depends on how much the students need me. I like it, but it's unpredictable – not sure if I have regular work yet this semester.'

As a freelancer, I sympathised, but said it sounded like he was doing good work. He agreed. As he ducked into his compartment, I pondered the trade-off between a full-time nine-to-five job and the sort of unpredictable but rewarding roles people sometimes chose for themselves. It had been a very long time since I'd worked in someone else's office, and I couldn't imagine returning to its regimentation and petty internal politics. And there was another key bonus to working for myself – I couldn't be sacked. Freelance work could decline in difficult times, but it never completely disappeared and there was always time to turn the ship around.

Passing east of Barrington Tops National Park, the landscape was becoming impressively mountainous again, the train threading its way between undulating slopes rising quickly on each side as we slid through cuttings and tunnels. It was still farming country, I could see, but the cattle did a bit of climbing.

After we passed through Gloucester, I followed Jacob's lead and changed into every item of warm clothing I had available: two shirts and a fleece jacket above cargo pants. I also put my boots back on. It helped, but I was still cold. Thank god I hadn't left the fleece behind in Melbourne, as I'd been tempted to do to keep the packing light. I'd kept it in the backpack for just this sort of aircon emergency.

Something I noticed on the XPT which I hadn't aboard the *Spirit of Queensland* was plentiful creaking sounds as we progressed, as if we were travelling aboard a ship. I liked the effect, the proof of constant motion toward our goal.

Past Maitland I spotted a cemetery, an old one judging from the many crosses leaning at an angle. There were horses in the area too, some of the first I'd seen on this journey, and dressage courses.

At 6 pm we pulled into Broadmeadow, a suburb of Newcastle. Two hours to go. It felt like we were in Sydney's gravity well now, the great city pulling all routes inexorably toward its centre. As sunset approached, we were running down its commuter routes past Lake Macquarie and the other Central Coast waterways, down irresistibly to Central Station. As we tracked through Newcastle's suburbs and the sky turned dark again, I glanced at a parallel road and saw a pizza delivery vehicle drive past. I knew we were nearing the end.

Circular Quay to
Garden Island
Sirius

I was delighted to find myself aboard the *Sirius*, en route to Garden Island in Sydney Harbour. One of the city's older ferries, it looked like it belonged in a museum of small and jaunty vessels. It was also the namesake of HMS *Sirius*, the flagship of the First Fleet, which had landed at Sydney Cove on 26 January 1788, founding the first British settlement in Australia. As it happened, an occupant of that vessel was the object of my short voyage.

Circular Quay had been as busy as always, crowded with tourists on land and ferries on the water. Those iconic vessels seemed to jostle each other as they came and went from the wharves, their movements resembling a pod of whales at play.

Garden Island was only a short distance to the east, though it was not technically an island: it had long been connected to the southern shore of the harbour via landfill. But as it was the home of a major naval base, comprising HMAS Kuttabul and the Royal Australian Navy's Fleet Base East, it was inaccessible by land to the casual civilian. During daylight hours the northern tip of the peninsula could be visited via the ferry which ran from Circular Quay to Double Bay. A small slice of Garden Island there had been given over to the Royal Australian Navy

Heritage Centre, a naval museum that was free and open to the public.

As we rounded Bennelong Point, the golden-brown glass on the front of the Opera House glinted in the morning sunlight. There were kayaks to starboard, sailboats ahead and a seaplane turning lazily to the north. The ferry passed Fort Denison, looking itself like a stone boat, then pulled in at the compact Garden Island landing. I was the only passenger to disembark, and the ferry quickly churned away in the direction of Double Bay. It was very quiet as I stepped ashore. I was still technically standing on the mainland, but I felt a touch like Robinson Crusoe washing up on his desert island.

Suddenly, a security guard appeared and gave me what I could only call a briefing, explaining where I could go, where I couldn't, what was open and closed today, and when the last ferry left. He indicated the limits of the publicly accessible area to the west, beyond which a hefty grey naval supply ship was anchored, but conveyed the impression that he'd rather I didn't go that way at all. Then he disappeared. He had mastered that trick that Bertie Wooster had noticed of his valet, Jeeves, of moving from place to place so silently that it appeared he was part phantom. I almost wondered if I'd imagined him.

Near the ferry landing were scattered various memorials. One panel described the life of Bungaree, an Aboriginal man who'd been befriended by Matthew Flinders and had accompanied him on his circumnavigation of Australia, thus, of course, becoming the first Australian to circumnavigate the continent. Another plaque outlined the career of an Australian submarine which had served at Gallipoli. Nearby was the entire bow of the former HMAS *Parramatta*, erected as a monument. Facing out to sea, it seemed like a chunky art installation. A memorial to the HMAS *Canberra* caught my eye because my parents had once travelled aboard its civilian namesake the SS *Canberra* from Fremantle to Melbourne. I'd later visited the shipyards in Belfast where it had been built. The SS *Canberra* had had an interesting career, being converted from an ocean liner to a cruise ship, appearing in the James Bond movie *Diamonds Are Forever*, and being used as a troopship in the Falklands war. The HMAS *Canberra* had been critically damaged by the Japanese at the Battle of Savo Island in 1942. The names of the 84 lost crew were listed neatly in four columns on a plaque, and I was moved by the simple verse beneath them:

> They have no grave
> But the cruel sea
> No flowers lay at their head
> A rusting hulk is their tombstone
> Afast on the ocean bed

I walked around to the Heritage Centre. All I could hear were waves lapping at the shore, an aircraft passing high above and the hissing wake of the *Sirius* on its way back from Double Bay to Circular Quay. I was starting to enjoy the Robinson Crusoe vibe, though my Man Friday in the form of the security guard had vanished. I hadn't expected the museum to be deserted at 10 am on a Saturday, but naval history was presumably an acquired taste, and on this perfect sunny day most people had other activities in mind. I imagined, as with MacArthur's old offices in Brisbane, the place was busier with visitors during the week.

I entered the Heritage Centre with a cheery 'Good morning!' to the figure behind the front desk. But it was Man Friday, and I suspected he was unimpressed with my lack of recognition. I feared I hadn't made a friend there.

Dutifully I nosed around the museum, though what I'd come to see was in the garden above it. The displays were intelligent and well organised, imparting snippets of naval history. I learned that Britain's Royal Navy had operated an Australia Squadron until 1913, and that in 1922 the Washington Naval Treaty had limited the size of navies worldwide. It had been assumed, reasonably, that the competitive build-up of armed forces before

World War I had helped make the conflict inevitable, hence the impetus for disarmament. Objects were on display behind glass cases: a tompion decorated with the red lion of Tasmania, once used as a stopper to protect the guns of HMAS *Hobart*; a hat captured from an Imperial Chinese Navy officer in 1900, with a broad conical shape and decorated with gold trim; a crushed engine cylinder from a kamikaze plane which had dive-bombed HMAS *Australia* in 1945.

By trial and error, I worked out how to take the lift up to the garden, on a rocky ledge level with the museum's roof. It was even quieter there, with only birdsong breaking the silence. Sydney's greenery didn't have the fully tropical look of Queensland's, but it seemed more tropical than Melbourne's – a hint of the equatorial in its dark green shades and bright flowers. I was seeking a set of carved initials, which I assumed would be on a tree. They were actually inscribed in big bold letters on a rocky outcrop, right at the top of the garden. They had been placed there one day in 1788 by three crew members of the original *Sirius*. The three sets of initials read, 'W.B. 1788', 'I.R. 1788' and 'F.M. 1788'. I was interested in 'FM', belonging to Frederick Meredith. He was Narrelle's great-great-great-great-great-grandfather through her mother's side of the family, which made us in-laws of a sort. It was the only set of initials where there was consensus as to the person's identity, as the First Fleet's crew had contained multiple matches for the others. I sat on a nearby bench and looked out at the harbour. It was stirring to be in the same spot those men had sat that day in 1788, perhaps wondering if the new settlement they'd help found would work out. It was touch and go in those early days. Though the settlers had established a garden here, giving Garden Island its name, their attempts to grow fresh vegetables were unsuccessful. In late 1788 the *Sirius* left to fetch emergency food supplies from the Cape of Good Hope, and didn't return until seven months later.

I could see why the three men had come up here. It was a beautiful spot with a view of the harbour, presumably twinkling with reflected sunlight that day, as it was today. It wasn't difficult to imagine the trio scrambling up the steep slope, then smoking a pipe or drinking a tot of rum (my imagination was reaching a bit) while wondering what would become of it all. I texted Narrelle a photo of the initials. She hadn't taken that close an interest in the family history, but was pleased to see them. In return texts she said that knowledge gave her a stronger feeling of connection with Australia's early days. Not that British settlement hadn't been a disaster for the Indigenous population – clearly it had – but the knowledge of her roots instilled extra confidence, she felt, to stand up for reconciliation and against any intolerance advocated by more recent arrivals.

A steep flight of steps took me down to the ferry landing. As far as I could tell, I was still the only visitor. I'd been warned the ferries might not stop if no-one was visible, so I stepped onto the landing. It was a floating structure and regularly disturbed by the wake of passing vessels. By gripping the railing I could imagine myself at the bridge of a naval ship in motion, preparing to repel boarders.

'There's a submarine over there,' said a voice directly behind me, making me jump. It was Man Friday, again manifesting noiselessly. I wondered if he'd started out in naval black ops. He was much friendlier now that I was leaving, giving me tips about my onward journey and warning me off the expensive private ferry that pulled in just before mine was due. I mentioned I was going to head to Double Bay rather than back to Circular Quay, and catch a bus from there.

'Double Bay, double pay,' he said.

'Because you need double the pay to afford to live there?'

'No, because everything costs double.'

Which amounted to the same thing.

As the sleek modern ferry *Saint Mary MacKillop* paused at the landing, I left Friday behind to startle the four new visitors who'd just stepped ashore.

####

On the walk from Double Bay's wharf to the main road, I saw what he meant. It was a pleasant residential suburb that appeared wealthy in that over-tidied way of well-to-do areas. A shop on my left bore a large sign reading, 'We hear you ... retirement postponed!' I looked inside and saw a gleaming interior filled with old-fashioned toys and smart children's clothing, the shop assistant clad in pristine white. I assumed the sign meant the locals had strong-armed the owners into continuing to supply their hobby horse and teddy bear needs. I clearly wasn't the only person finding it difficult to move on from a vocation.

I needed a new notebook. I'd been given a few of the smaller Moleskine notebooks at travel events in the past, and on this trip had found they were the perfect size and sturdiness for this kind of travel, where I needed to make notes at a moment's notice. To my horror, I'd become one of those posers who wrote things in Moleskines as if they were Hemingway. At least I was actually writing about travel in mine, rather than jotting down shopping lists. It occurred to me that Double Bay would be the ideal place to procure a pretentious notebook, so I dropped into a local newsagency and bought a knock-off version for ten dollars less than the usual Moleskine price. I even got a further three-dollar reduction because the strip of elastic around the notebook had stretched with age. One didn't always pay double in Double Bay.

The number 325 bus wound its way slowly up the hilly road toward Watsons Bay, which sat at the top of a peninsula separating harbour from ocean. Above the road towered the houses of the rich – some old-style brick edifices, others bristling with glass, but all built as high as possible to catch water views. Aside from their well-watered gardens, they had the aspect of luxurious fortresses. As we laboured uphill, a group of four women came aboard, sympathetically attired in shades of orange, red and pink. I had a feeling they were using the bus as I was, for an inexpensive self-guided tour.

From a stop in Vaucluse I walked downhill to Parsley Bay Reserve. There was something I wanted to look for there, connected with the history of exploration, that had been on my mind since that near miss in visiting Burke and Wills' final camp near Normanton. I wasn't sure yet why it felt significant, but it did. At the bottom of the street I stepped into the reserve – a long, flat, grassy park between two rocky slopes. On this Saturday it was busy with families and groups of friends enjoying the sunshine. In the centre of the lawn was a couple throwing a frisbee, next to a small group which was inflating a pink raft with a flamingo-shaped head. Beyond them, running straight as a ruler above the waterline, was a cable suspension bridge which provided pedestrian access across the bay. It was an elegant addition to the natural setting – like the Sydney Harbour Bridge and the Opera House, the best architecture on the harbour enhanced rather than diminished the efforts of Dame Nature.

I ordered a sandwich from the Parsley Bay Kiosk (hung with a hand-painted sign stating 'A little piece of paradise') and got talking to the man at the front counter. He was a Singaporean on a working holiday visa.

'I love Melbourne!' he said when he heard where I was from. 'Australia is very popular with Singaporeans. In Singapore you can feel boxed in – all the rules. Here it feels more easygoing.'

Leaving the kiosk, I looked around for evidence of an event described in a book I'd read the previous year titled *1912: The Year the World Discovered Antarctica*. It was a fascinating read, detailing several expeditions which had taken place around the same time. The least well-remembered was the Japanese expedition led by Lieutenant Nobu Shirase aboard the *Kainan Maru*. Forced back from the icy continent by bad weather on its first attempt, the expedition had sailed into Sydney Harbour and taken refuge for several months here in Parsley Bay, aided by a sympathetic professor from the University of Sydney, Edgeworth David. It was a remarkable story, as were all the Antarctic expeditions – but this one contained the added drama of a temporarily stranded group of Japanese explorers living in an Australia that was wary of Asians, and a heartening friendship that reached across cultures. When the expedition left for its second attempt in late 1911, Shirase made a gift of his samurai sword to Professor Edgeworth David. That sword now hangs in the Australian Museum.

Beyond a lonely picnic table behind the children's playground I found a commemorative plaque set on a low concrete plinth. It marked the Parsley Bay sojourn of Shirase's team, and had been placed here ninety years after the Japanese expedition had reached as far as eighty degrees south, though not to the pole itself. Explorers had now appeared twice in my travels: first Burke and Wills, then Shirase. They made me ponder. Was turning back before disaster better than achieving success followed by disaster, as had happened to Robert Scott? But my thoughts were having difficulty cohering as I panted my way back uphill to the bus stop. Sydney had some annoyingly steep hills, I thought, but that was the price of having such a beautiful harbour, an inrush of water that had drowned mountains.

On the bus to Watsons Bay there was a notice declaring that State Transit was hiring bus drivers. 'Do you want a $70k starting salary?' it asked. I fancifully pondered the idea. The money was appealing, but not the job. It would involve paying Sydney prices for accommodation, and dealing with the hills and humidity. And driving a bus, which I also couldn't do. The notion was something of a non-starter.

At Watsons Bay I wanted to have a quiet beer at Doyles pub, which had been a waterfront fixture since the 1880s. But the front bar was heaving with weekend crowds, so instead I walked through the interior to Watsons Boutique Hotel. It took some chutzpah to use the word 'boutique' in a name, considering its misuse by marketers over the years. It had a back bar that was much quieter, so I ordered a schooner of IPA. It was second nature to order schooners now. Why would anyone order a middy (Sydney's equivalent of Melbourne's 'pot') when there was so little difference in price? It struck me that the varying beer glass sizes had a parallel with the different rail gauges I was encountering – another reminder that Australia had started as six separate colonies. Though we'd been a nation for over a century, differences endured. People often took pride in those quirks, moreover, at least at a jokey 'potato cakes' (Victoria) versus 'potato scallops' (New South Wales) level.

Sydney, for some reason, also contained many men who looked exactly like the larrikins you saw going off to war in old newsreels. One walked past me now – sandy-haired, lean, in a blue singlet with eyes squinted as if against the sun. I almost expected him to start a game of two-up. This look had been an idealised vision of the typical Australian man for so long, disseminated through advertising and pop culture, that it had skewed representation of what Australia really looked like nowadays – diverse and multicultural to a level beyond even other nations built on immigration such as the USA. A few years earlier I'd met up with an American musician of Chinese heritage in Hawaii, when I'd been writing an article about the local bar scene. After I suggested he visit, he'd paused a beat then asked me if there were many people of Asian origin in Australia. That note of hesitation was possibly reflective of a lingering international view of the nation as mostly white and largely racist. The place had changed hugely, but we still had a lot to live down.

The pen I was using for note-taking ran out, so I fished around in my daypack for another. Travel writers are given a great number of pens by tourism authorities and businesses, and I'd been burning through them on this trip. So far I'd disposed of Juneau (Alaska), Via Rail (Canada) and Barcaldine Regional Council (Queensland). Now I was onto Seattle. As long as I remained a travel writer, I would never be short of a pen.

After my beer I followed the coastal path to Camp Cove, where the first governor of New South Wales, Arthur Phillip, had stepped ashore before sailing on to Sydney Cove. There was probably a plaque somewhere among the sunbathers, but I walked on. I wanted to swim at Lady Bay Beach. It had been made a clothing-optional beach in 1976, a remarkable turnaround since women had been occasionally arrested on New South Wales beaches for wearing bikinis as late as the 1960s. I was a big fan of communal nudity when it came to bathing, and I'd written travel stories about such traditional baths in Korea and Germany. I liked the easygoing German attitude toward nude bathing. In the outdoors it felt like freedom, a temporary sloughing off of one's identity in order to merge with nature. Lady Bay was a small beach surrounded by rock walls, without much shade. There were people in and out of the water, other people passing on the trail above, and boats floating by to the north. I doffed my gear and entered the water. It was cool, not cold, and refreshing on this humid day. The seabed was rocky rather than sandy, with unexpected dips and rises. I was enveloped by liquid once more, but feeling reinforced by it, rather than about to dissolve. The tropics were behind me, and all my baggage was up on the beach. As I bobbed around on the border of harbour and ocean, a tall-masted sailing ship passed in the hazy distance, an apparition from the colonial past.

Dulwich Hill to Central
Dulwich Hill line

I was staying at a hostel, Railway Square YHA. Not only was this on the western edge of Sydney's Central Station, it was built along a former platform used for delivering mail – the hostel styled this as Platform 0, as it lay alongside Platform 1 and was lined by mock carriages which acted as extra dorms. The adjacent former post office was now an apartment hotel. I'd stayed at this hostel many times over the years when visiting Sydney. If I wasn't being hosted by a hotel chain for work reasons, it was an affordable place to stay with good transport links because of the proximity of trains and a bus hub. Until 1961 the square had also been served by trams, before Sydney foolishly wound up its original tram network. I also liked the atmosphere in hostels' common areas, a friendly informal vibe which made it easy to fall into conversation with travellers from around the world.

A short walk south led to the former Regent Street Station. The temperature had hit forty degrees, which seemed excessive for 18 March, well into autumn. It was also a windy day, so it was like strolling within a fan-forced oven. I'd seen this distinctive building many times from arriving trains, but never from the street. It was behind a locked fence, but there was plenty to see. You might take it for a church or chapel, but there was something macabre about its Gothic styling. That architectural styling had actually been an apt choice. This had once been a railway station for a special clientele: the dead. When it opened in 1869 it had been known as Mortuary Station, and until 1938 had acted as a receiving station for the dearly departed, conveying them and their funeral parties to Rookwood Cemetery in Sydney's west. The immediate predecessor of Rookwood had been the Devonshire Street Cemetery, which after closure in 1867 had been demolished and the dead relocated in order to build Central Station. Its replacement was sited well outside the city centre, with the Parramatta railway line allowing access via a spur from Lidcombe Station (originally named Haslam's Creek Station). In the days before mass ownership of private transport, it was a dignified and efficient way to lay the deceased to rest, especially considering the 17-kilometre distance between the city centre and the cemetery. Victorian-era folk had a fascination with Gothic design, and Mortuary Station's architects had gone with the flow. Gothic to the nines, the station had pointed arches aplenty, along with an octagonal tower with a slender spire on top. Intricate carvings on its sandstone surface depicted cherubs and stars. This being Sydney on a hot sunny day, the sandstone glowed in the sunlight and took on an almost cheerful appearance, in strange contradiction of its original purpose. It was such a remarkable building that it was a pity it wasn't used for some public purpose: as a gallery, or a museum. Anything but the use it was put to from 1986 to 1989, when a pancake restaurant had operated on the premises, feeding diners in railway carriages. It had been called the Magic Mortuary. The building put me in mind of the Morbid Anatomy Museum I'd visited in Brooklyn, New York, a few years before. That fascinating place showcased funerary art, forcing visitors to confront our own era's awkwardness with the subject of death. Perhaps with the addition of a sympathetically designed annexe, something similar could be created here. Carvings on the two gateposts depicted an hourglass with wings, flying toward the sun. The symbolism was obvious, and blunt. The

Victorians confronted death better than we did, with honesty.

Further south-west, past Redfern Station, lay Carriageworks. After my visit to Grandchester Station in Queensland, I'd decided to visit significant railway sites along my journey where I could, to see what had become of them. This vast cultural centre sat within the former Eveleigh Carriage Workshops, which from 1888 to 1989 had maintained New South Wales' train fleet. On arrival I walked down to the entrance via an enormous open-sided shed, at the far end of which I could see a man playing racquetball against a brick wall. He was so far away he seemed to be part of an optical illusion, as if seen via the wrong end of a telescope. The Carriageworks building was a cavernous space, criss-crossed with rails embedded in concrete, with big skylights above. Its main daytime use was as an art gallery. Upon entering I walked into Katharina Grosse's sprawling installation *The Horse Trotted Another Couple of Metres, Then It Stopped*. This big piece consisted of 8,000 square metres of fabrics hung from near the ceiling, and gathered together across the floor. This raw material Grosse had then painted in a riot of streaky colours, and visitors walked across the result. It was delightful to be within and stepping upon its long folds, swallowed up within the work, and part of it. The art and the building complemented each other, soft and flowing against hard and geometrical. Inside the work, a young woman was making model-like poses while leaning against a column, as a man took photos of her with a big camera. This artful self-consciousness was a neat fit. I was about to leave when another work, *Constellations* by Marco Fusinato, caught my attention. It appeared to be a high white wall, set at a diagonal to the building. When I walked around the other side I found an attendant, and a baseball bat chained to the wall. Along its surface were breaks and indentations.

'What you do is hit the wall as hard as you can with the bat,' she said. 'You only get one go.'

I did as she suggested, pulling back and swinging, imagining the wall as the material incarnation of Queensland's wet season. I struck it with a resounding crack, setting off an enormous boom, as if a gigantic anvil had been dropped from a height.

'There are microphones and speakers inside the wall,' she said. 'They amplify the blows.'

That was deeply satisfying, as if all the frustrations of Far North Queensland had been channelled into one violent moment. I wished I could have another go.

Wilting in the heat, I planned a final rail jaunt that would deliver me back to the hostel. Catching a train from Redfern to Dulwich Hill, I transferred to the Dulwich Hill light rail line. This was the only tramway currently in operation in Sydney, though a second line was being constructed from the CBD to branch towards Randwick and Kingsford. The city had had an extensive tram network up until the 1960s. The old saying 'to shoot through like a Bondi tram' was a relic of that era, and captured the colourful nature of Sydney's earliest tramways, for its first motorised trams were hauled not by electricity, nor underground cables. They were, remarkably, steam-powered – or perhaps remarkable only to us in hindsight, as steam was a tried and true method of powering vehicles along rails back then, though not usually rails set within streets.

The steam tram had arrived fifteen years after a death had shaken confidence in the horse-drawn trams that had run along Pitt Street. In 1864 Isaac Nathan had died beneath such a tram, as bluntly described in an article in the *Maitland Mercury* of 19 January:

> Mr. Nathan, who lived at No. 442,
> Pitt-street, a few yards distant, alighted
> from the car at the southern end, but
> before he had got clear of the rails the
> car moved onwards, and the deceased
> gentleman was unhappily crushed
> beneath one of its wheels.

Isaac Nathan was no anonymous Sydneysider but a notable citizen who had had an intriguing life. Born in 1790 in Canterbury, England, he was the son of a Polish refugee, Menehem Mona, a Jewish cantor who believed himself to be the son of the last king of Poland. Young Isaac was apprenticed to the London maestro Domenico Corri at the age of nineteen, then eloped with novelist and fellow student Rosetta Worthington in 1812. Perhaps it was this impulsive nature which endeared him to the 'mad, bad and dangerous to know' poet Lord Byron, who wrote poems to be fitted by Nathan to traditional synagogue music, resulting in the acclaimed *Hebrew Melodies*. Nathan also gained royal clients, acting as music librarian to King George IV and teaching music to the monarch's daughter, Princess Charlotte. With Lord Byron fleeing Britain in 1816 and the princess dying in 1817, Nathan's connections started to fray. He claimed to have been sent on a secret mission in 1837 by King William IV, and thus to be owed 2,000 pounds by the government. The prime minister of the day, Lord Melbourne, refused to disburse the cash, even though (or because?) Nathan had once fought a duel to defend the honour of Lady Caroline Lamb, who had been married to Melbourne but had run off with – who else? – Lord Byron. In short, Isaac Nathan was a seriously interesting individual well before he set foot on Australian shores in 1841, in an attempt to reinvent himself after financial ruin. Setting up as unofficial music laureate for the young colony, he created compositions for historic milestones and tragedies, including *Leichhardt's Grave* upon the disappearance of the explorer Ludwig Leichhardt on an outback expedition in 1845 (he survived, only to disappear permanently three years later). He also wrote *Don John of Austria*, the first opera to be wholly composed and produced in Australia, which was staged at Sydney's Victoria Theatre in 1847. He even experimented with the inclusion of Aboriginal music in his compositions. Then he died under a tram, the first person ever to do so in Australia. It seems strangely fitting that his death should be as dramatic as key events of his life: discordant, but somehow fitting the overall composition. I wouldn't choose to die under a tram myself, but it seems morbidly appealing to depart in a way that strikes a memorable coda to one's life, rather than in a fog of dementia or expiring after a slow decline. Sadly, he left this world a few years too early to enjoy a post-mortem train ride to Rookwood Cemetery. But perhaps a rail-borne exit would have been in poor taste.

Though Nathan's tragic death hastened the demise of the horse-drawn tram, the city's horse-drawn buses soon had new competition in the form of the steam tram. Its introduction now seems like a series of happy accidents. Firstly, as part of the never-ending competition with Melbourne, now revelling in the 'Marvellous Melbourne' era of gold-fuelled prosperity, Sydney decided to host an international exhibition in its Royal Botanic Garden. Taking place in 1879, it would pip by a year the Victorian capital's own such exhibition, to be housed in the grand Royal Exhibition Building (which still stands today and was Australia's first UNESCO World Heritage cultural listing). The timing was a clever coup, but there was a problem – how to transport to the exhibition the expected crowds of attendees from Sydney Terminal, the city's main train station at the time, which lay just to the south of today's Sydney Central Station. The solution, another happy accident, was a tram line along Elizabeth Street. As the new tramway was intended as a temporary measure, having vehicles able to move under their own power would be preferable to the laying of major infrastructure such as power poles or underground cables. Thus the third happy accident occurred: the decision to adopt steam traction as the answer to Sydney's people-moving needs. Luckily, the Baldwin Company of Philadelphia, USA, had the ability to construct one hundred steam trams per month, and these hissing engines were coupled to double-decker passenger carriages built in New York. The result, to judge from contemporary photographs, was ungainly but fascinating. In the front was the 'steam motor', resembling a squat version of a steam train, with a large circular lantern at its front and a low black funnel directly behind. The two-level passenger carriages towered behind the motor, with a canvas roof on top above longitudinal benches and striped canvas blinds that could be dropped down the sides. The steam trams were an immediate hit, and became indispensable rather than temporary in the public mind. Deputations from the suburbs pressured the government for their own tram lines, and a network began to form, with early extensions to Moore Park and Randwick Racecourse (interestingly, both places to be reached by tram again via the twenty-first-century extension to Sydney's light rail). Not that the steam era was without its share of injuries. In his history of Sydney's steam trams, *Juggernaut!*, David Burke quotes an 1882 poem from *Sydney Punch* which includes the lines:

> Maiming its victims, day after day
> Through human bodies hewing its way!
> Who could contrive a more devilish
>   sham
> Than we have in our horrible
>   Juggernaut tram?

Notable victims included George Oakes, a member of parliament who in 1881 impatiently stepped onto the Elizabeth Street tracks just as a tram had passed, not realising that another was right behind it. He was pushed out of the way by the quick-thinking fireman on the second tram, but died as a result of his head hitting the asphalt. Despite such tragedies, the steam tram network expanded across Sydney from Leichhardt in the west to Bondi and Coogee in the east, and to Botany Bay in the south. The eastern route allowed would-be bathers to go all the way by rail to Bondi Beach, far better than the present-day necessity to change from train to bus at Bondi Junction. The zippy steam tram between the city and Bondi, which reached up to 80 km/h and spawned the immortal 'shoot through' tag, first reached the beach when the line was extended there in 1894. In the beginning the

Bondi branch trams were infrequent on weekdays but plentiful at weekends, bringing the sands within reach of the average worker for a four-pence ticket.

The steam trams were soon joined by electric trams, which covered a vaster area as Sydney expanded in the twentieth century. At the network's maximum extent in the 1930s, there were tram lines in areas as far-flung as northern Manly, western Ryde, southern Rockdale and La Perouse, and on the harbour's eastern edge at Watsons Bay (having just been out there by bus, I found it hard to imagine how trams handled the hilly terrain along the way). It was all gone by the early 1960s. The last steam tram trundled through Parramatta to meet a ferry at Redbank Wharf in 1943, and the final electric tram ran along the La Perouse line in 1961. Though some steam trams and electric trams were sold or preserved, most notably at the Sydney Tramway Museum in Loftus, the bulk were scrapped and burnt. Like many cities around the world now rebuilding tramways at great expense, Sydney would come to regret that folly. Melbourne was regarded then as backward for keeping its trams, but the boot is on the other foot nowadays; that's one aspect of the eternal rivalry where Sydney will never catch up. Though, to be fair, it did find a good use for the site of the redundant tram depot next to Circular Quay: for the Sydney Opera House.

To celebrate the city's colourful tramway heritage as part of my Sydney interlude, I had only one choice of line to ride. And it was a ring-in of sorts, having been a heavy rail line for most of its existence. The Dulwich Hill light rail line (badged as L1 in anticipation of its forthcoming companion line, L2) had not carried light rail vehicles until the very end of the twentieth century. It had been constructed along a redundant goods line opened in 1855, which had linked Central Station with factories and other industrial facilities. From 1997 to 2014, the light rail route had been progressively extended until it had reached its current terminus in the suburb of Dulwich Hill, where it intersected with a suburban train station of the same name. I'd used this tram line many times at its eastern end, where it wound from Central Station past the hotels and restaurants of Darling Harbour. I'd even once written a travel article about highlights near its stations. But I'd never ridden its entire 13-kilometre length. Mouthing a brief homage to the memory of Isaac Nathan, and to the more lively spirts of those long-ago Bondi daytrippers, I boarded the modern light rail vehicle at the terminus and we set off into what was, for me, tram terra incognita.

As I'd suspected, the newer western section mostly served residential neighbourhoods, though there were industrial landmarks along the way. At Waratah Mills we passed the eponymous flour mill, whose distinctive silos were now part of an apartment complex. The Lewisham West stop lay next to another mill complex, which was covered in scaffolding. This former flour mill had been built for the company Mungo Scott in 1922, with silos added in the 1950s. It had been placed here to take advantage of the freight line, and had kept grinding grain until 2009. Now it too was being converted to housing. Interestingly, its suburb, Summer Hill, had been an upmarket residential area in the 1920s. It had then transitioned to being a working-class suburb, presumably because of the freight line and the industry it attracted. Now it was being re-gentrified. The mill redevelopment's website implied that it would be thrilling to live inside the former silos. But would it? Not for the first time, I felt that 'exciting' was the English word most abused by marketers. Or possibly 'iconic'.

We had a long pause at Lilyfield, once the tramway's terminus, during which the driver left the doors open and the air conditioning struggled. When we resumed we passed stops more familiar to me: Glebe, where the bookshop Gleebooks was a mainstay; The Star, Sydney's hideous casino complex; Convention, where I'd come and gone the previous month for a travel trade event; and Capitol Square, next to the Capitol Theatre which staged big-budget musicals – I'd once seen *The Lion King* there with Narrelle.

The stretch from Convention was once paralleled by Sydney's monorail, a textbook example of a white elephant in the same way Australia's rail gauges were a textbook example of poor infrastructure planning. Built in 1988 over the objections of those who desired a light rail system to service the redeveloped Darling Harbour area, it had underperformed from the day it opened. As it had no interchange with any train stations, running in a loop connecting the CBD, Chinatown and the harbour, it wasn't very useful. The monorail stations were also awkward to reach, being high above the streets. They were a reminder of a key advantage trams had over other public transport – because they ran at street level rather than through tunnels or overhead, they were quick to exit. London's Underground system gave a quick ride between stations, but it could take ages to rise from its platforms to the street. With a tram you were out and on your way. Now Sydney's monorail, which I remembered being under construction when I visited Sydney in 1987, was a fading memory only five years after it had stopped operating. Friendless and unloved, it had been bought in 2012 by the New South Wales government, specifically to be demolished. Now it was as if it had never been; I suspected its very existence would feature in trivia-night questions before too long. Its memory lived on fitfully through its scattered monorail cars, two of which had been installed at Google's Sydney offices for use as meeting rooms. There were also a few remaining cavities in city buildings which had once been stations, and whose ownership and future uses were unclear. They'd probably make good bars, given their elevated views.

At the end of the route, the tram swung onto an elevated turning loop which brought it up to Central Station's Grand Concourse. This had been designed for Sydney's original tramway, so it seemed fitting that it should be used by its successor. The loop was closed, and I was back at Central.

Central to Redfern
309 bus

'I told Tony to go for the Tigers, but he said "Are you mad, love? They're playing the Storm."'

Two women on the bus were discussing rugby, a closed book to me as I'd grown up in Western Australia and had lived in Victoria for twenty years. Aussie Rules was the code I understood, and the only Tigers I cared for were based in Richmond, the Melbourne suburb where I'd lived when I moved east.

I had time to kill before meeting with Richard Graham, a local tour operator who I'd met on a travel writing trip to Sydney several years before, so I ate breakfast at Redfern cafe Yellow Fever, a Vietnamese eatery with an eyebrow-raising name. Its menu matched a trend I'd noticed in Melbourne in the past few years: the traditional cuisine of Asian countries blended with Australia's independent cafe culture. When it worked well, it produced interesting food and great coffee. Yellow Fever's interior was generic modern cafe – concrete floor, timber benches, stools with angular struts, a prominent espresso machine – but pages from Vietnamese newspapers were plastered across one wall. The short menu stood out, presenting what Sherlock Holmes would call 'certain points of interest.' There were banh mi and rice bowls for lunch, but at breakfast the most innovative choice was the VB Roll, filled with crispy Spam, egg, sriracha mayo, pickled carrots, cucumber, spring onion, coriander and soy sauce. I temporarily exempted myself from vegetarianism for research purposes, and ordered it. It was delicious, with a contrast of textures between the crunchy vegetables and the soft egg. It even worked well with black coffee. I ordered a long macchiato, and was asked how I wanted it. The question threw me. The 'long mac' is Australia's most inconsistently prepared coffee. I regularly ordered it out of curiosity, to see what would arrive: how high it would be, how integrated the milk, what type of container it would be in. This one was what I thought of as the 'classic' preparation: it came in a glass, about half full, with the milk lightly resting on top. It was good.

I walked to Richard's house on Lawson Street and knocked on the door. Richard opened it, and I found myself being introduced to four strangers. In addition to Richard there was his wife, Bérangère, two American tourists, and a tour guide called John. Richard's company, My Detour, specialised in intimate small tours which often incorporated his home in Redfern. It seemed I'd arrived as a tour was about to depart. Richard and John were staging an orientation for the two visitors John was about to take on a tour, discussing how the Indigenous society encountered by the first British settlers was fundamentally different from their own.

'There was governance, not government,' said Richard. 'No fences, no walls. When the British came, they were like a square peg in a round hole.'

I thought of my HMS *Sirius* great-great-great-great-great-grandfather-in-law, up on the rocks on that day in 1788, wondering if the new colony would be able to grow food to survive. The Aboriginal people it had displaced had no trouble surviving off the land, yet the newcomers seemed unable to learn from them.

The tour moved out with John in the lead, and I was left with Richard and Bérangère in their compact living room. It was packed with art, much of it with Indigenous elements. A portrait of Captain Cook caught my eye, the famous face broken into Picasso-esque fragments.

I'd met Richard seven years before, when he was starting up his company. He offered tailor-made tours of Sydney, a mix of walking and driving, often in a smooth EH Holden which he kept in sleek condition. I'd written a piece about his tour of Redfern for the *Sunday Age*.

I'd dropped in to Redfern once or twice since then, and was curious to hear Richard's thoughts on how the district was changing. Redfern seems to me a quintessential Sydney suburb, even though (or perhaps because) it's nowhere near the coast. Working-class, ex-industrial, now gentrifying, and full of terrace houses on leafy streets. It's also famously identified with its strong Aboriginal community.

Richard praised the 'City of Villages' policy being pursued by the Sydney City Council under Lord Mayor Clover Moore. Inner-city suburbs such as Redfern and Glebe had been designated as urban villages, he explained, and work had then begun to regenerate local parks and institute neighbourhood festivals. As proof of its success, he took me around the corner to Charles Kernan Reserve, which had been refurbished in 2010 and was named after a long-time council worker and resident who had raised funds for locals in need.

'My daughter practically lives here,' he said, pointing to the children's playground behind the lawn. But he had recently found a syringe there, and had put up a sign warning others to watch out. The area still had its issues.

'It's not unique to Redfern nowadays though,' he said. 'Everywhere has that risk.'

We stepped into the communal garden at the back of the reserve, where Bérangère had been harvesting vegetables earlier. Richard pointed out a clump of warrigal greens, a native plant which had been eaten by the crew of the *Endeavour* to ward off scurvy. 'It's like kale,' he said.

We walked to Wilson Street, which ran above the busy railway line, and Richard gestured toward it. 'This is where it's going to happen, a growth corridor from here to Erskineville.' He, like other locals, was concerned about the pressure lofty apartment towers would place on the narrow streets. 'You're building onto 1870s infrastructure, in a way.'

The railways had always been present in Redfern, where they'd been the backbone of its industry. Sydney's first main station had existed not far north of the current Redfern Station, before it had been re-established closer in. As a result, there were railway assets scattered everywhere.

We passed a derelict shed which was slated to be replaced by housing, then paused by a set of stunningly renovated former railway offices, still inscribed with the initials NSWGR, for New South Wales Government Railways. With its verandahs decorated with iron lace, and its institutional look, it put me in mind of a Victorian-era school or hospital.

'They've done a great job, but what are they going to do with it now? We don't know,' he said. In a city which had long had a problematic relationship with developers, there was little trust when it came to reuse of old buildings, or the quality of new ones.

What was driving this frenzy of development was, of course, money. Redfern had once been a working-class suburb with a reputation for petty crime, but was now perceived as a distinctive neighbourhood in a prime position near the Sydney CBD. And of course it had excellent transport links – nearly every commuter line passed through the station before reaching Central. 'Getting off at Redfern' had once been slang for the withdrawal method of contraception, as it involved stopping just before the final destination.

'When I bought my place in 2004 it cost $470,000,' said Richard. 'Now it's worth $1.5 million. If they go ahead with the growth corridor, it could hit $2.5 million.'

We were walking down Caroline Street toward the location of The Block, the enclave of Aboriginal-managed housing which had been synonymous with crime and other social problems from the

1980s. Its dilapidated old terraces had now been razed, pending redevelopment as a mixed-use site known as the Pemulwuy Project, but plenty of old houses remained in the neighbouring streets. Some were the worse for wear, others were in the throes of renovation.

'Who wouldn't want to live here now?' asked Richard, pointing out the three-storey Victorian homes, narrow but attractive. 'Back in the day you wouldn't buy in this part of Redfern, and if you had, they would've only cost $250,000.'

Bad news took time to disperse, however. 'Taxi drivers still say to visitors, "Don't go to Redfern." It still has that reputation.'

Walking past The Block's northern edge, Richard pointed out student housing, rented by students attending nearby universities. Turning, we saw The Rabbit Hole Organic Tea Bar.

'You used to come down here to score drugs, now you score organic tea,' he grinned.

Around the corner was Cake Wines' cellar door, and a cool-looking cafe called Henry Lee's. 'The sort of place that charges you $18 for poached eggs,' said Richard. 'Good food though.'

We paused at a nearby ex-factory building in the process of renovation, and he shook his head at the matter-of-factness of it all. 'You'd be wary of coming down here in the old days.'

Nearby had stood Tony Mundine's famous gym, Elouera, closed in 2017. A row of remaining terrace houses had featured in ABC's TV drama series *Redfern Now*. Opposite these, behind the site of the former gym and its big Aboriginal flag mural, was a long grassy area beyond a high fence. A tent embassy had been set up here a few years before by locals opposed to redevelopment. We stood next to this contested patch, where the distressed houses of The Block had once been, and watched a video clip on Richard's phone about the Pemulwuy development which would be built here. It looked good, a collection of contemporary buildings intended as a modern village. Shortly I would be talking to Mick Mundine, Tony's brother and the driving force behind the project. It was interesting to see what was planned while standing in the actual space. Richard had a positive view. 'What I admire Mick for is he's stayed true to his values.'

We paused at the corner of Eveleigh Street, opposite Redfern Station. Richard mentioned that in his early days in the area, there was always a campfire burning at this corner. 'If you were feeling brave, you'd stop and have a yarn with the guys around the fire, then head home. That was Redfern.

'The people here are the best: everyone takes the piss out of themselves. The eastern suburbs are full of people too concerned with what sunglasses they're wearing, what car they're driving. In Redfern you're still accepted for what you are.'

Richard had no Indigenous ancestry but he spent a lot of time with Aboriginal locals, including at a men's group in Glenbrook. 'I've learned a lot,' he said.

I waved Richard off to his train – he had an afternoon tour to lead in the CBD – and walked to my meeting with a PR firm on the other side of the tracks. In its slick modern offices above Gibbons Street, I was meeting Mick Mundine and Lani Tuitavake, respectively CEO and COO of the Aboriginal Housing Company. Having visited Redfern more than once in relation to travel writing, I'd become interested in both its Aboriginal and rail heritage and wanted to learn more, and this seemed the perfect opportunity as I was visiting Sydney without firm commitments. I often said that being a writer gave you a licence to be nosy, and strangely people responded well to that inquisitiveness. So I'd got in touch with the company earlier in my trip and asked if I could interview someone about the AHC's Pemulwuy Project. There might be an article in it, if not for a travel section then perhaps as a newsy profile. From what I'd seen and read, the project was going to include commercial and retail, as well as housing. Why not make it all housing?

'It's practically rebuilding our community,' said Lani. 'We're unlocking its economic base to be able to sustain our need for housing. Housing and Redfern and railways all come hand in hand for us as a community. You get off at Redfern Station, and you're almost on The Block. You're home.'

'The location of the station must add to the land's economic value,' I said.

'I'm not a map person, but get me to a landmark and I know where I'm going,' said Lani. 'You get off at Redfern Station, you look across the road and there's a wall with murals and Eveleigh Street: you're there. It's close for the families and childcare, and for the students in our student housing. They'll subsidise the ongoing affordable housing.'

Being a fan of Victorian terraces, I asked why they were putting up new buildings. Couldn't they have renovated the old houses instead?

'No,' said Mick, firmly. 'They really were old stock. We renovated them for years; it was a band-aid job all the time. And as you know, The Block became a vicious cycle: drugs, crime. It was time for a change.

'This is what we're doing with Pemulwuy – changing the future for the next generation of children so they live in a good environment and don't have to worry about drugs, crime, alcohol. That's what it's all about. What we're building now is solid, on solid foundations. Not just for our people and the next generation, but for the general community. With the Pemulwuy Project, we want everyone to be welcome.'

'Over the years it seemed like we were a little oasis on our own,' added Lani, 'but we're part of the bigger community. It'll be a meeting place.'

Because they knew I was interested in the railways, Lani and Mick had brought along Gadigal Elder Charles Madden, otherwise known as Uncle Chicka. He had a long connection to the area.

'I was here when the Second World War was raging. I lived just down the road when the Japanese mini-subs entered the harbour. That's when we were packed on a train and sent up bush,' he said.

'After the war I did construction on the railways. I drove vehicles most of the time, from jeeps to buses to concrete wagons, and concrete pumps.

'Redfern in the early days was probably the industrial hub of Australia. All the industry was around here, that's why Redfern Station was so popular. If you worked around Botany or Rosebery or Zetland, you could catch a tram on the hill here which would take you out. And you could walk to Waterloo in twenty minutes.'

'Was there always a big Aboriginal community here?' I asked.

'We were just down the road on The Block, and the streets all around,' he said. 'When I left school in the bush, there was no work up there. You wouldn't get a job in any of the shops. You might get a job on a sheep or cattle station, which would be way out and the pay wouldn't be much.

'But after the war there were jobs everywhere in the city, so the men came back and worked in the factories,' he continued. 'People also came from everywhere to work at the carriage works. My mother and auntie used to work as train cleaners there. In the early days most of the goods came in from the country and were loaded in Alexandria near the pub. That was all casual work, so a lot of Kooris worked there too.

'There was plenty of work, and Aboriginals all lived around here. In Caroline Street you could go to sleep and leave the front door open, no-one went near you.'

This was new to me. I hadn't envisioned railway work as empowering, but for Uncle Chicka's generation it had allowed a measure of urban independence.

'But not in the 80s and the 90s,' said Mick. 'That's when it started to turn. It became a very vicious cycle, but that's part of the journey. This is a new journey for us now.'

'Once the project's completed, it'll strengthen the younger generation's resilience,' added Lani. 'There's a generation that haven't seen anything other than buildings being demolished, drugs, alcohol. For us, this is an opportunity to inspire others.'

I mentioned the 2004 riots, which had taken place after a seventeen-year-old Aboriginal boy, Thomas Hickey, had come off his bicycle and been impaled on a fence, dying the next day. It was alleged that his bike had been clipped by a pursuing police car, while the police said he had lost control while riding. On the evening of his death, 15 February 2004, a riot erupted after Aboriginal youths from across Sydney gathered in Redfern in protest. Bottles, bricks and Molotov cocktails were thrown as the violence spread through the area around The Block. Even Redfern Station was damaged, briefly being set alight.

'That was a turning point for us, but also a wake-up call for the state, that something needed to be done,' said Lani. 'It was important for us to not only look at the economics, but to look at rebuilding our community. It's part of the identity of Redfern.'

The AHC had been buying land and houses from the 1970s onward, and in 2009 drew up the plans for the Pemulwuy Project. Its website emphasised its financial independence from government funding, which Mick thought was crucial.

'It's empowering ourselves, and showing everybody we can do it,' he said. 'We've got land, and it's time to invest in our land. We want to show people we can do it. If we can get out of that vicious cycle on The Block, anyone can do it anywhere.'

'The bulk of the housing will be affordable housing, tied to employment,' said Lani. 'And we're the only developer in the area that's building three and four bedrooms, so it's clear we're there for families.'

I hoped it would work out. There had been community opposition to the project from the beginning, and renewed controversy a year after my visit when a twenty-four-storey tower for student accommodation was approved for the site, up from the sixteen storeys originally proposed. Aside from question marks still hovering over the later construction of sixty-two affordable dwellings for Indigenous residents, there was concern that the higher tower would overshadow Redfern Station.

'Is there a distinct urban Aboriginal identity?' I asked, as the conversation drew toward a close.

'This is something we've talked about,' said Lani. 'It's important to maintain the culture, whether there's family here or family in Country. We've added the South Sydney Rabbitohs, the

Redfern All Blacks football club, there are all these things which make up the identity of an urban Aboriginal person. Even the railway tracks here are blackfella tracks. [But] you don't really see anything that says that. We're not just "fare evasion".'

'We're building a brand-new gym too,' said Mick. 'It's time for a change. As Aboriginal people, we're going to make the change ourselves. And you know what? We own the land. Land is power, brother.'

After the interview I backtracked to Henry Lee's for lunch, because I'm the sort of person who likes cafes that charge $18 for poached eggs. It was set within a courtyard beneath a glass roof, surrounded by walls of chipped brick and pitted concrete. Potted plants broke up the gritty vibe, and a tree grew in a corner. It was relaxed on a weekday afternoon, even serene. A waitress told me the building had once been a hosiery and leather-goods factory. On the cafe's website, it said, 'We are passionate about flavour, seasonal produce, art, culture, coffee + living a self-sustaining lifestyle, supporting artisanal, creative + small batch producers.'

The menu was almost a parody of gentrification, with dishes containing a riot of elements. To make amends for my earlier Spam misadventure, I ordered a vegan dish, The Good Son. It contained turmeric EVOO flatbreads, curried chickpeas, coconut yoghurt, mango and coriander salsa, pickled cucumber, banana, coconut, tamarind dressing, chilli and burnt lime. And it did indeed cost $18.

It was delicious. But dining in this fine style, on the streets that had erupted in riots just fourteen years earlier after Thomas Hickey's death was hard to get my head around.

After eating, I ordered the Aztec Chilli Hot Chocolate with almond milk, and realised I'd be in Melbourne in less than twenty-four hours. Melbourne was the midpoint of my rail trek, but also home, with Narrelle, my friends, the trams, the laneways, the coffee, all waiting for me.

I should have been missing home, but I'd been too busy to focus on it. Aside from Narrelle, I'd been communicating with no-one and hadn't posted to social media. I felt like I'd vanished around the far side of the moon and was about to make a re-entry from orbit. Whenever I was undergoing a long travel-writing journey, there was a point in the middle where I transitioned into 'flow', a feeling that I had always lived on the road and always would live on the road. As Kerouac wrote, the road is life. But it – or its rail equivalent – was about to bear me home.

Sydney to Melbourne
XPT

The Grand Concourse at Sydney's Central Station was everything I wanted for the start of a long train journey. Opened in 1906, the concourse is a lofty space with a curved roof, walls of brick and stone, and stained-glass windows. It's a sweeping statement of confidence in railways, down to the bust and plaque honouring nineteenth-century engineer John Whitton as 'the father of the New South Wales railways.' This is a fair call – when Whitton had arrived in the colony in 1856, only 23 miles (37 kilometres) of track were in operation. By the time he stepped down in 1889, this had increased by 2,171 miles (3,494 kilometres), stretching as far west as Bourke and Hay, and to the borders of Queensland and Victoria. One of Whitton's many achievements was the establishment of a standard-gauge network throughout New South Wales. Throughout his career there had been pressure to build narrow-gauge branch lines off the standard-gauge main lines, as a way of saving money on construction costs. Whitton ably resisted this misguided aim. He couldn't stop other colonies from adopting ill-advised gauges, but by God he could stop his home colony from having nightmarish break-of-gauge situations on country journeys. Not that Whitton had had an easy ride in his career. The station's plaque made mention of the Railway Bridges Inquiry of 1884–1886, which had heard accusations against

Whitton of poor design and the use of substandard materials. The inscription concluded, 'Whitton retired in 1890 and suffered broken health and a constant feeling of unappreciated service until his death in 1898.' It was a curious foreshadowing of the fate of Western Australia's famous engineer C.Y. O'Connor, a contemporary of Whitton's. I'd be learning more about him later.

Central Station was a terminal built for grand journeys, for desperate missions, for tearful goodbyes by loved ones waving lace hankies as they ran alongside departing trains. The only thing missing was a suitably portentous place to eat, though a sign featuring photos of old station dining rooms promised 'A new dining experience, coming soon!' Whatever emerged from that redevelopment would be a vast improvement on the refreshment facilities at the original Sydney Terminal, built to serve the colony's first railway line which opened to Parramatta in 1855. That station, between where Central and Redfern stations stand today, was an embarrassingly humble iron structure within which one Henry Dudley leased a room from which to provide refreshments in 1856. Unfortunately, the authorities had forbidden the operation of stoves within the building, so Dudley thought laterally and established a refreshment tent nearby. Dudley had evidently been cursed by the catering gods, as his tent was repeatedly set alight by sparks from passing steam locomotives, and was occasionally toppled by high winds. In 1857 he was given permission to erect a simple iron building at the Chippendale entrance to the station, which must have seemed a great improvement on the tent. This new structure was promptly damaged by a storm. When the line was extended to Campbelltown, the first extension to be overseen by our boy John Whitton, Dudley hoped the increase in passenger traffic would finally lead to healthy profits. On the opening of the line, however, the fares increased considerably, causing travellers to cut back on tea and pies. The land around his building was then leased to timber merchants, who surrounded it with a fence, leaving it poorly ventilated. Dudley accepted the decrees of fate and abandoned his doomed business in 1859, later seeking compensation from parliament. The first attempt to refresh the rail travellers of Sydney had not ended well.

In 1917 the New South Wales government took over the catering within its stations, by which time it operated refreshment rooms across the state. The jewel in the crown of this operation was Sydney Central, where more than 200 staff served diners in dining rooms and bars, and at kiosks and fruit stalls on the platforms. It was a far cry from the sad little convenience store which was the only food option I could see in the present day.

Above the concourse hung a clock with Roman numerals, next to a large departure board with screens divided into suburban, intercity and regional services. On the final screen was listed '20.42 Melbourne'. My train was departing from Platform 1, next to the carriage dorms of the YHA hostel where I'd been staying. On the platform I found a large plaque erected in 1970, when Sydney and Perth were joined for the first time by a single standard-gauge train. How glorious the rail future must have looked back then, when cross-country airfares were still dauntingly expensive. That was still the case in 1984, when I took my first ever trip from Perth to Sydney – by bus (once was enough; after that, I flew).

Across the platforms, I could see each had a hanging sign saying 'CENTRAL' in large block letters. They stretched out like an optical illusion, one behind the other. On an adjacent bench to mine were two women and a young child. They weren't sure if they were travelling in seats or berths, so I looked at their tickets and confirmed they were in the sleeper section. Out of curiosity, I asked the young mother why she was taking the train to Melbourne rather than flying.

'I'm not good at aircraft,' she said, with a note of apology. 'I need sedatives to fly.'

'It's more fun this way, anyway,' I said.

It was a still, humid evening on Platform 1. Anticipation hung in the air, as if fate was about to deliver something special.

What it delivered was Mr Singh.

I met him the moment I stepped into our cabin, in which he had drawn the top berth. 'I travel down to Melbourne every three months,' said my travel mate. 'I live right here next to Central Station, so it's easier than flying.'

Mr Singh was originally from Punjab in India, and worked as a migration agent. I had guessed he was a regular, as the attendant who'd taken our breakfast orders had recognised him.

The complimentary breakfast supplied to sleeper passengers was fairly basic, but you got to choose your spreads. I went for Vegemite.

'Ah, you are Australian,' said the attendant, who I guessed was also from India.

The two-berth compartment, technically known as a twinette, was the same as the one I'd sat in from Brisbane, but the night-time experience was different. Mr Singh and I each had a pile of plastic-wrapped items stacked on the middle seat: a snack pack, a toiletries bag and a towel.

Later the berths would be folded down, and the shower within the adjacent bathroom could be used. In fact it had been so hot that day in Sydney, I ended up using it that evening to lower my body temperature.

Unlike my Brisbane-to-Sydney jaunt, there would be little scenery to enjoy on this trip. It was already dark when we left Central, and the only brightly lit places that could be discerned through the reflective windows were the suburban stations we passed: Redfern, Sydenham, Wolli Creek.

Mr Singh and I engaged in desultory chat about India and travel, but mostly he was happy to look at his phone. I continued reading *Affection*, in which a plague-stricken Townsville was becoming a tense place for the hero.

Occasionally we'd pass a two-deck Sydney train running along a parallel track. They weren't very full this late on a weekday. I could see people reclining, reading, thumbing their phones. I wondered idly who they were, where they were heading, what they'd be doing when they got there, what they'd be having for dinner, when our trains diverged and they passed out of my life.

I opened the plastic snack pack. Inside it was the following: popcorn, biscuits, water, a mint, crackers and chutney.

It was odd eating a sachet of chutney with crackers but without cheese, and there were only two crackers so some chutney was left over. Perhaps cheese had been the victim of a budget cutback.

By mutual agreement, Mr Singh and I asked the attendant to put the beds down at about 9.30 pm, after we'd dutifully munched our way through the snack packs.

Lying in my berth, I watched an episode of the 1966 science fiction TV series *The Time Tunnel* on my iPad. In that episode, the time-tossed heroes Doug and Tony were thrown into the time of Kublai Khan, and had to grapple with heavily made-up English-speaking Mongolian warriors, and threatening stock footage of marauding hordes. Television was far more innocent – and unsophisticated – back then, but it had helped form my personality at an impressionable age. I'd not considered it until recently, but I wondered whether the space–time-travelling show *Doctor Who* had partly prompted a yearning for travel, along with those half-remembered steam trains of my childhood years.

Then I tried to sleep. There were two recessed slots next to my berth. One was probably designed for spectacles and neatly held my headphones in their pouch. The other was a broad slot likely intended for a book, and by luck was exactly the length of my iPad. It was difficult to sleep, though Mr Singh seemed to be managing it. He was very quiet, not a snorer. On this train I was lying perpendicular to the train's direction of motion, which meant a lot of rocking – and not like that of a cradle, more a washing machine. As a result I tossed and turned, trying to find the ideal position and never quite managing it. I sneaked to the loo a couple of times during the night, as that jostling seemed to be agitating the bladder. I felt like I hadn't slept at all, then I looked at my phone at one point and it was 4 am. We were about to arrive at Albury.

I dressed and wandered down the train to the cafe, through the first-class seated area. In the darkened carriage the sleeping passengers looked as if they'd been the victims of a terrible plague, their bodies arranged at grotesque angles.

The train stopped and, coming across an open door, I stuck my head out to view the long colonnaded platform at Albury Station. For a regional station, Albury is rather magnificent – a colonial-era edifice with a clock tower, verandahs decorated with iron lace and waiting rooms with arched windows and high ceilings. Its platform is equally spectacular. At 455 metres long, when it opened in 1883 it was the longest in Australia. Covered by a long colonnade of Grecian pillars supporting a metal roof, it's still an attractive place to board or alight.

The reason for this splendid platform was, of course, the gauge problem. From 1881, when the New South Wales railway line first reached Albury, passengers had to transfer between Albury and Victorian Wodonga via stagecoach. Then in 1883, Victoria's broad-gauge North East line was extended across the Murray River to meet New South Wales' standard-gauge Main Southern line at Albury. It's hard to imagine the excitement that at the time was stirred by the opening of a railway line, now that trains are a daily convenience and aircraft a useful nuisance. But the meeting of these lines was a very big deal indeed. The official record of the event, snappily titled *The Union of the Railway Systems of New South Wales and Victoria*, sets the scene:

> On the day of opening, the border
> towns of Albury and Wodonga were
> astir from an early hour. The special
> trains from Sydney were loaded with
> passengers, and the traffic between
> Albury Station and the various
> hostelries, to which the travellers
> drove immediately on their arrival,
> gave to the streets an appearance of

activity and excitement which they
never before assumed. Lines of flags
and banners were stretched across the
principal streets ... The railway station,
an exceedingly handsome structure,
was decorated most lavishly with
bunting; festoons of evergreens were
hung along the platform front, and
the supporting pillars of the verandah.
Poles bearing huge flags of different
nations were erected ... In short,
advantage was taken of every point
where decorations of any kind could
be displayed.

(I first read this passage seated within the grand Queens Hall of the State Library of Victoria, and it amused me to imagine its uncredited author subtly throwing shade in that mention of Albury's streets possessing 'activity and excitement which they never before assumed', and of the Sydney visitors dashing to the pubs, presumably in pursuit of a few quick ones.)

A public holiday had been declared in Albury for the opening, which was officiated over by the colony's governor, Lord Loftus. Bands played, an address of welcome was read out by earnest local councillors to the governor, and in the mid-afternoon a train from Melbourne crossed the Murray River to deliver his Victorian counterpart, the Marquess of Normanby. Quite the gathering of toffs.

The keynote event was a banquet, eccentrically held in the railway's engine shed, which had been extravagantly redecorated for the occasion. The central touch, above the governors' seats, was a depiction of two women representing the two colonies and clasping hands: Victoria holding a sheaf of corn, New South Wales a shepherd's crook. The symbolism was hard to miss – yet again, the needs of agriculture and trade had played more of a role in building an Australian railway than the abstract desire to move people at speed. As far as I could judge from *The Union of the Railway Systems*, these symbolic women were the only female attendees at the banquet, which was a veritable blokefest of dining, drinking and speech-making. I tried to imagine the raucous scene at a table distant from the speakers, awash with beer and wine and drunken good spirits, and it was not a pretty vision. It made me consider what a male-dominated thing the railways had been, and how seldom women were included in its official story. Yet at every point in its development there were women playing a part, not least by holding together the households of those men who ended up with their names on plaques and in the history books.

One symbolic connection with a real woman's hand was a small wheelbarrow affixed to a wall for the occasion. It had been used by the daughter of then Governor FitzRoy when she turned the first sod in the construction of New South Wales' first railway from Sydney to Parramatta, which later extended to Goulburn. Presumably it glinted dully in the novel illumination of the electric lights rigged up for the occasion, as many toasts were proposed and answered.

In his speech, the Premier of New South Wales, Alexander Stuart, remembered the sixteen-day clipper voyage he took between Melbourne and Sydney in 1852, the clipper becalmed for six days of it, and spoke of the railway as the harbinger of a union between all the Australian colonies. So many speakers after him supported so warmly that cause, often referencing the success of Canada, that it's almost a surprise to note that Federation was still two decades away. The Premier of Victoria, James Service, was typical in his support for the cause: 'I verily hope to see the grand Dominion Parliament established in my lifetime, and I mean to be a candidate.' He didn't make it, in the end, dying in 1899 – but by then Federation in 1901 was near-certain. As a symbol, then, the meeting of the rails at Albury was more than a practical development – it was a potent new beginning. Except ... though people could now travel by rail all the way between Melbourne and Sydney, the break of gauge still required a change at Albury. The lengthy platform, at least, sped the transfer of passengers from one train to another. It wasn't until 1962 that a standard-gauge line all the way to Melbourne was opened, allowing a single train journey. That occasion was also well attended by the people at the top, including Prime Minister Robert Menzies and Governor-General Lord De L'Isle. Australia would soon grow out of the habit of appointing British aristocrats as the monarch's representative – Lord De L'Isle was the last – but it wasn't quite there yet.

As for literary royalty, the great American author Mark Twain had passed through here by rail. In his 1897 travelogue *Following the Equator*, he marvelled at the lunacy that had created such an inconvenience as a break of gauge between Australia's two greatest cities:

> Now comes a singular thing: the
> oddest thing, the strangest thing,
> the most baffling and unaccountable
> marvel that Australasia can show.
> At the frontier between New South
> Wales and Victoria our multitude of
> passengers were routed out of their
> snug beds by lantern-light in the
> morning in the biting-cold of a high
> altitude to change cars on a road that
> has no break in it from Sydney to
> Melbourne! Think of the paralysis
> of intellect that gave that idea birth;
> imagine the boulder it emerged
> from on some petrified legislator's
> shoulders.

Beyond the platform was a short section of disused broad-gauge track which had been left in place, as an exhibit of rail gauge folly.

The train quietly pulled out, and a few minutes later we were crossing the Murray River, invisible beneath us in the dark. I was back in Victoria. Returning to my berth, I napped. The next time I checked the time it was nearly 6 am, and still pitch-black outside. I followed my 'hit the showers first' policy and dressed, wondering idly when I could ask Mr Singh to reinstate the lounge in place of the berths.

A knock on the door heralded the first instalment of breakfast. The XPT catering department continued its mix of old school and plain odd, by producing a plastic bowl of cornflakes with peel-off lid, a small carton of milk and a spoon whose bowl was the size of a thumbnail. Together they constituted an IQ test, to be passed by not spilling anything on oneself. The second instalment was a box containing two slices of white toast, Vegemite, butter and a cup of hot water with supplied coffee bag. Attempting to consume any of this while lying in my berth was tricky. The cornflakes alone were a minefield. After I'd eaten as much as I could manage, I realised I could restore the lounge seat without disturbing Mr Singh, by levering up my berth alone. He was happily seated cross-legged on his berth, the old hand, eating his toast like a pro.

The sun finally rose to reveal a cloudy day. A train operated by V/Line, the state railway company, played hopscotch with us on a parallel track as we approached Melbourne's outskirts. It was filthy, and packed with long-distance commuters heading to the city. At Roxburgh Park, one of Melbourne's outer suburbs, a huddle of people was waiting for a local train to work. One of the traveller's greatest pleasures is watching other people go to their nine-to-five jobs while you're not. Though I was, in fact, working. And going home, which was where I usually worked.

We passed Middle Footscray Station, beyond which were the grounds of the Footscray Trugo club. Trugo was a purely Victorian invention, and a product of the railways. When workers at the railway workshops in Newport had spare time in the 1920s, they'd used materials at hand to create a new game. Improvised mallets, resembling those used in croquet, had been used to hit thick rubber rings along a grassy surface toward a goalmouth. The rubber rings had once been used as shock absorbers on buffers. Trugo's popularity had waned as the number of railway workers diminished, and as age took its toll on players. Nine clubs were still active, and there was hope of harnessing its heritage appeal to revive it in the gentrified inner city. In Footscray, with its own dedicated ground, it had recently been adopted by a new generation, tapping into the 'I was into it before it was cool' factor beloved of hipsters. I hoped it would survive and prosper.

We slid through the industrial backblocks of Melbourne, across the Maribyrnong River, past towering stacks of shipping containers. I had my first sighting of a tram as it crossed the La Trobe Street bridge. I felt buoyed when returning from a long trip and sighting my first Melbourne tram. If returning by air it usually happened soon after arrival, as the number 59 tram route terminated just a few kilometres from Melbourne Airport at Airport West (a suburb named after the older Essendon Airport, not the current main airport at Tullamarine).

As we passed the glass-and-steel architectural fancies that were the new office buildings of Docklands, I asked Mr Singh why he really took the train rather than flew. Was he afraid of flying?

'No. If I fly, I wouldn't get to my Melbourne office before noon. This way I'm there when it opens. I like to be on time.'

That was more than could be said of this train, which was running half an hour late.

'Perhaps I'll get to the office at nine-thirty today, rather than nine,' allowed Mr Singh. He had a certain degree of flexibility after all.

####

Narrelle was waiting for me on Platform 1 of Southern Cross Station, her hair a new and interesting shade called Vampire Red. By chance the XPT had arrived at the exact moment the *Overland* was departing, the train I'd be catching to Adelaide a week in the future. We watched it go, then walked beneath the undulating roof of the station, out onto Spencer Street. A short distance away was Higher Ground, and a real breakfast.

Higher Ground is my go-to cafe for long-distance rail trips, as it lies so close to Southern Cross Station. It's very Melbourne, a slick modern cafe-bar with seating on multiple levels, within the cavernous interior of a former power station. With its high timber ceiling and natural light from big arched windows, it's a beautiful space in which to eat.

The menu was another example of the collision of cafe-style brunch dishes and international flavours. I ordered the spiced cauliflower scrambled eggs with curry leaf and roasted chilli on flatbread; Narrelle the heirloom tomatoes on olive toast with stracciatella, fennel, dried olive and verjuice. Vegemite toast this was not.

Around us were seated groups of friends, men in suits, a young Asian family and a couple speaking in French while eating avocado.

I smiled at Narrelle. I'd missed her, and I'd missed my city. This was my food, these were my people. It was good to be home.

Royal Park to Moonee Ponds (via Brunswick West)
58 tram and 508 bus

Along Victoria Street on the edge of the Melbourne CBD, I could see remnants of the nineteenth century's Marvellous Melbourne era, in particular the elegant bulk of the Royal Exhibition Building beyond the treetops of Carlton Gardens. There was also evidence of the city's twenty-first-century prosperity, in the cranes constructing office towers and apartments. It had been two weeks since I'd boarded the *Gulflander*, and this vista could not have been more different from that of Normanton at the end of the wet. In Melbourne it was the height of autumn, the city's best season, when its famous climatic unpredictability eased to produce sunny, temperate days.

One of the city's classic W-class trams, its wooden body painted green, chugged up La Trobe Street past me. It was a potent visual reminder that I was in the one Australian city that had retained an extensive network from the tramways' glory days before the coming of the private car.

It was proof, to me, that Melbourne was different. When I'd first moved to the city from Perth in the 1990s, I'd been fascinated by the survival of things that had long vanished in other cities: the trams, the sprawling Queen Victoria Market and various grand colonial buildings. The city seemed to instinctively value its past; often I'd look up while walking its streets and notice old, weathered signs which no longer served a purpose but which had never been removed. For many years a hand-lettered sign on the corner of Elizabeth and Bourke streets listed tram routes which no longer ran, and an almost unnoticeable small sign high up on a pole on Collins and Swanston gave a potted history of the Colonel Collins the street was named after (for all I know, it's still there). And of course there were the now ignored 'Ladies Only' signs spelt out in stone in front of benches next to St Paul's Cathedral.

To me, the trams were the most fascinating of these survivors. The retention of an old sign could be explained as a benign oversight, but a tram network was a big, complex thing that had to be consciously maintained. How had it remained when, as in the poem 'Casabianca', 'all but him had fled'? I knew one factor had been the leadership of Sir Robert Risson, a former military man who was chairman of the Melbourne and Metropolitan Tramways Board during the danger period (for the trams' survival) of the 1950s and 1960s. He steadfastly resisted attempts to downgrade or chip away at the tramways, and was recognised as an active and organised leader. He once climbed onto the roof of a tram in his homburg hat after being challenged to demonstrate safety procedures by a union leader, following the death of a driver trying to replace a trolley pole that had come off the overhead power lines. But Risson also had his share of good fortune. Over a century before, government surveyor Robert Hoddle had laid out unusually broad main streets in Melbourne's city centre, a full 99 feet (30 metres) wide, which would later accommodate both cars and trams with relative ease. Hoddle had defended that width to his boss, Governor Bourke, on the basis of health and convenience, and as the price of his victory accepted the Governor's insistence on a series of 'little' streets only 33 feet (10 metres) wide, which alternated with the main east–west streets. Then, in the 1940s, bus services which had replaced then defunct cable trams down

Bourke Street were judged to be a failure, and that led to new trams coursing down that major thoroughfare by the mid-1950s. That one development meant that a large proportion of the tram fleet was fairly new in the 1960s, which neutralised the reason often given in other cities for closing down tramways – that they would be too expensive to upgrade to modern standards. When, in 1975, the very first steel-framed Z-class trams were built, as successors to the timber-framed W-class workhouse, Melbourne tram enthusiasts could rest easy. The trams were here to stay, and other Australian cities would come to rue their decisions to remove their own tramways, later partly rebuilding them as 'light rail' lines in places as diverse as Sydney, the Gold Coast and Adelaide.

Thinking fondly of the W-class, I reached another survivor of the city's golden age: a compact neoclassical building set on one of the triangular plots of land that occurred wherever the river-aligned CBD street grid met the compass-aligned inner-city grid. This was the headquarters of the Royal Society of Victoria, the organisation that had sponsored the expedition led by Burke and Wills. It was still housed in the same building, over a century and a half later. I had a meeting with the society's Burke and Wills expert that I'd arranged on the fly after coming so close to their final camp near Normanton, and I intended to ask some proving questions. I just hoped I wouldn't be shown the door for engaging in ungentlemanly conduct.

Before that might happen, I needed to find the door. What appeared to be the front entrance facing Victoria Street, framed by two neatly trimmed poplars, was actually the tradies' entrance. The correct door, with Australian and Victorian flags suspended above it, was on the other side of the building.

I needn't have worried about my reception. My mind's eye had pictured Dr Douglas McCann as having the character of an impatient and masterful Victorian-era African explorer, perhaps along the lines of Conan Doyle's Dr Leon Sterndale. In reality he was a softly spoken science educator with greying hair, practically dressed in a white shirt and shorts. For the expedition's 150th anniversary he had contributed to the RSV's publication *Burke and Wills: The Scientific Legacy of the Victorian Exploring Expedition*, which had looked beyond the drama to the expedition's original premise. Dr McCann ('Call me Doug') took me first on a tour of the building's exterior. It was a structure of two halves. The Victoria Street section, built in 1859, was indeed the original front entrance. The other half of the building had been constructed in 1953, when the Royal College of Surgeons had needed a home. Doug pointed to a long crack between the two halves of the building, high up on one side. 'The problem is, the newer section wants to go south. We've had to underpin it twice; cost a lot of money.'

I thought of suggesting that an inclination to head south might be karmic payback for sending Burke and Wills north, but thought better of it. I'd been heading south myself, after all, though from here on my route would be largely westward.

Instead I listened to Doug's outline of the RSV's history, as we circled its headquarters. The building had been designed for free by architect Joseph Reed, for which service he received life membership. The Cornish-born Reed was a great colonial overachiever, having designed such landmarks as the Melbourne Trades Hall, the Melbourne Town Hall, the stately home Rippon Lea Estate and the grand Royal Exhibition Building over the road from where we stood. This last structure was built for the Melbourne International Exhibition in 1880, and later played host to the opening of the first Federal Parliament in 1901. With so much of Reed's iconic Melbourne architecture extant and loved, I was put in mind of the dedication given to the great London architect Sir Christopher Wren: 'Reader, if you seek his monument, look around you.'

'He missed out on designing Parliament House, though,' said Doug. 'That stung.'

As we finished our circumnavigation at the main entrance, I noticed the garden bed next to the steps had been replanted with native vegetation. This led to a discussion of Baron Ferdinand von Mueller, the great German-born botanist who had been director of the Royal Botanic Gardens across the Yarra River, and president of the RSV in the year it had received its royal charter.

'After the gold rush, there was a critical mass of people interested in science and engineering,' said Doug. 'And the Victorians also believed in the moral uplift of education as an essential part of civilisation.'

Thus the Royal Society had seen part of its mission as educating the public, and held many open lectures. It still did now, he added, though they were usually oversubscribed.

On an inside wall hung photographs of RSV presidents, starting with Redmond Barry who had chaired a predecessor society in 1854. I always thought of Barry as 'The Hanging Judge', because a quarter-century later he would sentence Ned Kelly to death by hanging. Kelly was executed, as it happened, six weeks into the Melbourne International Exhibition, and just around the corner at the Melbourne Gaol. That had been a busy news year in Marvellous Melbourne.

Walking along the photo wall gave the impression of travelling forward through fashion history. The beards grew progressively shorter, then contracted to moustaches, and bow ties gave way to neckties as the twentieth century advanced. Eventually, in 2010, came the first female president, Lynne Selwood.

Next to these later presidents was a cabinet containing nardoo seeds, both raw and ground. It was these which were baked into a kind of bread by the Aboriginal people encountered by Burke and Wills in their last desperate days. The dying explorers tried to do this themselves, but without realising that the grain needed to be soaked to remove toxins. This lack of knowledge hastened their demise.

Around the RSV's interior I also saw photographs dealing with Antarctic exploration, the final chapter of the great era of land-based explorers which ended with World War I and the coming of aircraft. It occurred to me that Antarctic exploration was an activity the RSV could be proud of, without the ambiguities of the Burke and Wills disaster.

We settled down in the Cudmore Library. This resembled a writer's fantasy of a Victorian-era library with a touch of Harry Potter: towering wooden shelves filled with hefty leather-bound tomes, the walls punctuated with Corinthian pilasters and the odd crack caused by the southward drift. We sat on blue-grey chairs in soft natural light, only the faintest of traffic noise penetrating into this sanctum which, I felt, would always be a piece of nineteenth-century Melbourne. I wanted to ask Doug some hard questions about the Burke and Wills expedition, and the RSV's role in its mismanagement. This was where I might get chucked out, and possibly blacklisted by polite society.

'Burke and Wills succeeded in getting to the north coast, but most of the expedition's members died on the way back,' I said. 'So was it a success or a failure?'

'That's an interesting question, because it was certainly an absolute failure in terms of its original goals,' Doug replied. 'It was to be a scientific expedition, but of course it was also very political. There was enormous support from the public in Victoria, and they were interested in the land that was available up there that hadn't yet been claimed. The Queensland border actually was not where the Queensland border is now, it was further over [to the east].'

Doug was referring to an anomaly that had existed when the colony of Queensland was first carved from New South Wales. Its western border had been proclaimed as the 141st degree of longitude, not the 138th where it lies today. This created an isolated chunk of New South Wales which could be up for grabs, a possibility the movers and shakers of Melbourne had taken seriously.

'It was open slather, and there were good reports of the area from maritime explorers,' he continued. 'Leichhardt had been through the top bit, as had [Augustus Charles] Gregory. Von Mueller had actually had gone with the Gregory expedition, so there was a lot of excitement about claiming the land. Queensland was being settled and land was being claimed left, right and centre there.

'A lot of Victorian people who financed the expedition did later claim land in Queensland, right across. But of course they had to fight a frontier war to get total ownership. It was really an invasion.'

I clearly wasn't going to be shown the door today, as Doug was being franker than I might have expected from a spokesman for the RSV. Presumably enough time had elapsed for the society's 1860 shortcomings to feel less personal, and his science background prompted honest analysis. Thinking of that background, I asked him if the expedition at least had some scientific achievements.

'There was a certain amount of science done, and some of it was highly successful,' he said. 'In fact, the plants that were brought back by expedition member Dr [Hermann] Beckler were put into the herbarium [founded by von Mueller in 1853], and von Mueller processed and named those plants.

'But also the meteorology was interesting. [Cooper Creek] was the first inland meteorological station in Australia, but it also was the first to record the Coriolis effect, which is the way that the winds in a twenty-four-hour period rotate in opposite directions in the southern and northern hemispheres.

'But altogether seven people perished. Grey and Burke and Wills died, out of the four that went to the Gulf. King alone survived. We had one person who went all the way up and all the way back, so it's a success from that point of view. You've got to remember that,' he said, cutting the expeditioners some slack.

'When they came back, it was an absolute tragedy. The news hit Melbourne on the day of the very first Melbourne Cup race, believe it or not. It caused depression right across the city. They were seen more like fallen soldiers who'd died in battle.

'They went into this really elaborate thing of making them heroes. Because the Royal Society was very vulnerable. They were the ones who had financed this and didn't really follow up properly. A royal commission was held, incidentally, and everybody ran for cover.'

I contended that we regularly reinvent heroes to suit the times, giving the example of Scott of the Antarctic. He had been another brave adventurer who had failed to return alive from a great expedition.

'Exactly,' said Doug. 'And I think that's when Burke and Wills were partly forgotten. The whole Scott thing took over, and of course in the First World War we had Simpson and his donkey, and that totally changed the scene.'

Returning to the Burke and Wills expedition, Doug pointed to its questionable leadership.

'The problem is, Burke didn't want them to do the science. He just wanted to get there and back to prove he'd made it. He was an absolute mistake as leader. He had no experience. The one thing I'll say about Burke – he was bloody determined, and they knew that, and he did make it. He was, I think, a fairly driven sort of person. He saw this as his chance for glory.

'His brother was reputed to be the first person to have died in the Crimean War. Burke went back overseas to try to get into that war, but it was over by the time he got over there. So he always felt like he wanted to be a hero.'

I sensed there was a lesson in this for me, of the disaster that could befall someone who was only interested in glory. Also something about the worth of being practical, of not trying to achieve too much with too few resources.

'It was a very slow-moving expedition,' said Doug. 'Then they tried to speed it up by getting rid of all their gear, and it ended up a race in the end. It really was a disaster.'

'In Burke's case, and in Scott's, you've got someone who's driven, who succeeds in the primary goal but then dies on the way back,' I said. 'And then you have more cautious explorers like the South Australian John McDouall Stuart, who cut short expeditions that got into trouble, and who was finally successful.

But there's something romantic and heroic in succeeding but dying on the way back, isn't there?'

'Exactly,' said Doug. 'I think the reason it will always have that interest is because of the tragedy. It's not because of the success. But I think it's a salutary lesson in hubris. That's what the other states said of us before it even took off: "those smart-arse Victorians". We had half Australia's population back then; we were the centre of the action. It was the end of our innocence, the end of an era.'

I pondered his remarks, seeking lessons. Was it better to labour quietly and successfully, or aim for great things and perhaps perish in the process? Common sense suggested you couldn't enjoy your fame if you were dead, so you'd be better off sticking to what you knew. But what if your chance was slipping away from you? What then? Would that make a risky adventure more worthwhile?

I thought my time with Doug was over, but he had other ideas. He led me outside to his small car, and drove me through the congested streets of Carlton to Melbourne General Cemetery. The resting place of the great since 1853, it contained the graves of many Victorian premiers and four Australian prime ministers, along with a memorial to prime minister Harold Holt, whose body was never recovered after he disappeared while swimming in 1967.

Doug drove into the cemetery and parked the car. Shortly we were standing before the tombstone of John King. He had been the one member of the expedition to survive, because of the care of the Yandruwandha people of South Australia. I was stunned to realise he had been only thirty-three years old when he died in early 1872, which meant he was just twenty-one when he joined the expedition. What a life.

I noted his grave was well-kept compared to the neglected headstones and plots around it. While I made notes, Doug leant down to pull a few weeds from the edge of the gravesite. King's short later life, marred by the psychological scars of his trials on the expedition, clearly resonated with enough people for his resting pace to be cared for.

We returned to the car and drove onward through the expansive forest of stone pillars and angels, passing the Elvis grotto, an odd concrete-and-rock memorial to the legendary singer. Funny to realise the King died just over a century after John King. Culturally, it seemed a gulf of millennia between the high Victorian era and the 1970s.

Burke and Wills' remains lay buried beneath a huge monument. At 36 tons (36.6 tonnes), said Doug, it had been the largest block of stone quarried in Victoria at the time. Before they'd been interred here, their coffins had lain in state within the RSV building, attended by large numbers of Melburnians.

As is still the case with deaths of the great and good, such as Princess Diana, the period leading up to the funeral had been filled with public displays of grief. The two explorers' scant remains, retrieved from the wilderness, had been laid within glass-topped coffins at the RSV building for the public to view. As *The Dig Tree* relates the emotion-charged scene:

> Such was the public obsession with Victoria's dead heroes that up to 7000 mourners a day queued to see the remains. Those with enough influence were actually allowed to climb up beside the coffins and handle the bones. Pickpockets ran through the crowds and stalls sprang up outside the hall selling food, drink and commemorative handkerchiefs. More than 100,000 people filed past the bodies.

The base of the memorial was carved with this legend:

COMRADES IN A GREAT
ACHIEVEMENT
COMPANIONS IN DEATH
AND ASSOCIATES IN RENOWN

I was struck by the rough-hewn nature of the huge block, still bearing the marks of its excavators. It was as if they'd been trying to convey the natural ruggedness and vastness of the outback. Sitting here, with the roofs of Melbourne University's colleges visible over the surrounding trees, it seemed like a potent manifestation of the remote and unknown.

Our final stop was the Burke and Wills memorial cairn in Royal Park, the biggest of the inner-city parks with 181 hectares containing a zoo, sporting facilities and native trees. The cairn marked the spot where the expedition got underway on 20 August 1860. It was a circus of a departure, with thousands of onlookers getting in the way while the party tried to stow far too many supplies on far too few horses, camels and wagons. The location still lay among bushland, though next to a busy road – Doug and I had to wait a few minutes before being able to cross. The cairn was another rough-edged memorial, but with an odd shape. Its concrete-and-basalt body tapered to a point, on top of which was a wider, roughly spherical rock. It had something of the look of an old-fashioned perfume bottle. I wondered if the designer had had in mind a boab tree, with its bottle shape.

'The two brave leaders perished on their return journey,' read the inscription on the cairn. Despite the traffic noise behind us, there was something mournful about the monument in its setting of dry yellow grass and gum trees. I said goodbye to Doug and walked west through the park. I wasn't through with the doomed explorers yet.

Though the morning had started out cool it was now mid-afternoon, and it felt hot in the direct sunlight. Royal Park looked parched at the start of autumn, and particularly dry after my weeks in the wet tropics.

I wanted to catch the number 58 tram south through the park. This was my favourite stretch of tramway in Melbourne, where the rails abruptly left the road system and tracked through native bushland to connect with Melbourne Zoo and the suburbs beyond. The first time I'd even taken this ride, I'd been delighted by the unexpected juxtaposition of that most urban of transport, the tram, with a landscape that looked as if it belonged in the back of beyond. It seemed curious that anyone had been allowed to build a tram line through the middle of this recreational space, which had been laid aside for public use as early as 1845, just a decade after the establishment of Melbourne. From 1880 to 1923 a horse tram had carried pleasure-seekers from Royal Parade to the zoo, so it wasn't as if that institution was under-serviced. But as Melbourne's tramways were consolidated under a government-owned board in the 1920s, an opportunity arose for the long-suffering residents of Brunswick West, separated from the city centre by the park, to push for a new tram route. The resulting line snaked across Royal Park to carry passengers down to William Street in the Melbourne CBD, almost accidentally creating the city's most scenic tram route.

My intention was to transfer from the 58 tram to a number 59 heading north. Thus I would be roughly following the route of the Burke and Wills expedition on their first day, when they progressed a mere 11 kilometres north to the town of Essendon (now the suburb of Moonee Ponds). Fate, however, now decided to lay a Burke-and-Willsian obstacle in my path.

The tram, still within Royal Park, died. The driver couldn't get it to restart, and before long there were three trams backed up and we passengers had to abandon ship. Since this was the first transport cancellation I'd had since leaving North Queensland, I was doing well. Crossing to the northbound platform – where, ominously, there was an empty stone horse trough – I caught a tram going back in the other direction. A good thing about Melbourne's inner-city public transport system was that there was always an alternative route to wherever you were going, though it might involve the indignity of catching a bus.

I alighted from the 58 tram in Brunswick West. By chance I set down opposite St John's Church, which I'd visited years ago when the Melbourne Science Fiction Club had met in its adjacent hall. The street it was on was the type of scrappy shopping strip you found in the inner suburbs away from the major roads, dotted with practical local businesses and cheap eats (Con's Fish & Chips was on the corner).

On the number 508 bus to Moonee Ponds there were two notices about passenger behaviour toward drivers. One read, 'Thanks for being nice', while the other said, 'We wear your words.' It seemed the authorities were hedging their bets on whether reward or guilt was the best way of encouraging good behaviour. Maybe it was also a comment on the quality of bus passengers, I imagined in my snobby pro-tram way (to be fair, there were plenty of dodgy passengers on trams too).

Queens Park in Moonee Ponds was a picturesque manicured park of the Victorian-era variety, with expertly placed trees and numerous war memorials. It was in fact Victorian to its bones, having been established for Queen Victoria's diamond jubilee in 1897 and named for her. In Burke and Wills' day it had been a natural waterhole, a convenient stopping place for those headed north to the Mount Alexander goldfields. The expedition had camped here on its first night. As I'd started my journey in the vicinity of its final camp near Normanton, where Burke had carved 'B/CXIX' on a tree for Camp 119, I wanted to see what evidence remained of Camp 1. Entering the park from the south, opposite the old Essendon Courthouse, I wasn't sure what I was looking for. The grounds were full of monuments. Near the entrance was a soaring war memorial which put me in mind of a decorative rocket ship, and on a nearby bench was a plaque commemorating a beloved local doctor who'd died in 2004. The trees lining the path each remembered a soldier – I spotted 'Weary' Dunlop's name on a plaque beneath one, which reminded me of the time I'd visited the official memorial to the wartime Thai–Burma Railway near Kanchanaburi in Thailand. A curious plinth-like monument near the lake was dedicated to local men who'd fought in the Boer War. One inscription referred to a 1902 rockery, but on the other side there was a newer inscription saying the memorial had been re-erected here on the accession of King Edward VIII. There couldn't be many monuments referencing that monarch anywhere in the world, I thought, seeing as he'd abdicated within eleven months of taking the throne.

This was getting me no closer to relics of Burke and Wills, so I walked to the Moonee Ponds Bowling Club ('Established 1891') on the western edge of the park. This bore a sign referring to its Burke and Wills function room, a promising portent. I stepped into the club bar. No bar staff could be seen, but four grizzled old blokes were drinking beer by the front window.

'Are you looking for someone, mate?' asked one of them.

Well, I was. When I explained I was writing something connected to the explorers, one of them confirmed that they'd camped here the first night.

'Then Burke buggered off home and shagged his missus,' he added. This was colourful but inaccurate, as the leader had galloped back to Melbourne that night to witness a final performance by an actress with whom he was infatuated, Julia Matthews, in a production at the Princess Theatre.

'He should know,' said one of his friends, nodding toward my unreliable informant. 'He's old enough.'

They also pointed me to the nearby median strip in Mount Alexander Road. Here I finally found a monument to that first night, a round-topped chunk of stone marking 'the first camping site of the Burke and Wills Expedition.' It lay beneath the shade of a gum tree, as the site no doubt had back in 1860. With nonstop traffic on either side, it was hard to imagine that scene. But here they had slept uneasily to the braying of horses and camels, at the first stop on a hard road that led to the Gulf of Carpentaria.

And there was more. In the north-western corner of the park, a small garden of native plants had been established. Among them were four metal sculptures of camels. On a large stone at one end was a plaque, bearing what amounted to an essay on the expedition. I found this level of detail very moving. At the very bottom of the plaque was a quote from Wills, something he had told a friend before leaving Melbourne:

> 'I have only one ambition, which is
> to do some deed before I die, that
> shall entitle me to have my name
> honourably inscribed on the page of
> history. If I succeed in that I care not
> what death, or when I die.'

I found I felt much the same. Life isn't about quantity, it's about quality. And that quality doesn't have to be fame, but the knowledge that you've made a mark somehow, left an imprint on society. In Wills' case, I supposed he had got his wish.

####

'You can tell this is *taamia*, not falafel,' said Narrelle. 'It doesn't taste the same.'

'It's made from fava beans, I think.' I'd recently written an article on African food in Melbourne, and had been looking up falafel variants in Egypt and other North African countries.

After leaving Moonee Ponds I'd met Narrelle at a new Egyptian restaurant in Northcote, an inner-city neighbourhood which had run the gamut from working-class district to hipster hub to overpriced real estate in recent years. High Street was the kind of shopping strip on which you'd find former retail shops that have been transformed in cafes or bars, while retaining their original names (the bar 'Joe's Shoe Store' being the prime exemplar).

The restaurant, Pharaoh, was tastefully outfitted with a vaguely Art Deco look. What was catching our attention was the bowl of crunchy strips of Egypt's answer to falafel, which reminded us of the two years we'd spent teaching English in Cairo in the 1990s. Back then we'd bought *taamia* sandwiches from a street stall. The bean patties had been served within flatbread, with salad and pickled vegetables and a tahini sauce. They cost about twenty-five cents each.

The food at Pharaoh was upmarket Egyptian street food, and completely vegetarian. The table was scattered with dips, bread and baked dishes that reminded us of the down-to-earth versions we'd eaten in Egypt at a fraction of the price. *Koshary* was the cheapest of the cheap food in the Egyptian capital, a mess of carbs: lentils, pasta and rice cooked with tomato sauce and onion, with sauces splashed on top. The Northcote take on the dish was much the same, but with much higher quality ingredients and the addition of haloumi.

Our two years in Cairo had been formative. We'd moved there specifically to teach English, but more broadly to have an adventure. There was nothing like living in a culture so different from your own to stimulate your ability to comprehend and adapt. Those years had consolidated my love of travel, and its capacity to shock the traveller out of complacency. It hadn't been an entirely happy time, but we'd survived it and grown from it. Travel wasn't after all about happiness, but stimulation. Egypt had been endlessly stimulating. I wanted to return, but I had no idea when that might happen. For now, this food-inspired nostalgia would have to do.

Melbourne to French Island
Frankston line, Stony Point line, *Naturaliste*

Narrelle and I caught the 7.45 am train to Frankston. Again I sensed a hint of our early-morning departures to Alexandria all those years ago, though Frankston wasn't at that level of exotic. A suburb in Melbourne's south-eastern sprawl, it had for many years had a bogan reputation, though it was now much like any other outer-suburban hub. It had a core of bland commercial buildings, though with the benefit of a location on the vast Port Phillip Bay.

We departed from Flinders Street Station, the grand terminus which had been built in 1910 in French Renaissance style. It was a railway station on an impressive scale: Platform 1 alone extended over two blocks from Swanston to Queen Street. In its heyday its interior had been a hive of activity, with office space supplemented by a ballroom. Rumours suggested the latter space was now mouldering, unloved in the era of privatised rail. An even better rumour suggested that in some imperial drafting room the plans for two great railway stations had been mixed up, and Mumbai had received our station while we had built theirs. That was unlikely, but I did wonder whether Flinders Street Station's opening in 1910 was a response to Sydney's Central

Station having opened in 1906. The two cities had long been rivals, and by the first decade of the twentieth century Melbourne was heading downward while Sydney was on the way up, about to reclaim its crown as Australia's largest city (a century later the situation would be reversed, with Melbourne's population set to surpass Sydney's again in the 2020s).

The suburban train swayed through the maze of tracks to the east of the station. When the railway authorities had rationalised this complex interlacing of rails in the early twenty-first century they'd found sections that dated from the nineteenth century, still in their original positions.

We passed the Melbourne Cricket Ground and the National Tennis Centre, paused at dowdy Richmond Station, then crossed the Yarra River on the long haul south to the end of the line.

I rarely caught a train out of the CBD this early on a weekday. The carriage was crowded with private-school kids in crisp school uniforms with blazers. They made a lot of noise for 8 am, but soon disembarked for their schools in the wealthy suburbs just beyond the inner city.

There was a stretch of the line before Ormond Station where the train ran down an unfenced strip between suburban streets, with palm trees and houses on each side. Palms, I'd been told, were emblems of the exotic to the people of the Victorian era, and they survived well enough in Melbourne's climate. There were two in the laneway nearest our apartment, Somerset Place, which the council had planted in a fit of whimsy a few years before.

We dived beneath ground level for the new stations at Ormond (which I later discovered was named after the captain of the *John Bull*, which brought immigrants to Melbourne in 1840) and McKinnon (reputedly named after a nineteenth-century settler). Near-identical underground concrete bunkers with red, orange and yellow panels for decoration, they had been built by the current state government in order to replace level crossings, but it was a pity they had so little ornamentation. Railway stations had gone from being symbols of civic pride to functional boxes.

It was a beautiful day. Blue sky with a hint of thin white cloud, warm but not humid. Textbook Melbourne autumn weather. The houses of the middle-ring suburbs I could see from my window were a mix of weatherboard and brick-and-tile, along with recent creations of concrete and glass. They all looked very respectable.

The station at Mentone (named somewhat unexpectedly after the French Mediterranean town of Menton) was a quiet rebuke to its newer associates, a neatly maintained weatherboard structure that was a local landmark. Ten stations to go. The Frankston line seemed to go on forever, taking over an hour to travel from end to end.

A group of three 'authorised officers' boarded at Mordialloc – a station with an Indigenous name, meaning muddy creek or little sea in the Boon Wurrung language. AOs were basically ticket inspectors, and had earned a bad name for themselves by using strongarm tactics against passengers suspected of being fare evaders. This trio was the soul of civility, happy to scan our Myki cards through our wallets rather than having us fish them out.

We crossed Mordialloc Creek and from this point ran close to the shore of Port Phillip Bay for the rest of the journey to Frankston. These days it seems unthinkable to have given over prime waterside real estate to a railway, but in the nineteenth century the rails took precedence. Many of the suburban houses at this point encapsulated the Great Australian Dream – being archetypal brick-and-tile homes as depicted so memorably by artist Howard Arkley – with the bonus of being located near a beach. In these areas the local shopping strip usually ran parallel to the rail line, with shops on one side and the tracks on the other. This meant shop signage could also advertise to passing train passengers. At Chelsea a boldly painted sign read 'Chelsea Body Care: Traditional Chinese Massage for Ladies and Gentlemen', and at Bonbeach I saw shops we no longer had in the CBD because of soaring commercial rents: a coin laundry, and a fish-and-chippery. Though Chelsea clearly took its name from the London district,

Bonbeach, I learned, had been voted into existence in 1926 in a referendum held by the Department of Railways. Its folksy name suggesting a 'good beach' fitted with the vaguely bucolic real-estate-agent-friendly names of several other twentieth-century stations along the Frankston line: Parkdale, Aspendale, Edithvale.

We were very close to the bay now, its water visible as the train passed each perpendicular street. Just before Carrum (derived from another Boon Wurrung word, meaning boomerang), we crossed above the Patterson River and I saw a small recreational boat heading along it to the larger body of water.

Then we arrived at the end of the line: Frankston. As once before in Queensland, I was surprised to discover no-one was sure about the origin of the suburb's name. Logic suggested it was named after a prominent early settler in the area, Frank Liardet, but in 1916 the Liardet family insisted it had been named for the Irish-born settler Charles Franks, who had been killed by Indigenous people in 1836 in far-off Werribee, reputedly the first European settler to die in that way. As if that wasn't enough confusion, a third theory claims the town was named after heroic British army general Sir Thomas Harte Franks, in common with other military-related place names in the area.

Whatever the truth, we didn't linger, stepping across to Platform 3, which seemed an afterthought or even a mild embarrassment, being narrow and lacking in shade. It was the northern terminus of the Stony Point line.

This line was an anomaly. It was part of Melbourne's urban public transport system, with the same fares, but was served by diesel railcars operated by long-distance operator V/Line. Designed in the 1990s for short country routes, these railcars operated as suburban trains on this run. In practice, the only difference was locked onboard toilets. Why this essentially country service along the Mornington Peninsula had survived through the years, when so many regional branch lines had been scrapped, was a mystery. There was a fair amount of industry at Hastings, which occasioned freight, and the naval base HMAS *Cerberus* at Crib Point was a consideration. When it had opened in 1920 as Flinders Naval Depot, railway was still regarded as an essential adjunct to the movement of troops.

At 10.10 am a single railcar eased in next to the platform and we boarded. The interior was that of an old country train: luggage racks, heavily cushioned seats, a water dispenser with tiny paper cups. Next to me was seated a man in a high-vis vest and bike helmet, leafing through a copy of the *Australian* newspaper.

A man in a wheelchair was waiting for a ramp to be provided so he could board but, tiring of the delay, he stood up and wheeled it on himself. 'I don't need special treatment,' he said to no-one in particular.

The train snaked through the residential fringes of Frankston, then broke free into countryside, the single set of rails lined by spindly gum trees with twisted trunks. We were cutting across the peninsula from west to east, and although it seemed rural I could see it was also an extension of Melbourne, with small towns that acted like dormitory suburbs for commuters.

At Somerville, Narrelle spotted an attractive Mechanics Institute among the shops, with Art Nouveau lettering. At Tyabb there was a landmark packing store whose voluminous interior was occupied by a popular antiques emporium. At Hastings we finally glimpsed Western Port Bay, whose waters we would soon be crossing.

Morradoo Station caught my eye. When I'd first come to Melbourne it had been known prosaically as Stopping Place Number 15. It had been renamed in 1996 after a local competition, in which a student had suggested the original Aboriginal name of nearby Crib Point.

We passed the naval base, and the waters beyond shimmered. Two noisy children with startlingly blond hair started wandering the aisles. As their parents both had brown hair, the kids put me in mind of the ring-ins in John Wyndham's novel *The Midwich Cuckoos*. At Stony Point we left the train and they stayed aboard for the return trip to Frankston, perhaps using it as a cheap family joy ride.

Stony Point Station resembled a shed. The only businesses here were a kiosk and a caravan park, on either side of the line. I felt a strong urge to check into one of the park's cabins and hide out for a week, reading. Stony Point was the perfect place for a recluse: tiny and overlooked, though served by regular trains. But we were moving on. There was an hour to kill before our ferry to French Island, in the centre of Western Port Bay.

#####

It was a long walk along the jetty to the ferry, past serious-looking maritime vessels including the *Seahorse Spirit*, a chunky vessel with a low stern, used by the Royal Australian Navy to train recruits. Fishermen near the end of the structure were trying their luck.

I was surprised to see how far the bay's mudflats extended, almost to the end of the jetty. Clearly it was essential to stick to the designated shipping channels in the bay, for fear of running aground. Seabirds hung around the edge of the flats where they met open water, pecking away at exposed lifeforms.

We sat on the open top deck of the *Naturaliste*. This was a new ferry which had only been operating for a few months, replacing a squat predecessor. This vessel had elevation. The bridge, directly ahead of where we sat, had a raised, cushioned pilot's seat with views all round.

The ten-minute crossing to French Island felt like a leap into mystery. Named Île des Français by a French expedition led by explorer Nicolas Baudin in 1802, it had been the home of diverse enterprises over the decades, including farms and a prison. Some 70% of the island is now the French Island National Park, and only a hundred or so people live on the rest of it. Because it's an unincorporated area, there's no shire council and no rates to pay, so the residents are largely self-sufficient. It's not uncommon to see cars driving by on the island with no licence plates. Though it's only 60 kilometres south-east of central Melbourne, it feels as if it's a remote territory. All this piqued my interest, but until recently it had been difficult for a non-resident to explore the island. There was no bridge from the mainland, so cars couldn't be taken across except by an expensive barge, and the unsealed roads weren't gentle on bikes. The ferry could drop you at the Tankerton Jetty on the island's west coast, but there was no township there and no public transport. The only shop on the island was a general store a few kilometres east of the jetty.

In December, however, the ferry had been upgraded and a company sharing its name, Naturaliste Tours, had started operating day tours using a four-wheel-drive vehicle. It was this tour we were joining.

Our guide, Matt, met us at the land end of the French Island jetty, alongside a 4.8-tonne vehicle which looked as though it was descended from a tank. An 'OKA', it had originally been built for use by the Western Australian mining industry. Getting into the front passenger seat required me to haul myself upward by gripping an overhead handle. This was a rare occasion on which I could identify a precise use for the weightlifting I did at the gym, and was thankful for it. Narrelle sat in the main body of the vehicle along with the six other tour members.

Matt, a marine biologist by training, gave us a verbal sketch of the shore life of the island. It had some of the southernmost seagrass in the world, he said. It also had some of the world's southernmost mangroves, the same plants which had prevented Burke and Wills from actually setting foot on the shore of the Gulf.

He confirmed that locals looked after their own affairs. 'They maintain a rubbish tip and handle recycling,' he said. 'Anyone who does live over here is fully off the grid.'

We drove north a short distance. Led by foot to Fairhaven Beach, we could see the salt marsh stretching back from the coastline had dried out in the hot weather. 'We haven't had a drop of rain here lately,' said Matt.

On the mainland was a point called – in classic Australian descriptive style – Sandy Point. From there, said Matt, sand had been blowing across the water to the island for thousands of years, building up the beach on our side.

There were signs of the industrialised world across the bay: a bright orange flame burning waste products at the oil refinery at Crib Point, and around to the south-west the rooftops of Cowes, the main town on Phillip Island. From HMAS *Cerberus*, said Matt, one could occasionally hear the sounds of naval target practice.

On our side of the water we could see the island's jetty and the collection of cars parked around its end. 'People park them there for the day when they're using the ferry,' he said, 'and sometimes people leaving the island permanently dump them there.'

Industrial elements aside, it was an appealing view from the beach, one of overlapping colours: the green vegetation of the mainland, then the blue channel, the blue-brown mudflats, the white sandy beach, and the strangely fuchsia-coloured plants of the salt marsh. On our way back to the OKA, Matt pointed out a low succulent with chunky fingers, which was called pigface. He bit off a piece, and so did I; it was salty, then bitter, but full of water.

Back in the vehicle, he explained that Western Port, though east of Melbourne's Port Phillip Bay, gained its name from George Bass's charting of Australia's east coast. 'It was at the edge of his survey, so from his perspective it was west.'

One of the main marsupials here, the koala, had been introduced to the island and was free of chlamydia, which had torn through the mainland population. The French Island koala numbers were getting out of hand, however, and there was a program to resettle some of them on the mainland. There was also a plan to introduce the tiny eastern barred bandicoot to the island, but that depended on first ridding it of feral cats. 'There's a program to catch them. The trappers swear by using KFC chicken as bait,' said Matt.

Remembering what had happened when a similar project in New Zealand had rid an island of cats – that the rat population had soared – I wondered how feasible that would prove to be.

The tour had access to the national park, so Matt jumped out and unlocked a gate, which doubled as a firebreak. 'Fire is the greatest threat on French Island,' he said. 'So much risk, so little capacity to fight it.'

My fellow tour members were most interested in the natural history of the island, but I was intrigued by the human story. As far as could be determined, Aboriginal people hadn't lived permanently here, but had used it as a seasonal place to camp.

The first settlers in colonial times came in 1842, a duo who burnt mangroves so their ashes could be used to make glass. They'd described their time on their island as fairly grim. From 1847 farmers grazed sheep and then cattle, to moderate success given the relative aridity and the need to swim cattle across the bay to market.

We stopped at the sea of reeds that was the Pobblebonk swamp ('We can't go in too far because of snakes'). It was named after the colloquial term for the eastern banjo frog, derived from its distinctive call. When we asked about the trees around its edge, Matt said there weren't many on the island that dated back to colonial times. That was due to the next industry established on French Island. From 1878, chicory, widely used as a coffee alternative or additive, was grown and dried in local kilns. These required a large amount of firewood.

'On French Island there was a firewood mentality,' said Matt. 'Everything got burned.'

I was starting to see a pattern, one which mirrored colonial exploitation of nature and capitalism in general. Because French Island was relatively difficult to exploit, its land remained cheap. But because its land was cheap, it encouraged experiments in exploitation. There was always someone new willing to give it a go, no matter how wacky or ill-advised the idea.

The OKA ground up to one of the island's high points, the Pinnacles, about 90 metres above sea level. On its level top was a huge rusting trapezoidal frame covered with horizontal yellow panels. Narrelle and I exchanged a glance. We had been joking earlier about the French Island locals having a wicker man stowed away for over-inquisitive visitors. Was this it?

'This was a navigational feature for ships, before the era of GPS,' said Matt. Well, that was his story.

Matt pointed toward the mainland, where we were surprised to see the black form of a submarine riding high in the water. This was the former HMAS *Otama*, an Oberon-class submarine which the navy retired in 2000. It had been sold to a group which wanted it for a local maritime museum, but nearly two decades later not much had happened.

The next of French Island's curious enterprises was the McLeod Prison Farm, which had opened in 1916 and remained operational until 1975. In looking this up on my phone I happened upon an old newspaper story from 1952 which described an escape from the island, during which four prisoners stole a dinghy from the Tankerton Jetty and rowed it to Crib Point. There they stole bicycles which they rode to Frankston, where they stole a car. My first reaction was that they must have been impressively fit. For a while after the prison had closed, it had been run as a holiday camp. Recently it had been bought by a Chinese investor with ambitious plans for tourist accommodation. Despite this, it was hard to imagine it being developed into a resort, given the formidable logistical and planning difficulties presented by the island. Not to mention its history of knocking optimistic enterprises on the head.

Another was the 1960s proposal to build a nuclear power plant. As part of the push for this, the State Electricity Commission of Victoria and other interested bodies had bought up land, depleting the resident population. Given the low price of coal and increasing opposition to nuclear power by activist groups, the power station never happened.

Heading east now, along one of island's more navigable roads, we spotted a lone emu in a paddock. Matt had no idea where it had come from or why it was there alone; I received the impression from his reaction that emus weren't native to the island. French Island still had its secrets.

We turned off along Saltmine Point Road (a tribute to another failed industry), and spotted the tents of a glamping outfit in the distance as we descended through a grassy slope to Blue Gums Homestead. An abandoned farm with decaying buildings and a chicory kiln preserved under a new roof, it was an eerie place with an outstanding view over the bay. 'It's too "snakey" here to get out,' said Matt, and we were happy to go along with that. As yet another example of the history of failed experiments on the island, it had a tangibly melancholy air.

The location did present a stunning vista, including the low, compact form of Elizabeth Island just offshore, available to buy as freehold. I looked at its long-exposed surface and frowned. I liked the idea of living on an island – who didn't? – but it would need more facilities and connectedness than that.

I asked Narrelle – a novelist as well as a freelance business writer – whether the island was giving her inspiration for fiction. She said it was yielding crime story ideas by the minute.

The tour finished with the group leaving the bus and walking 500 metres or so along a road lined by manna gum trees. We were looking for koalas, who fancied this type of vegetation. We spotted six or seven of the marsupials by my count ('Seven or eight,' insisted a fellow tour member, an older woman with an authoritative air, and I yielded the point). Eight was the record, said Matt, adding, as an afterthought, that a specific clan of eight might live in those trees.

On the timber deck outside the French Island General Store, the realisation set in that we weren't going back to the mainland. We'd waved the tour group goodbye after they'd paid a quick visit to the store to buy its home-made choc-tops. We were staying overnight.

The deck's 'Enjoy your stay' sign had broken off, and was lying face-up on the ground. By the road, a group of locals was dealing with an automotive problem, with jump leads linking two cars.

French Island wasn't really remote – Melbourne was just over the horizon – but it *felt* remote. One glance at the store's Telstra phone box with a solar cell array sprouting from its roof fuelled overexcited *Mad Max* / *Wake in Fright* imaginings.

I remarked to Narrelle that there was a fictional sub-genre, especially on screen – of 'Gothic' small towns where the residents were strange and secretive, possibly cult-like, and the stranger feared to tread. Its manifestations were shaped by local culture. In the UK, the town would be a traditional-seeming village off the main roads, where the locals secretly hewed to pagan beliefs and rituals (see *The Wicker Man*). In the USA, the town would be a typical Main Street town, with twisted, homicidal, insular residents (see multiple *Twilight Zone* episodes). In Australia, these places were always located in the liminal, heat-crazed outback, a reflection of our communal historic fear of that so-called 'ghastly blank' that had first drawn and then killed Burke and Wills. The remote regions of the continent ably represented forces at odd with material civilisation. But did those villages of the damned make their own choc-tops? Narrelle went inside to buy one, and I got talking to a local who was sitting on the deck with a small dog.

'Do the dogs here ever go after snakes?' I asked.

'This one's too young to try,' he said, in a measured Aussie drawl, then added, 'The other day I got into my campervan and there was a 1.5 metre tiger snake stretched out there. No idea how it got in.

'I don't kill them,' he said. 'They're part of the ecosystem.'

'I don't go into their home in the long grass,' said Narrelle, who'd emerged with the ice-cream.

'So I guess that snake shouldn't have got into my van!' he said with emphasis. I wasn't sure for a moment if he was angry with the snake. Then he smiled.

We spent the night at the cottage next to the general store. Aside from the glamping tents, it was the only place to stay on the island. A former eco-lodge near the jetty was under renovation, but not operational yet. I cooked dinner with ingredients I'd brought from Melbourne in my backpack. Afterward we sat in the garden on metal chairs, looking upwards. A smear of light lay across the north-eastern edge of the sky, the lights of the great city reminding us of its proximity. But above us was a spectacular sight, a mass of stars which arced up and over. I could see Orion straight ahead. When we stood and looked back over the roof of the cottage, we were rewarded with the Southern Cross and the broad stripe that was the Milky Way: a glimpse into the burning heart of our galaxy. I'd been used to that sight as a child living on a farm in Western Australia, but had gone years without seeing it as an adult.

Sitting in the quiet night, the stars above us, I felt calm for the first time that week. It had been more difficult than I'd expected being back in Melbourne but still on my long journey, home but not home, trying to mesh new research with familiar people and routines. Now that we finally had the time to talk at length, we chatted about my project. And about my travels in general.

The typical travel writing research trip I usually undertook was several weeks, often across a few different countries (as an example, in 2016 I'd travelled from Hamburg, Germany, via Denmark and Poland to Ukraine, spending a night at the end of the trip in Chernobyl). These trips resulted in a bounty of raw material that could then be harvested into individual travel articles; that 2016 trip had produced about twenty-five such published pieces over the following years. However, planning such a mammoth undertaking required liaison with several national and city tourism promotion organisations, along with hotel firms, tour companies and other relevant players. The beauty of this thorough itinerary planning was that once I was on the ground, I knew exactly where I had to be each day and it ran very smoothly. However, piecing together that itinerary before departure felt like herding cats. It could be – well, always was – stressful. And that stress could slosh over into our home life.

After talking about this we sat quietly, reflecting. The past few years hadn't been an easy period in our lives. Narrelle's mother had passed away in 2014, then in early 2015 I'd had a health scare when I'd lost a small amount of sight in my left eye. Then late that year, just after I'd returned from a long rail trip up the west coast of the USA, our cat Petra had died. I'd been particularly close to her as we'd brought her home from an animal refuge the same week I'd taken up freelance writing in 2004, and we'd been workmates for the almost 12 years since. The loss had rocked me, and the grief took a long time to diminish.

For her part, Narrelle had been traumatised by the mass murder that had happened in 2017 in Melbourne's Bourke Street Mall, when a drugged-up psychotic driver had driven a car at speed through the pedestrian zone, killing six people and injuring dozens. As it happened, Narrelle – in her freelance business-writer persona – had been working in a corporate office above the corner of Bourke and Elizabeth Streets that day, on the driver's destructive route, and we lived just half a city block away from the mall. For a long time afterward, the mounds of flowers left on the GPO building's steps in memory of the victims were a colourful and dreadful reminder. The experience had left Narrelle brittle and easily angered.

Still, here we were.

'When you rang me about the wet-season rain causing train cancellations at the start of your journey, I was worried about you,' she said. 'You were so distressed. But there was nothing I could do to help but listen.'

Listening was something. It was more than something. And we'd tackled big challenges together in the past.

We sat for a while in companionable silence, admiring the stars. Then I asked Narrelle, who'd recently had a short story published in *Sherlock Holmes: The Australian Casebook*, what mystery she would give the great detective to solve if he'd visited French Island in his nineteenth-century heyday.

She thought for a moment and said, 'A body found in the chicory kiln. Dead, and dried out.'

Next morning the weather had turned cool and cloudy, threatening rain. We had breakfast at the general store, whose manager, Tanya, was delighted we'd enjoyed the night sky so much. Tanya introduced her dad, who was stacking the fridge, and the rest of her family in the kitchen. It made sense that such an isolated business would be a family affair.

As we waited for our meals, locals arrived to pick up parcels from the post office counter, or to buy groceries. The shelves carried practical items like sealant and firelighters alongside foodstuffs. Against the postal counter leaned two enormous sacks of chicken feed. When I dropped off the key to the cottage, I asked Tanya how they stocked the general store.

'I take our courtesy bus across to the mainland and load it to the brim with groceries,' she said. 'It can be tricky logistically – you have to think about things like melting ice-cream – but it gets done.'

It was raining steadily as the departure time approached for the ferry back to Stony Point, and a breeze was blowing. Good news for the arid island, but I was glad the weather had held off until we'd seen that crisp star field.

Tanya's dad, Neil, gave us a lift to the jetty, and we talked about life on French Island.

'I've been the postman for years, so I know everyone,' he said. 'And the island does draw its share of loners.

'I don't live for possessions myself, I'm happy doing what I do.' That included fencing, which at first I thought was the sport, but then realised meant building fences. For a man in his late sixties he was doing well, I thought – active and occupied.

While I peered out across the bay, Narrelle and Neil talked about curious incidents on the island. Just the previous week a woman who was about to be evicted had vanished, her car and possessions abandoned on the beach. No trace of her had yet been found.

I remembered the prison escapees from 1952, and wondered if she'd stolen a dinghy or swum to Crib Point. Or, as seemed more likely, if there was a tragedy waiting to be discovered.

The rain fell heavily as we waited for the ferry, which was moving toward the jetty with glacial speed. I stepped outside the shelter beneath the mauve umbrella I'd bought in Cairns, so the pilot could see there were passengers waiting.

'Yes,' said Neil behind me. 'This island's full of mysteries.'

Melbourne to Adelaide
Overland

The spires of St Patrick's Cathedral stood out against the lightening eastern sky as I caught the number 86 tram through the city streets. It was 7 am, but – thanks to daylight-saving time enduring through those last days of March – still dark. An autumnal chill had enveloped Melbourne, and all the passengers were in dark colours, wearing jackets. Remembering the first law of travel, I bought coffee from the cart outside Higher Ground, then carried it across Spencer Street.

Like Sydney's Central Station, Melbourne's Southern Cross Station is a splendid place to begin a long-distance train journey, especially on a weekday morning with the peak-hour pressure building. Long-distance stations should be grand and momentous, and with this new station building, completed in 2006, they'd got it right. The roof high above the platforms undulated in great waves, putting me in mind of the profiles of blue whales. The view across the platforms, serving both country trains and suburban ones, suggested volume and scope, that the railways still mattered in Victoria. It was a small enough state for that to be true. The longest rail journey one could take was about four hours, and the only Victorian city I'd ever flown to from Melbourne was far north-western Mildura.

The *Overland* train was waiting at Platform 2, its exterior standing out with cobalt blue trim above streamlined steel, and a badge featuring a running emu. Standing on the platform, I chatted to the crew member minding the door. She'd be working on the *Indian Pacific* in a couple of days, so might encounter me again on the next train on my list.

It wasn't hard to pick the *Overland* as a privately run train, operated by Great Southern Rail. Shortly to be renamed as the more mystical Journey Beyond Rail Expeditions, the company also ran the *Indian Pacific* (from Sydney to Perth) and the *Ghan* (Adelaide to Darwin). The staff had a distinctive uniform of neat light-brown jacket and striped shirt topped off by a stockman's hat – an iconic Aussie nod to tourists. They were briskly efficient in ticking our names off the boarding list at the gate to the platform, and let us board the train a good half-hour before departure. Once we were on, however, they locked the door. I had to ask to go out again on the platform to take a photo, when there was still twenty minutes until departure. On the *Spirit of Queensland* the crew had resembled genial housemistresses; on the XPT they'd been as casual as cafe waiters; and on the *Overland* they were mother hens, making sure you didn't stray. As I was considering this, the XPT from Sydney pulled in next to us on Platform 1, neatly replicating the crossover from the previous week. I wondered if there was a Mr Singh alighting on today's train, marching off for breakfast and a check-up on his Melbourne office.

The sun had risen. On the platform to the west I could see a purple V/Line train waiting to head to Geelong, and beyond it the constant inbound/outbound shuffle of blue suburban trains conveying workers to the daily grind. Yet again I felt the pleasure of watching people commute while I wasn't. Beyond the station were the quasi-futuristic office blocks of Docklands, one featuring jagged slots of colour between slate-grey triangular windows.

We pulled out on time at 8.05 am and quickly passed the Docklands towers, the stadium, the old goods sheds and the observation wheel, which had malfunctioned in the severe summer of 2009 and taken four years to rebuild.

The train crept slowly to the west of North Melbourne Station, passing random railway detritus: rails, small trucks, vast spools of cable. Outside one shed were arranged neat rows of train wheels, looking like giants' barbells.

An announcement over the carriage speakers gave an orientation to the train. I heard, 'Unless you are leaving at an intermediate stop, you will not be permitted to leave the train.' That sounded strict. Could they hold us against our will?

We crossed the Maribyrnong River just north of where Lonely Planet used to have its headquarters – I could see the building from my window. I'd visited the publisher by bus, back in the days when marked-up maps from research gigs were delivered by hand.

The voice was now talking about the locks in the onboard loos, which needed to be activated separately after the door was closed. Not checking this 'could lead to an extremely embarrassing situation.' We couldn't have that. It did make me wonder about the unintuitive design, which I'd encountered in other company's trains as well.

'Our journey today will cover eight hundred and twenty-eight kilometres at an average speed of eighty-five kilometres per hour.' Not for us the super-fast trains of Asia or Europe, but that was actually faster than the average achieved by the *Spirit of Queensland*.

I was happy to again be on the move. There were two classes of service on the *Overland*: Red and Red Premium, basically economy and premium economy. Those classifications, odd in isolation, fitted with the Gold and Platinum classes aboard the *Indian Pacific* and the *Ghan*. Both of those had had Red seated classes until a few years before. The people at the back of our train were in Red, which had four seats across in a two-two configuration. This was more or less the public-transport section, its fares kept competitive with those of flights between the two cities.

Both the Victorian and South Australian governments contributed to the budget of the *Overland*, so it was possible to buy a Red seat from V/Line. In years when a South Australian football team made it into an AFL grand final, GSR stacked on extra carriages and ran the longest versions of the train ever seen.

Red Premium had only three seats across, in a one-two setup. These were comfy padded seats with a lot of leg room, and tables that unfolded from the armrests. The decor echoed the Australian bush, with the pattern of the two-tone green carpet hinting at twining vegetation.

The standard-gauge route through Melbourne's western portside districts passed through a grab bag of industrial heritage. In West Footscray we saw a faded Uncle Tobys sign on a huge silo, and big former woolsheds.

Tottenham Station's platform was lined with commuters looking at their phones, seemingly marooned on an island in a sea of tracks which formed the marshalling yard known as Tottenham Yard. The yard had declined in use since the line to Adelaide had been converted to standard gauge in 1995, and the suburbs around it were steadily gentrifying. We passed the old Bradmill factory, which had produced denim until the start of the twenty-first century. It had been decaying for more than a decade, waiting to be turned into a new housing estate. Not far past it loomed the container tanks of the Shell petroleum terminal at Newport. No matter how gentrified the west became, it was impossible to ignore such vast reminders of its industrial base. Newport also housed the sizeable railway workshops which had been opened in 1882, and within whose walls Trugo had been invented.

Past the hellish vista of the Mobil refinery with its tangle of metal pipes and smoking vents, we picked up speed as we neared the end of the suburban rail network. Again I felt as if each great city had a gravity well which drew objects toward it, and from which it was hard to escape.

I went to the loo (remembering to lock it). When I returned, we were on the flat volcanic plains between Melbourne and Geelong, the granite peaks of the You Yangs range to the west. I always thought of this stretch as 'The Wasteland', it was so low and empty, as if a void between the two cities. Above The Wasteland a Cathay Pacific jet was flying low, but such was our relative speed and trajectory that it seemed to hang in the sky motionless, like a giant white balloon on a string.

A crew member came through the cabin to take breakfast orders. I was surprised to discover that meals and soft drinks were included in the fare. This was a recent innovation, she said, to bring the *Overland* into line with the meals-included policy of its sister trains.

'We'll be travelling through Geelong's industrial areas, but don't be fooled – it's a beautiful city,' came an announcement. This was fair warning, as we would only call at North Shore Station before making a westward turn, skimming the northern edge of the city. I'd wondered why the *Overland* took this indirect route via Geelong, rather than heading west via Ballarat, but I suspected it was the standard-gauge line which dictated the itinerary. It had been slow progress this far, as we'd had to wait for a freight train early on. We'd reached North Shore after ninety minutes, a distance V/Line trains covered in sixty minutes with multiple stops.

I got talking to the passenger across the aisle. Rhys was a graphic designer who'd grown up in Zimbabwe and now lived in the UK. He was of Welsh heritage, and his father had worked on what was then Rhodesia's railways.

'They used to train air force pilots in Rhodesia during the war, so my dad worked there as an armourer – they loaded ammunition onto the planes. He'd been a fitter and turner above a mine in Wales, but he met a girl out there and stopped on, and got a job on the railways.'

Rhys was going to join the *Indian Pacific* from Adelaide to Perth the same day as me, though we might not see each other there, given the length of the train. But why wasn't he indulging in the full *Indian Pacific* experience from its starting point in Sydney?

'I've just been to the Grand Prix in Melbourne with some friends,' he said. 'It was easier this way.'

He could have flown, but his dad's job in the railways had filtered down as an interest to his son. And he far preferred trains to boats.

'I don't like cruises,' he said. 'Especially the big ones. You'd hardly know you were at sea.'

When he learned I wrote regularly about train journeys, we compared notes on our best rail experiences around the world. One of my favourites, I told him, had been Amtrak's *Coast Starlight* sleeper train between Los Angeles and Seattle, passing ocean and mountains, and stopping off at San Francisco and Portland. That had been a special trip: talking with fellow passengers, exploring four very different cities, meeting up with friends along the way.

West of Geelong we passed an old cemetery at Inverleigh, then a paddock with dirty-looking sheep and big black crows, contrasted against the dry yellow grass. Interstate friends might joke about it raining in Victoria all the time, but this was the driest landscape I'd seen on my entire trip. When I'd first taken this train, years before, it had been in spring and the scenery was dominated by the bright yellow of canola crops.

'This is the least visually interesting time of year to travel this way,' confirmed a passing crew member. 'Later in the year there's lots of colour.'

At Ararat, a brief announcement mentioned its history of being 'the only Australian town to be founded by the Chinese,' without adding the backstory.

Which was this: the Victorian government had tried to dissuade Chinese miners from joining the 1850s gold rush by slapping a large landing tax on them. In response, the Chinese had instead landed at Robe in South Australia and walked 500 kilometres or so, all the way to the goldfields. On one such trek they had struck gold at the site of Ararat, and stayed on. Narrelle had been on this train some years before, had heard the same announcement, and had been inspired to use Ararat in her Sherlock Holmes novel set in Australia.

'We're now coming up to Stawell, the largest town close to Grampians National Park. The Stawell Gift is held here each year.'

Here was the anagrammatical partner to Sawtell, which I'd passed in New South Wales. The Gift was Victoria's answer to the Mount Cooroora race and the richest foot race in Australia. Held almost every Easter since 1878, the next would take place in a few days time.

Before we reached the town we passed through Great Western, which for a long time I'd associated only with a brand of sparkling wine, not realising this was where it was manufactured. A banner for the company that produced it, Seppelt, was draped along the side of an old railway building as we passed.

The station at Stawell took up a scrappy broad area between streets. On one side I could make out a pub – the National Hotel – with attractive Art Nouveau lettering on its facade. A number of pubs must have been built or renovated around the start of the twentieth century, as I'd encountered several with this style of signage. I'd passed one the previous week while sleeping aboard the XPT: the North Eastern Hotel in Benalla, located near the railway station. I had a soft spot for the North Eastern, as I'd once visited it for the *Age* newspaper's Sunday Lunch column. For this component of the travel section, I'd visit a great country restaurant by rail, be fed an excellent complimentary lunch, then write a few hundred words about the experience and get paid for it. It had been a sad day when that column was cancelled.

Stawell was named after Sir William Stawell, a Royal Society figure who had been heavily involved in the planning of the Burke and Wills expedition. He'd also been the state MP for Melbourne, the state electoral district I lived in. Nowadays the seat was held for the Greens by a woman, Ellen Sandell, which might have surprised Sir William.

We passed silos, old brick buildings and disused sidings on our way out of town, and a business called Split 'N' Stawell which sold air-conditioning units. As the town passed by I could once again see the rugged Grampians ranges (known to the local Djab

Wurrung and Jardwadjali people as Gariwerd), which had been quietly looming to the west, ghostly beneath a bluish haze – the last gasp of the Great Dividing Range which I'd been following since I'd crossed it outside Cairns. Then the gum trees thickened, hiding it, only to open on an ageing farmhouse with an old train carriage in its backyard. At which point lunch arrived. Mine was baked moussaka with Napoletana sauce, bocconcini and basil, presented in a metal pannikin on a board, with metal cutlery. Posh.

There was more evidence of German settlement as we passed through Lubeck, whose European namesake I'd visited two years before. This incarnation had avoided being renamed amid the anti-German sentiment of World War I, though I had no idea why. The Victorian Places website I checked later mentioned that the first church in the town had been shared by Methodists and Presbyterians rather than being Lutheran, so perhaps there wasn't an enduring sense of German heritage to the place. Some 140 people now lived in the area. Towns in this Wimmera region of Victoria were never big: even Horsham, the major centre, held only 17,000 people. I remembered reading that sheep farming didn't require many people compared to other industries, and that was how Victoria had started, founded by settlers from Tasmania looking to make money from wool.

'This looks a lot like Africa,' said Rhys as he gazed out the window. I hadn't been further south than Egypt myself, but it did match the idea of South Africa I'd gained from movies set there: dry and sparse and open. (A month later I'd be in South Africa, invited as part of a media group, but that email hadn't landed yet. For the record, it did often resemble western Victoria.)

I got talking to Rhys about politics, and Robert Mugabe, and the fraught period when Rhodesia had declared independence from Britain to forestall a black-majority government, sparking a guerrilla war. I'd had a similar conversation with a black Zimbabwean at a hotel gym in Manchester the previous year. He had shaken his head at Mugabe's staying power. The president had been ninety-three at the time, and had not yet been deposed. We didn't get into the details of his family's involvement in that era, but Rhys too shook his head as if remembering a difficult time. 'Certainly it could have been handled better.' A verdict for almost every power struggle in history.

After we passed Horsham there were more tiny localities at which the train no longer stopped. I couldn't find out why Pimpinio had been given its name, but its Wikipedia entry included the droll comment, 'They also have a cricket side, who have had a bit of success.'

Dimboola, our next stop, was revealed to be named from a Sinhalese word which meant 'land of figs', by a district surveyor who'd lived in colonial Ceylon. By coincidence there was a Dimbulah Station called at by the *Savannahlander* in Queensland, though that name apparently derived from a local Aboriginal word meaning 'long waterhole'. Dimboola was also the title and setting of a famous play about an Australian bush wedding, which had premiered at La Mama Theatre in Melbourne in 1969. Written by Jack Hibberd, the first production of *Dimboola* had been directed by a twenty-four-year-old Graeme Blundell, who'd also starred in the play, and subsequently became a successful actor.

From Dimboola we tracked north of Little Desert National Park. A British colleague of mine had written that there were so many national parks in Australia you suspected they were overdoing it, until you visited and realised each one was stunning. This park, an elongated oval stretching almost to the South Australian border, ranged from seasonal swampland to mallee heathland, and was home to the threatened ground-dwelling malleefowl.

At intervals we passed enormous silos, a legacy of wheat growing. At Kiata the silos seemed to amount to the entire town. A marvellous thing had happened to the region's silos in recent years: their tall blank faces had been turned over to street artists who'd created murals that now towered over the flat plains. The Silo Art

Trail now included six silos over 200 kilometres to the north of the railway line, bringing tourism to the region. The first of these, in the small town of Brim, had been painted by the respected artist Guido van Helten in 2015, and featured four local farmers in a black-and-white photorealistic style. It had been an instant success. In 2016 I'd met van Helten at a street art festival in Benalla. A few weeks later I'd been walking through the base of an abandoned cooling tower at Chernobyl, Ukraine, when I saw a piece of art that was obviously his: a painting of an emergency worker who'd responded to the 1986 nuclear crisis there. Small world.

At Nhill the unseen announcer told us that the oldest wheat silo there, installed in the 1920s, could hold 135,000 bushels of wheat. A bushel is eight gallons, equivalent to just over 36 litres. So that was a lot of wheat. Nhill was also home to the Australian Pinball Museum, I discovered – an unexpected fun fact.

At 2 pm we were served pear-and-walnut tarts, and a herd of sheep on the left were startled by the train into an ungainly gallop. The *Overland* only passed this way twice a week, so they could be forgiven for being surprised. The previous year I'd read a report of a car colliding with the *Overland*, and wondered how they'd managed to do it. Being in the precise place to collide with so infrequent a train in an area this vast seemed like threading the eye of a microscopic needle.

I was alert now, camera primed, as we were about to breeze through Serviceton and I wanted a photo of its train station. Located on the border between Victoria and South Australia, it was an outsized structure which had contained facilities for customs checks in the days before federation, when the colonies had levied import duties on each other. It loomed, I clicked, it was gone.

The train no longer stopped at Serviceton, but it had a significant place in Australia's rail history. In 1887 the railway from Bordertown in South Australia had joined up here with the line from Dimboola, creating Australia's first intercolonial (later interstate) railway. Because Victoria and South Australia had both used broad-gauge track, there was no break-of-gauge problem. On 19 January 1887 the *Intercolonial Express* (now the *Overland*) had run its first service between the two cities, using jointly owned rolling stock. For 120 years the train had been a sleeper, conveying passengers neatly between the two state capitals to arrive at each end at 9 am. As a glossy marketing brochure I found in the State Library of Victoria pointed out in its promotion of the 'new' *Overland* in 1952:

> Passengers between the two capitals
> leave after dinner ... and, after a
> journey in which they can really sleep,
> arrive on the following morning.
> Business and professional men using
> the *Overland* have the whole of the
> departure and arrival days at their
> disposal.

A touch sexist, that 'professional men' line, as was the depiction of women in a black-and-white photo in the brochure, chatting within the ladies' powder room in the second-class sitting car. It sounded classy, though:

> The powder rooms are a new feature.
> They have full-size mirrors, stools
> and chairs for six (in second-class,
> four) and are decorated in the modern
> manner.

Powder room party, anyone?

Half a century after that brochure was published, I'd occasionally seen the train's sleeper carriages at rest at Southern Cross Station. Then, in 2007, the train was relaunched as a daytime-only service each way, with the hope of attracting tourists for the views, and more passengers from the towns in between. Running only three times a week, however (nowadays twice-weekly), it proved a difficult service for locals to use effectively. With the removal of federal government subsidies for concession train travellers in 2016, the *Overland* became reliant on funding from both the Victorian and South Australian state governments to underwrite its operating costs. As I'd approached the border in early 2018, I'd had no idea of the crisis that was about to befall this cosy arrangement. In November that year the newly elected conservative government of South Australia would decide not to renew its subsidy, prompting the Victorian government to temporarily top up its contribution to keep the train running. A year later, cancellation would again loom as that deal ran out. In the midst of a revival of long-distance rail travel in Europe in response to climate change, the future of Australia's oldest interstate passenger train was dangling by a thread. But with South Australia's state election only just concluded, I'd had no inkling of this impending predicament.

Not long after leaving Serviceton, Rhys spotted a sign on the right saying, 'You are now entering South Australia', and I smiled. I'd had three state border crossings so far on the trip: the first to a beautiful dawn over the Border Ranges, then crossing the dark Murray River after Albury, and now here, in the midst of dry plains after the end of a long hot summer.

Now that we'd been travelling for a few hours, I felt weary. Two days before, I'd hosted a gathering of my friends at Whitehart, a bar behind our apartment building in the laneway of the same name. As a result I was still feeling the after-effects of a hangover, but it had been fun. As I'd been absent from social media since flying to Cairns, I'd had plenty to talk about. In the Facebook invite I'd promised them, like Othello, tales:

> ... of the Cannibals that each other eat,
> The Anthropophagi and men whose
>   heads
> Do grow beneath their shoulders

The further I was removed in time from my trials in the tropics, the better they became as a story. That was how travellers' reminiscences had always worked, ever since Herodotus had returned home to Halicarnassus with images of Egypt's pyramids shimmering in his memory.

At Bordertown, 17 kilometres west of Serviceton, we were told it was the birthplace of 'Australia's longest serving Labor prime minister, Bob Hawke.' The more interesting story was about the border itself. In the early nineteenth century, two successive surveys had attempted to mark the boundary between South Australia and New South Wales, with Victoria not yet in existence, as conflicts were arising between pastoralists expanding from both west and east. The 1847–1849 Wade–White survey was beset by drought and hardship, ending with White staggering to safety after the death of his horse. With improved instrumentation, Wade and White's border was proven by an 1868 survey to lie 3.6 kilometres too far west of the intended 141st meridian east of longitude. This created a very long and narrow rectangle of apparently mislabelled territory, extending from the Southern Ocean to the Murray River. It comprised almost 1,300 square kilometres of land, most of it by then leased out by the Victorian government. Both sides refused to back down, and this area became known as the 'Disputed Territory'. Eventually, more than sixty years after the errant survey, the matter was referred in 1911 to the newly created High Court by the new state of South Australia. The court ruled in favour of Victoria: 'facts on the ground' trumped scientific precision. Thus Serviceton Station was now located entirely within Victoria, rather than in the Disputed Territory as it was when built as a joint project between the two colonies. I had passed this landmark with the smug ease of a conqueror. On each side, sheep breathed the free Victorian air in what I imagined to be an exalted state.

Heading into South Australia, I visited the cafe car, where I got talking to a woman from Adelaide who'd just led a tour group to the International Flower and Garden Show at Melbourne's Carlton Gardens.

'It's more fun on the train as a group,' she said, when I asked why they'd chosen to travel that way.

She had a point. A group travelling together on an aircraft would be hampered in their sociability by the tight space. On a train, they had the luxury of moving around easily, even gathering in the cafe car. It was a more social means of transport, by its very nature.

I returned to my seat to find the crew serving a caramel slice and weak coffee. Why train coffee was always brewed weak was an enduring mystery. After sipping and wincing, I glanced out the window to notice a metal pipeline had appeared on my left, faithfully following the railway, diving beneath side roads as it did so. This was a water pipeline running from Tailem Bend ahead of us on the Murray River, supplying small towns such as Keith. The terrain was becoming slightly hillier now, as if the earth had settled into gentle waves topped by low twisted trees. A narrow horizontal disc of blue sky ahead of us was framed by cloud, the fanciful eye of a sky god.

We passed a tiny derelict station at Coomandook, which reminded me that South Australia had no state-run trains beyond Adelaide's suburban network. That seemed short-sighted; in Victoria the country trains had been upgraded in the past few decades and were often packed to the brim.

Two hours after crossing the border we reached Tailem Bend, and it felt as if we were finally in the outer reaches of Adelaide's influence. It was a sizeable, handsome town with an attractive station building. We crossed the Murray River via an impressive 1920s rail bridge, after having run above grazing cows in low paddocks which were presumably flood plains. After a day of dry grass, the town of Murray Bridge glowed green, with grassy parkland running down to the riverbank. This was the second time I'd crossed the Murray on my rail journey – the first being in the dead of night at Albury a week earlier. That seemed like months ago now.

From this point, the terrain became much hillier. It was a different world, still dry but with paddocks arranged along crinkled slopes. I wondered why the eye enjoyed hills so much, and deplored openness. Perhaps it was because hills hid secrets. The *Overland* now wove through cuttings which must have been hell to create. At Nairne there was a lovely station building, built to last, though the trains that had stopped there hadn't.

Soon I saw my first grapes in the wine country of the Adelaide Hills, and many houses arrayed with solar panels. There were more frequent homes along the line, and dappled sunlight fell across the train as trees grew close to the track. A lone black-faced sheep looked up at me from a small yard, but I suspected this was more likely to be horseriding country.

There were more grapes and dams and tightly packed stands of native trees, and more frequent picturesque defunct stations. There was road traffic too, the first of any amount since we'd passed Geelong. It was the end of a working day, and the city lay just over the hills. When we entered the first tunnel, then the train creaked and squealed around the frequent bends through the hills, I knew we were almost in Adelaide.

I glanced out across a valley to a garden of reds, greens and yellows, autumn starting to work its magic on the leaves. There was a house with broad verandahs set high above it on a slope, and it looked idyllic. The vegetation became greener and denser as we progressed, the cuttings deep and branches almost brushing the train. It was difficult to see the landscape as a whole now – it had closed in around us, drawing in the broad dry paddocks to these leafy green hills. I glimpsed the derelict Mount Lofty Station near the top of the range, then it was gone. At last we were sliding down through the Adelaide suburbs, past the densely arranged houses and the peak-hour traffic, finally pulling up at the long platform of Adelaide Parklands Terminal. All change.

Adelaide to Belair
Belair line

The Pullman Adelaide was the most upmarket accommodation of my entire trip (after this I'd be back in youth hostels). Its decor attempted a balancing act of being modern and uncluttered while suggesting luxury. The breakfast room had stylish lampshades and a samovar for tea – the first time I'd seen this Russian-style hot-water urn in a hotel since I'd stayed in one in Białystok in eastern Poland that received many Russian guests.

An unwritten law of travel writing (rule number three?) was that the most comfortable hotels you stayed in were the ones where you had the least time to enjoy the facilities. The most extravagant would be visited as part of a media group that would check in at 10 pm and check out for an early tour starting at 8 am. There were suites in foreign countries with entire rooms I'd never set foot in. In this case I'd checked in at 10 pm after dinner, and been up early to catch a suburban train.

It was cool and sunny on this autumn morning, and I rejoiced. Goodbye to the extreme heat of the recent weeks, and the humidity. This temperate climate was similar to that in which I'd grown up, and it was buoying. I walked to Adelaide Station along North Terrace, delighted to see new tram tracks being constructed. Though Adelaide had dismantled its tram system like so many other foolish cities back in the 1950s, one line to the seaside suburb of Glenelg had been retained. When I'd first visited the city, it had run vintage carriages as a tourist attraction. In the years since then, the tramway had been reinstated as a key part of the public transport network, with extensions added through the CBD. The north side of North Terrace was lined with cultural institutions: the Art Gallery of South Australia, the South Australian Museum, the State Library of South Australia. Their neoclassical facades were prim, proper and self-contained, reflecting South Australia's self-satisfied pride in being the only Australian colony not to have received convicts.

A long ramp led down from the street to the station's platforms. Though the ticketing hall at its end had a decorative barrel roof, the approach to it seemed furtive, and the platforms dark and depressing. Once the entire building above had been the central railway station, but now it housed a casino. It was the first indication I'd had of Adelaide's railways being unloved, but not the last. I was the only passenger in the front carriage of the 9.56 to Belair. We trundled slowly out of the station past the modern buildings at the west end of North Terrace, including the South Australian Health and Medical Research Institute with its striking metallic points, resembling a robotic echidna. The first suburban station we passed, Mile End, was a windswept platform with a battered metal shelter that would be rejected for a bus stop.

On the way south the train passed Adelaide Parklands Terminal. The *Overland* carriages were still parked at the platform. One of the biggest blunders affecting rail travel in the state had been the 1984 relocation of long-distance trains to this station beyond the CBD. It was poorly connected to the rest of Adelaide's public transport, with passengers generally needing to use taxis to arrive and depart there. City authorities in recent years had talked about returning long-distance trains to Adelaide Station, and I wished them luck. Arriving in the busy heart of the city, and walking out to North Terrace with its distinctive architecture, would be far preferable to arriving at this Parklands dead end.

The train moved slowly south, and at Mitcham I finally saw an attractive station, an old brick-and-stone building. In one window was a black-and-white photo of a man in uniform, with the caption, 'I was Mitcham's last stationmaster.' Then, just before Springbank Road, we passed a ghost station, a sad decaying platform covered in dead leaves. This had once been Clapham, closed when one side of the line was converted to standard gauge in 1995. Everywhere along this line I was sensing the decline of rail travel since its glory days.

I looked up from my notes and we were suddenly in spectacular hilly country with a ravine to one side, passing through stony railway cuttings. That had been very abrupt: suburbs one moment, rugged hills the next. With Adelaide it was remarkable how quickly you could depart the city. Unlike Sydney and Melbourne, it seemed to have no gravity well at all. The day before I had thought Tailem Bend the outermost point of contact between Adelaide and the country, so this expanse of pure bushland surprised me. A former station here, Sleeps Hill, had served quarries. It was long gone, and two railway tunnels beyond it had become disused when the line was rerouted in 1919. After the Japanese bombing of Darwin in 1942, an alarmed museum board had stored South Australia's most prized possessions there, stacked up on a purpose-built platform. It was a remarkable collection, including artworks, documents, delicate crockery from Government House, and forty-one insect cabinets containing drawers of fragile butterflies. I was retracing the route of the *Overland* in the Melbourne direction, heading upward into the Adelaide Hills via the Belair line, which was a single broad-gauge track. On the right I could see the standard-gauge line used by the *Overland* and freight trains. As at Clapham, this division between two gauges had rendered many station platforms redundant. At Coromandel Station I glimpsed its disused platform as a freight train came thundering past, laden with shipping containers.

At Belair Station I crossed to its own unused platform behind a young dad and his boy, fellow passengers off with bikes to enjoy the national park. A big timber shed there had once served as a waiting area, but now bird droppings were liberally scattered across the ground and seats. There was a certain Wild West look to the shelter, with its timber awning sporting a serrated fringe, and 'BELAIR' painted on its side in capital letters in an old-fashioned font. Within were pasted vintage posters for the *Ghan* and the Trans-Australian Railway, presumably a recent touch by the volunteers who maintained it. This was the end of the suburban network, and the broad-gauge tracks disappeared within a locked enclosure beyond the end of the station. On my side was a dainty timber signal box and an unkempt garden, and at the end of the platform a sign arched across the exit: 'THE NATIONAL PARK'.

Belair National Park had been around for a while. Proclaimed in 1891, it was Australia's second such park, after Royal National Park in Sydney. Such green reserves on the edges of cities – particularly those that could be reached by train – were a distinctive feature of Victorian-era culture. It was not yet an age for disporting oneself immodestly by the seaside, but it was an era of tree worship, a counterpoint to the industrial pollution of the towns and cities.

I stepped down into the park and read the introductory signage, from which I learned that 'Cyclists and walkers generally give way to horses.' Good to know.

The undulating grounds were crisscrossed by walking tracks through native trees, and the occasional access road. I walked along a track between grey box trees (*Eucalyptus microcarpa*), which the signage said were endangered. Under their grey peeling bark their trunks had an ochre tone, almost orange in places. Cheerful trees, I thought. There were several dead trunks along the first rise, some lying uprooted – victims of a storm, I assumed. Ahead of me walked a father and his daughter, occasionally disappearing from view then reappearing. Their bright modern clothing stood out strongly against the muted tree trunks, and I was reminded of McCubbin's great painting, *Lost*.

The track led me to Playford Lake, a large triangular body of water with an island at its centre, so crowded with eucalypts that they leant outward over the water. There were shelters and barbecues near the shore, and it was easy to imagine Victorian ladies and gentlemen escaping the city here in their highly unsuitable clothing. There was more than a whiff of *Picnic at Hanging Rock* about the scene. Humans had touched lightly here, in strong contrast to recreational areas of a similar vintage that I'd visited in Europe, with their beer gardens and promenades and carefully arranged gardens. It was very quiet by the lake, apart from birdsong. I'd moved beyond the range of Belair Station's platform announcements and there was no-one in sight. This was the most solitary I'd been on the entire trip, even compared with Normanton, and it felt a relief. The bustle of travel, the human interaction and the endless note-taking was exhilarating, but didn't leave much space for contemplation. Here, I had it. A big flock of cockatoos squawked overhead, and then what I thought were galahs. Above me another pair of unseen birds voiced a mournful downward call, as if they'd received sad but not entirely unexpected news.

I looped around to the east along a narrow track that followed the dry bed of the Workanda Creek, passing a couple with enormous cameras who were taking photos of avian life. Off the track I spotted a forgotten plaque beneath a tree, commemorating a 1937 Scout jamboree. I'd been in the Cub Scouts myself as a kid, but the only big outing I could remember from that era was a visit to Perth Zoo. Finally, off an arm of Echo Track, I encountered the railway once again. This time it was 25 metres above me, running along an 1880s embankment that had been built to take the railway through this difficult terrain. At the base of the embankment was Echo Tunnel, which looked as though it had been constructed by and for hobbits. This low arched tunnel allowed the creek to flow from the eastern side of the park via a narrow channel, with what looked like a raised walkway on one side. I stepped down to its mouth. Its roof was well below my height, though if I'd walked along the parallel dry creek channel it would have been more manageable. When I yelled 'Echo!' the tunnel produced a faint but satisfying duplicate. But I wanted to stay on the west side of the park, so I didn't head through. Instead, I backtracked and turned south.

It had been a huge job building the first stage of the Adelaide–Melbourne line through this terrain in the nineteenth century. The first section from Adelaide to Nairne had required eight tunnels, and two viaducts crossing gullies at Eden Hills. Three railway work camps had stood in the vicinity of the existing Government Farm which had been established to provide grazing for state-owned livestock, at the heart of what would become the national park. This caused tension between the farm's management and the railway workers, who were blamed for stealing and drunkenness. The worst incident was a murder in 1880, when one William Welch had done away with fellow railway navvy William Bell. As *The Express & Telegraph* newspaper of 2 November related the event:

> ... and from being sociable they
> started a discussion on the subject
> of religion, and hence, as Welch is
> a Roman Catholic and Bell was a
> Protestant, the views expressed were
> widely different. The effect of the
> liquor appears to have brought the
> men to angry words, and from words
> they proceeded to blows ...

At the southern end of Echo Track was Old Government House, once the summer residence of South Australia's governors. It seemed rich that the top toff had the use of not just one mansion but two. The well-proportioned sandstone building had picturesque gardens, but was only open on the occasional Sunday. I wasn't too bothered as I hadn't planned to visit. I didn't mind the odd glance around a stately home but I could take them or leave them; it was neighbourhoods that really interested me. Also, one of the aspects of this rail trek I was trying to stick to was not over-planning, as generally happened when engaged on a formal travel-writing trip. To some degree I wanted to go with the flow, to see what fate threw at me. Still, it was a pity that the grounds were locked; I could have made good use of a garden bench to take a rest.

What next? In my hurry to get going I'd forgotten to buy food or water, and my left foot was hurting. I suspected I'd twisted it on French Island upon getting out of the OKA. Then by chance I noticed a sign for the State Flora Nursery, which was hidden behind a nearby stand of trees. Established in 1886, it grew native plants for propagation across the state.

I asked the tall bearded man behind the counter what his top sellers were.

'At the moment? Probably kangaroo grass, red gums and blue gums.'

Who bought them?

'Not just householders,' he replied. 'Government bodies, or landholders wanting to repurpose an area. Sometimes farmers.'

'Isn't selling gum trees to farmers like sending coals to Newcastle?' I asked.

He smiled. 'It depends. Sometimes they realise they've gone too far in clearing a property, and want to restore the balance.'

I liked that sentiment. Perhaps we'd come some way as a society, from the era of almost total felling of rosewood trees at Rosewood.

It was cool and calm within the nursery, the occasional customer drifting through and examining the plants in the open-air yard. I bought a bottle of water from a vending machine and prepared myself for the next leg.

I was feeling flat today. Narrelle had been unwell with a bad cold when I'd left her, so I felt guilty, and also still mildly hungover. But the park was beautiful, and calming. I was glad I'd decided on it as an excursion.

From Old Government House a track led south past an adventure playground, deserted in the middle of this weekday. I was arrested by loud birdsong directly above, and looked up to see the multicolour forms of rainbow lorikeets perched on branches. I mentioned this to a couple seated on a bench nearby, and they pointed at a koala asleep in a bough of another tree. I was seeing more koalas on this trip than I had over the previous two decades.

From the grassy Gold Escort Picnic Ground, the Nookoo Track led to the southern boundary of the national park. My trek so far had had a lot of downhill slope to it, so my trained senses had suggested at some point some 'up' would reappear. This was that moment. It was a long slow walk up the track, more of a firebreak than a useful path, without the neatly levelled surface found in the more popular areas of the park. On my right, behind a fence, was a private property which I realised must be a golf course when I spotted a lonely high dry green. I reached Upper Sturt Road and followed it west to a bus stop. I had thought of travelling onward to one of the abandoned old train stations further east, but I now discovered that would require waiting at the stop for two hours. So I caught the number 195 bus to Blackwood, further in from Belair on the same train line, to have lunch. The first cafe I found had red flags flying, the word 'award-winning' on its signage, and the use of brioche for its burgers. I chose a simpler place that served a lunch special of fish and chips.

After lunch, I attempted to walk to the railway station and discovered that pedestrian access had been configured so walkers had to cross a fair distance from the main roundabout. It annoyed me when planners inconvenienced pedestrians for the benefit of motorists. I waited for a quiet moment, stepped across the road and boosted myself up and over the concrete planter box which was intended as a barrier.

Blackwood Station was everything Adelaide Station should have been: an elegant and well-maintained civic landmark, still in use for its original purpose. I crossed to the city-bound platform (the track split here so both sides could be used) and waited for a train back to the not-so-big smoke. For a change, I was meeting someone for dinner.

'I had it all: all the skills and the knowledge. Then I left and I had nothing, just like that.'

I was dining with Carolyne Jasinski at Bistro Blackwood, on the east end of Rundle Street. The South Australian Tourism Commission was shouting me the meal, and this was the place they'd chosen. It was a classy restaurant with an artfully casual style. The far wall bore a complex painting of a longhorn bull being hunted by a man with a spear. We sat at a diner-style fixed table while dishes with lots of native ingredients were brought to us. The restaurant was connected with an organisation that promoted the knowledge and use of Indigenous Australian foods. It had been set up by chef Jock Zonfrillo, a Scot with an Italian background who later achieved TV fame as a judge for *MasterChef Australia*. There were Scots (or Scotts: Robert, Mungo) popping up everywhere on my trip.

Carolyne's job was to host visiting journalists for the SATC, but I'd known her for years as a travel journalist at the *Advertiser* newspaper. She'd recently taken redundancy and found herself in a new arena where her precise knowledge of specific systems and procedures had lost its relevance.

'I didn't have to work, but I had to work,' she said. 'Or I'd go mad.'

I was wondering again about the Burke-and-Wills direction of working life in my fifties, and thought Carolyne might have something to add. I discovered she'd tried many different jobs in her life, sometimes between other occupations: even once as a fitness instructor. She'd recently started talking to cruise ship passengers on the subject of travel.

'I was nervous when I got up on stage on the boat the first time,' she said. 'But then I stood there, and thought "Oh yeah. This is me."'

Interesting food had been coming and going on the table during this conversation: charred organic banana peppers with cavolo nero; fire-pit-smoked pumpkin with rainbow chard, saltbush and macadamia nuts; a tomato salad with lemon myrtle ice. I was enjoying a glass of chianti that had been poured from a magnum; the bistro opened a different magnum at the start of each week. It was a far cry from the meat-and-two-veg meals of my childhood. It was also a far cry from the olive-and-processed-cheese rolls I'd been eating in Normanton three weeks earlier.

I confessed I'd thought about chucking freelance writing in altogether, but that seemed a waste of my experience and contacts, so I'd tried sideways movement instead: giving travel talks, leading small tours, researching this book.

She liked this approach. 'You're still using your skill set. As for me, I'm just trying everything. People throw things at me and I say, "Yeah, I'll try that." One door might close for a while, or stay ajar, but another might open.'

Carolyne had been trying to transition into freelance writing herself, having been a staffer for so long, but others' good intentions kept getting in the way. 'Every time I try to go freelance, people offer me a job.'

This was heartening, optimistic stuff, words I enjoyed hearing.

Maybe I needed to worry less about emulating Burke and Wills and emulate another explorer instead, their great contemporary rival from this very city. Maybe I needed to be more like John McDouall Stuart. Another Scot. That alone made Stuart worthy of consideration.

####

'When the time comes to go into the Lodge, the Tyler who sits outside the doors checks that everyone is a Mason.'

The next morning, I found myself inadvertently on one of the most boring tours I'd ever taken, including all those brewery tours, and a tour of a sulphur industry museum in Poland.

'The star on the floor lights up. The hanging "G" represents the Great Architect of the Universe.'

I'd intended to join a weekly tour of the Stuart Collection, a permanent exhibition devoted to John McDouall Stuart. The website of the John Stuart McDouall Society had said it was located within the Adelaide Masonic Centre's museum on North Terrace, and that there was a tour on Thursdays at 2 pm. What I'd failed to register was that it was a tour of the Masonic Centre itself, not the collection. We'd breezed past the cases and displays devoted to J.M.S. (as I was starting to think of him), with a brief mention of his exploits, then proceeded to examine Lodges of various sizes where the Masons still gathered. It wasn't going well. Our guide was recovering from an illness, so his voice wasn't strong. Also, the ceremonial furniture which should have been arrayed in the Lodges was out in the corridors, so he wasn't able to demonstrate its purpose or function.

'I don't know why all this stuff is out there. Maybe being cleaned,' he said.

To make things worse, one of our group was a visitor from Italy ('I used to be a tour guide in Washington') who frequently interrupted his delivery.

'There are only 2,000 Masons left in all of South Australia and the [Northern] Territory,' said our plaintive guide.

'In ten years this will all be a museum,' said Miss Italy of the Lodges.

'Well, I don't know what will happen to it.'

'It'll be a museum,' she said emphatically. So that was that.

It was a car crash of a tour, and all I wanted was to peel away to see the Stuart Collection. But I hung on because, well, it was a car crash and I was curious to see what might happen next.

A peculiar group had turned up to learn the secrets of the Masons. There were five of us: myself, Miss Italy, her partner, a genial youngish man from South Africa, and a silent young man from Adelaide. None professed to be a Freemason. If this had been an Agatha Christie story, one of us would soon be dead, victims of an intricate conspiracy.

I was amazed that this grand multistorey 1920s building on North Terrace could be operated by a society with so few members. The land alone would be worth a fortune. Maybe Miss Italy was right about the future museum, or perhaps it'd be redeveloped into apartments or tourist accommodation. The foyer had the luxurious feel of a grand hotel, with its Greek pillars and marble stairs. The architecture was lovely, but it was hard to be interested in the Freemasons. As far as I could tell it was a group of people who used ritual and costumes to add a little drama to their lives, and to create an in-group that might help them in their careers. An in-group from which women were excluded. And atheists, though their requirement that members profess faith in a supreme deity didn't specify any particular religion. It seemed dull and dusty and past its use-by date, which I imagined was why membership numbers were so low. Its members no doubt enjoyed the social side, but the rituals sounded like something from a bygone age. Which they were, of course.

Within the largest of the three Lodges, past the portrait of nineteenth-century Brother Thomas Fax with six fingers on his left hand ('They named the fax after him,' said the wisecracking partner of Miss Italy), the guide was explaining the secret handshakes and passwords as a relic from the days when not everyone could read or write. He had a reasonable point to make about these secrets: that they were rituals but they didn't intrinsically matter. But Miss Italy was having none of it.

'In Italy it is still secret, totally secret.' she said. 'Only when a man is dead do we find out if he was a member.'

Then she tried to gather our group together to save the guide's voice. 'Sir, come closer so he doesn't have to scream,' she said to the quiet local who had wandered off.

It was time to peel away. I made polite excuses, then took the lift down to the first floor. The Stuart Collection was explained in signage as 'Artefacts and memorabilia of the famous explorer John McDouall Stuart'. It was a collection of objects in glass cases, and captioned placards that seemed to have come from different exhibitions held at different times. It was worth seeing, nonetheless.

Stuart had been active at the same time as Burke and Wills, and his sixth and final expedition was in progress when the Victorian explorers had perished. Like Burke and Wills, he'd managed to find his way to the northern coast, in his case near the present-day location of Darwin. Unlike the Victorians, he'd managed to return to tell the tale, though he was so debilitated that he was carried home aboard a stretcher between two horses. By a macabre coincidence, the day of Burke and Wills' funeral in Melbourne coincided with the great civic welcome for Stuart and his companions in Adelaide. He'd come second in the race but had won the economic prizes South Australia had been seeking: new valuable grazing land and, better yet, the route of the new Australian Overland Telegraph Line. The following year, South Australia had annexed the Northern Territory and begun construction of the telegraph. Not all these benefits stuck. The Northern Territory was handed by South Australia to the Commonwealth in 1911. But by then the telegraph line had been built along Stuart's original route to the north, and was followed by the *Ghan* as far as Alice Springs when it commenced service in 1929. The key difference between J.M.S. and Burke was that Stuart was experienced and much better organised. Rather than relying on large amounts of provisions carried slowly aboard easily delayed wagons, he favoured taking fewer rations on faster-moving expeditions comprising just a few men and horses. It was a gamble that could have gone wrong, but it meant they were nimble and could spend less time in difficult terrain.

A photograph of Stuart, blown up to poster size in the exhibition, revealed a compact, heavily bearded man with an engaging stare, intelligent and observant. The glass cases included items used by J.M.S. and his companions. What stood out was a carved snake-shaped walking stick which was said to have been presented to Stuart by Aboriginal people, later transferred to a museum at his Scottish birthplace, then returned to the collection here. It was simple and elegant, and I liked to think of the long journey it had taken.

I was intrigued that it had taken forty years for South Australia to erect a statue of J.M.S., while the tragic Burke and Wills had received memorials immediately upon their deaths. As it was, Stuart had died not long after his great triumph. I'm not sure if it helped me in navigating away from the rocks in my own career, but I liked Stuart's blend of courage and good judgement. Unlike Burke, he hadn't let ego push him onward when the objective had clearly become hopeless. Judgement and courage were a good combination. I should try to channel that combo in navigating new ways to work, I thought, and to make a living from them. More broadly, the way explorers were regarded by the public reinforced what I'd long thought – that fastening one's identity to events whose significance or worth might shift was folly. I thought of the enduring self-deception of terra nullius, or the unresolved attitude in the American South toward the Confederacy – or, for that matter, the strident 'Anzackery' that was tarnishing the commemoration of Gallipoli. Look not to explorers for your saints, I thought; they turn out to be ordinary men with their own agendas in the end.

Adelaide to Perth
Indian Pacific

It was deceptively quiet when I returned to Adelaide Parklands Terminal, my Iranian-born Uber driver surprised at its very existence. The *Indian Pacific* was waiting at the platform – all thirty carriages, plus locomotive – but there was hardly a soul around. That was because the passengers who'd arrived earlier in the day from Sydney were still off on their Adelaide excursions. Some were tasting wine and having dinner in the McLaren Vale region, while others were tasting cheese in Hahndorf followed by a German meal with the additional treat of yodelling.

There were staff walking around, in the same uniform as the crew of the *Overland*, and despite the lack of passengers I was excited by the proximity of the streamlined carriages with their eagle emblems. The train was 774 metres long, weighed 1,450 tonnes and had 12,000-litre fuel tanks. This was one of the great train journeys, from this point heading across stark desert country, like a John McDouall Stuart expedition with softer furnishings and upmarket provisions. The stillness before its departure felt like the spontaneous silence that descended upon a theatre audience just before the curtains opened.

I was there far too early, of course. It was an unconscious habit of mine, always arriving too early for everything. I think it came from not driving, thus subconsciously building in extra time for public transport delays and becoming absurdly over-punctual when they didn't occur. But arriving early allowed time for contemplation, an endangered condition that's very valuable to a writer. Around 9 pm the Sydney passengers returned, and the terminal became full of movement and anticipation. I bumped into Rhys and he said he'd see me onboard, but I never did encounter him again.

I'd been on the *Indian Pacific* before, but this was my first time in a single 'cabin', the term preferred by GSR. It was quite a different layout. Each twin cabin had two berths, one above the other, and an en suite bathroom. The singles each had one berth, of course, with shared bathrooms and toilets at each end of their carriage. My cabin was compact but neatly designed, with an armchair facing a cushioned bench, and a small table between. To one side was a small sink and cupboard space, with more storage next to the armchair and beneath it. The bulge caused by the sink resulted in the carriage's central corridor having a wavy profile. This would be the perfect corridor along which to see, like Hercule Poirot, the retreating back of a mysterious woman in a red kimono; she would flicker between the wall's curves like an optical illusion. I wondered if the need to weave back and forth while walking through the carriage would accentuate the rocking motion of the train or counter it.

I heard cheerful conversations in the corridor as other passengers arrived. We Adelaide-boarding people were the new kids in town, and something that marked us out as newcomers was our berths, which were set up as seats rather than as beds.

'Their beds are made up because they've come from Sydney and they've already been asked what they want,' said a perceptive fellow newbie of the earlier passengers. 'We're the blow-ins.'

Before I turned in, I overheard a female crew member advising two women passengers to make sure they pulled their blinds down before dressing. 'Once I came back from a shower and realised too late we were passing a level crossing. At least those motorists would never see me again,' she said.

We pulled out of the station with a thump at 9.40 pm, and slid beneath a full moon past the darkened carriages of the *Overland* on the next track. The longest train trip of my entire journey was underway.

'I'm a vet pathologist at a zoo,' said Mary. 'We treat all types of animals. It's interesting work.'

Meals on the *Indian Pacific* were taken at booths seating four, and one's dinner companions were a matter of chance. For breakfast that morning I'd drawn Mary from St Louis, Missouri, as well as Frank from Brisbane and Robert from Melbourne. Small-world syndrome had already struck with Frank, as he'd once owned a Melbourne cafe at which I'd reviewed a live comedy show.

Mary was originally from Edinburgh but had developed a distinct American accent in her years in North America. 'I started in Canada and my work eventually took me further south,' she said.

As he was facing forward, Frank delighted in pointing out the fauna he could spot through the window. It was a good haul in this open country of green-grey saltbush, low scrub, twisted trees and red earth: several kangaroos, some feral goats, two emus and a wedge-tailed eagle. The eagle suddenly flew at one of the roos, apparently attacking it, which seemed strange – it was too large to be prey. (Or so I thought – I later learned that these huge birds, Australia's largest raptors, are known to kill smaller kangaroos, though they more commonly go for rabbits and hares.) At one point Frank said he'd spotted a small town, but we thought he was joking. Then a meagre settlement hove into view, six houses or so in a dusty circle with an unsealed track in and out. What did they do out there?

It was remarkable how dramatically the scenery had changed as we'd climbed northward from Adelaide overnight, as if an unseen hand had pulled it all away: city, cars, people, parks, shops.

Port Augusta was behind us now, as was the turnoff to the rocket testing base at Woomera. When we reached Tarcoola, train manager Bruce announced the town was named after the horse that won the 1893 Melbourne Cup, and that it was the railway junction from which the *Indian Pacific* and the *Ghan* diverged on their respective paths.

'If you take a hard right here, you end up in Darwin.'

I hadn't slept well, but that was normal for me on long-distance trains (someone had once told me, 'To sleep well on a train, you have to be dead'). The single berth, which had folded out of the wall across the armchair and bench, was comfortable enough, but the night had been punctuated by bumps and clanks and the occasional solid thump. Everyone who'd been onboard since Sydney, however, praised the smooth ride out of Adelaide. The bumpy condition of the rails in New South Wales was legendary, and the passengers remembered it keenly.

I'd set an alarm for a 6 am shower and had been impressed by the size of the bathroom, which seemed bigger than my cabin. Not that 6 am was entirely what it seemed. The previous night we'd been told to set our clocks back ninety minutes, a shift which corresponded to no official time zone. This piecemeal approach was designed to make the summer time difference of two hours and thirty minutes between Adelaide and Perth easier to swallow.

When we weren't sleeping or dining, a large proportion of the passengers were in the lounge car, with its comfortable seating and open bar. I spent nearly all my time there, as my cabin was four carriages away. In any case, when travelling solo my instinct was to be social. In the lounge I got talking to Anna, a young woman who worked for a German economic ministry but was based in Bangkok. We chatted about places I'd visited in Germany, and her home city of Berlin.

'It's getting expensive in Berlin,' she said. 'I'd like to get a little house outside the city for the weekends.'

I mentioned that Poles who worked in the north-western Polish city of Szczecin, which had once been the German port town of Stettin, had started buying old farmhouses within Germany from which to commute. When Poland had joined the European Union, Poles had worried about Germans buying up property in their former eastern territories. Ironically, it was now happening the other way round.

'I think that's a good thing,' she said. 'That part of Germany became depopulated after reunification, and Germans have had a bad view of Poles. I hope it helps them to live together.' As I'd lived in Poland and had a dash of German ancestry on my mother's side, I hoped so too.

A bird with a white body and pink underside suddenly flew past the train, quite close. Anna reached for a reference book that she'd found on the shelves at the end of the carriage, *The Slater Field Guide to Australian Birds*, and we looked through its pages. We decided it was a Major Mitchell cockatoo.

This was my first full day aboard the *Indian Pacific*, the second for those who'd boarded in Sydney, and I already thought of it as 'Desert Day'. We would shortly enter the emptiness of the Nullarbor Plain, and spend the entire day slicing through it.

Across the aisle in the lounge was Peter, a semiretired architect and lawyer. He was wearing a T-shirt I recognised from the California Science Center in Los Angeles, depicting the evolution of man from ape to human to astronaut. Peter travelled overseas twice a year, and had got into the odd scrape on trains.

'I was robbed on a train from Lausanne to Venice,' he said. 'They were gassing passengers, then going through their belongings. When we got to Venice there were lots of other travellers in the same situation at the police station. And they weren't all from the same train.'

Gassing! I hadn't heard about that for years. When I'd first researched Poland for Lonely Planet in 2006, we'd included a warning in the relevant guidebook about robberies on international sleeper trains. Dramatic stories had circulated of such robbers using sleeping gas or chloroform in the process, but this might just have been an urban myth that concentrated the traveller's mind.

Peter hadn't thought much of Los Angeles, though he'd made the mistake of staying in Anaheim. 'I wanted to go to Disneyland once in my life. I should've known better. If I'd gone when I was seven years old, that would've been fun.' I could've told him that. I'd been to LA five times and had never made the trek to see Mickey Mouse. I preferred hanging around the stretch between the city's Downtown and West Hollywood. For me, enjoying Los Angeles was about not trying to cover too much of its sprawl and not being too proud to use public transport, including its relatively new and impressive Metro trains.

The train had now passed into an area that seemed much greener, with many more trees and shrubs.

'That's because a cyclone came down the coast a few weeks ago, created a trough and dumped a lot of rain inland,' said Peter.

It underlined what author Sarah Murgatroyd had outlined in *The Dig Tree*, that life remains dormant in these harsh environs, then flourishes dramatically when water arrives. I vaguely wondered if Peter's cyclone had been my cyclone, the one that had been threatening to form in the Gulf of Carpentaria when I'd been struggling with Queensland's overloaded river systems. From another reference book I surmised we were now – possibly – passing through mulga shrubland, with low trees and bushes growing in distinctively red earth.

The lounge kept filling after breakfast, with groups forming over coffee. This was a distinctly social train, much more so than the previous ones I'd taken. As on a cruise, the passengers were relaxed and looking to socialise, an attitude aided by the inclusive nature of the fare, which covered all meals, drinks and tours.

'I taught maths,' said Chris from Geelong, a retired schoolteacher. 'One time I was teaching the class how to calculate the area of a circle and a girl said, "Why do I need to know this?"

'"One day you might need to calculate the area of a circle," I said, but she said "I'd just get my husband to do it."'

Chris shook her head. 'This was a small town. "Look around you, girl," I thought, "These boys aren't any brighter than you."'

That was a fair call about the boys, but also about the knowledge. As a traveller I'd used almost all the skills I'd learned in my life, mathematical and otherwise.

We were now on the Nullarbor Plain, the name being derived from Latin: *nullus* + *arbor* = no trees. It had been aptly titled. The largest outcrop of exposed limestone bedrock in the world, it was utterly flat and treeless, the plain bearing only low green-grey shrubs. I'd long divined that the common unit of comparison used in the media for large areas of land was either Wales or Belgium. On this basis, the Nullarbor's 200,000 square kilometres equated to 9.6 Waleses, or 6.6 Belgiums. It was a big, if empty place.

At 1 pm in our artificial 'train time' we arrived at Cook. This had once been a railway town, founded specifically to serve the needs of the Trans-Australian Railway, whose rails laid from east and west had met near here in 1917. Stretching from Port Augusta in the east to Kalgoorlie in the west, these 1,700 kilometres of rail had been an impressive engineering achievement, but also a symbol of nationhood. It was partly the promise of a railway connection to the east that had won over the voters of Western Australia in favour of federation in 1901, and its completion in the midst of the Great War must have seemed a vindication of the six Australian colonies banding together for their own economic reasons – but also for mutual defence. Visiting in 1911, Lord Kitchener had pointed out that Western Australia's isolation might make it a military weakness, but that this could be mitigated by a railway linking it to the east. What followed was a massive five-year project, involving up to 3,500 workmen labouring in the harshest desert conditions, served by special water trains hauling in the means of life. When the first passenger train west along the line departed Port Augusta on 22 October 1917, it carried among its passengers Sir John Forrest, the former Western Australian premier who'd championed the railway. As it pulled out, the town's mayor called for three cheers for 'the King, Sir John, and the boys at the Front.' A century later, at the mouldering station building in Cook, a sign above a dusty bench commemorated the linking of rails on 17 October 1917. The town lay on a 478-kilometre stretch of track which was the longest dead-straight section in the world, so the train was stretched perfectly straight in each direction as we disembarked, as if it were an immense ruler.

Cook was hot and dry and deserted. Until a few decades ago there had been a community here of 200 people, but the automation of services had seen it decline to a mere four residents. It was a microcosm of a larger challenge our society faced: the shrinking need for actual workers. The visit to Cook wasn't a tour, merely a maintenance stop so the crew could refuel the train and undertake other routine tasks. But GSR had dotted explanatory signage around the township, explaining what the numerous abandoned buildings had once been used for. There was a melancholy aura to many of the structures, whose community-building purposes had withered not that long ago. A memorial stone in the centre of town marked 'The Greening of Cook', a 1982 event in which volunteers had planted 600 saplings in the town. Not many had survived. By the old station building was a sign advertising the defunct local hospital: 'If you're crook, come to Cook.' Near the edge of the township was an open-air swimming pool, now filled in with dirt. The moodiest building was the former school. Next to it was a mural honouring Murray Sims, a long-time rail worker who had died in Cook.

'We had a lease at Mount Oxide, near Mount Isa,' said a woman with a cane as we walked back to the train after a warning siren had sounded. Word had gone round that I was a writer, and that had made people more forthcoming. Perhaps they liked the idea of talking to someone who would feel bound to listen to their stories.

'We didn't ever catch the train from Mount Isa, because my husband was a helicopter pilot. You wouldn't want to be flying with him when he was mustering cattle – those manoeuvres were pretty hairy.'

This woman had grown up in a tiny town on the South Island of New Zealand, she said, and had attended a school as meagre as the one here in Cook had once been. As we reboarded the train, she looked around at the dusty non-town and said 'I wouldn't want to get stuck here.' Others expressed the same sentiment in the lounge car. But I would. Give me one of Cook's abandoned houses with air conditioning and groceries for a week, and I'd get so much writing done. All writers yearned for a place they could write without distraction, and this would be perfect.

There was something powerful in how the Nullarbor reasserted itself the moment we left Cook. Through the train's windows, the world was again divided into two blue and grey-green halves, delineated by a precisely horizontal line; as if the landscape was merely a CGI effect, and an unconvincing one at that.

I was tired in the afternoon. Talking about my weeks of travel had brought on fatigue, so I had a shower to relax. I'm not sure why immersion in water was key to my relaxation, but it was. When I'd been at boarding school in Perth in the 1970s, I'd sometimes taken long showers on boring Sunday afternoons.

As I dried myself, it struck me that the *Indian Pacific*'s motion was nothing like the rocket I'd imagined the *Spirit of Queensland* to be. For one thing it could only reach a top speed of 115 km/h, compared to the latter's 160 km/h. But as it barrelled along the 478 kilometres of dead-straight track, rattling and clanking, it felt more like a moving town, an elongated settlement which moved through the landscape lightly, touching the world but leaving it unchanged. With the terrain so empty and the train so full of life, it put me in mind of Christopher Priest's novel *Inverted World*, in a which an entire city is transported through its landscape on rails, its population largely unaware of the fact. His conceit was that of an apparently infinite world set in a finite universe. We'd been travelling through the unchanging Nullarbor for five hours at this point, and I related to that.

About 5 pm, after we'd moved back the extra hour to Western Australia's time zone, an announcement informed us the train was about to take its first bend in many hours of travel. The train manager also commented on the unusually grassy patch we were travelling through, as some of that cyclone-induced rain had fallen here. At some point we crossed into Western Australia, but my fourth state border crossing went unmarked.

Dinner was taken outside the train at Rawlinna, another ghost town that lay next to a vast sheep station of the same name covering 10,000 square kilometres (that's 0.48 Waleses; 0.33 Belgiums). I was feeling antsy as we were led through two carriages as a group, to disembark and be marked off a list. The *Indian Pacific* crew shared the mother hen characteristics of their *Overland* colleagues, though in a place this remote it was understandable. Except for the short stop in Cook, I'd been aboard the train for almost twenty-four hours and was I dying to get outside. That was the problem with Desert Day: there weren't many places that GSR could use to devise off-train excursions. Tables had been set up in the space between the train and the derelict former post office and railway station buildings. It was a clever idea to dine under the sky in this forgotten corner of the outback, amplifying the contrast of the comfort aboard with the emptiness outside. Food was being catered from the train's galleys to the tables, with sunset succeeded by stars as we ate.

I was seated next to Derek, a bloke in an Akubra who worked for a Sydney company that recycled building materials. As we worked through the main course – lamb or fish with roast vegetables – we talked about his job.

'Bricks, stone, concrete – we crush it, mate. Makes good road surfacing.'

A man seated across from us heard this and chimed in.

'I collect bricks,' he said. 'I have a big pile of them outside the back of my place – my whole yard's full of them.'

For a moment I thought he was joking – he had a laconic delivery style that hinted he might be taking the piss – but when I asked about his oldest brick he had an answer.

'It's from 1865; the year is written on it. They were demolishing a house in Maitland and most of the bricks were going to the council's museum. I asked, "Can I have one?" A few weeks later, it turned up on my doorstep.'

Ian was concerned about Derek's job.

'Please don't crush too many bricks,' he said.

'Sorry, mate, it's how we make money,' said Derek. Then, thoughtfully, as if concerned for Ian's feelings: 'We never see those convict bricks anyway.'

I had started out thinking Ian eccentric, but his enthusiasm for bricks was strangely infectious. As he explained the origins and properties of his collection – some older bricks needed to keep damp, apparently, so it was fine to keep them in his backyard – I started to see the heritage appeal. Every brick had a story, as it were.

'Mind you, my family want me to put them all in a skip.'

'For storage?' I asked.

'No, to chuck them out!' said Ian with a smile, aware at least of how his hobby could look to others.

I asked Derek if he was proud of his recycling work.

'Well, we're going to run out of landfill eventually, right?'

After dessert I wandered to the far end of the tables, where the train crew were packing up. Fires were burning in cut-off metal drums, fairy lights were wrapped around a tree, and battery-powered lamps illuminated the tables. In this soft light, photos with the train as a backdrop looked atmospheric.

Back on board, no-one seemed eager to head to bed. Instead we gathered in the lounge, talking and drinking. It was good to have a strategy about how much time to spend in one's cabin or in the lounge. If travelling with a partner, or if your cabin was close to the lounge, it might be desirable to spend some private time in your quarters. But for single travellers, socialising was top priority. Assisting this decision was the fact that our carriage was the farthest from the lounge, so the most hassle to walk back and forth from. Walking the length of four carriages through narrow corridors on a swaying train wasn't something I cared to do more often than necessary.

####

On the final day I woke at 5.30 am and couldn't get back to sleep. I suspected I was still running on Adelaide time. Both showers were occupied, surprisingly, so I chatted to an American woman as we waited in the corridor, and waved to Frank as I passed him later. The singles carriage had become a community within our moving township, its citizens not as posh as those in the twin cabins but with hearts of gold.

Well past the desert now, the Western Australian countryside was lovely. The local gum trees had pale trunks and grew in red soil. In the soft morning light they looked stunning, and promising: heralds of a new dawn, the final hours of our journey from Adelaide.

'Where are we?' asked a woman joining the cluster of us waiting in the lounge for the dining car to open.

'In the middle of nowhere,' answered an American voice.

'That's basically our address now,' I added.

We were soon passing paddocks covered with the dry yellow stubble of harvested wheat, and I knew we were in the Western Australian wheatbelt. We'd just passed through Southern Cross. That was the second time I'd passed through a station of that name, having departed Melbourne's main station four days before, and the grain fields and silos of the *Overland* itinerary were also reappearing here in the west.

We were winding down. There were still eight hours to go till we arrived at East Perth Terminal, but everyone knew it was our last day on the train and had remembered we all had lives beyond drinking, eating and socialising. So the mood was a little subdued.

At 8 am I caught my first glimpse of Charles Yelverton O'Connor's water pipeline to the goldfields. C.Y. O'Connor had been chief engineer of the Swan River Colony in the late nineteenth century, and since boarding the *Indian Pacific* I'd been reading a biography of the man, *C.Y. O'Connor: His Life and*

Legacy. I had just finished the chapter wherein he had been hired by the Western Australian government and was about to leave his work in New Zealand, so I was yet to reach his career zenith. The pipeline and its associated dam, officially known as the Goldfields Water Supply Scheme, had become necessary when the gold rush of the 1890s had boosted the populations of Coolgardie and Kalgoorlie beyond the capability of the local rainfall to sustain them. Into this arid region O'Connor had designed and begun to construct the world's longest water pipeline of its day, eventually transporting water across 530 kilometres from the outskirts of Perth to Kalgoorlie. It was an outstanding achievement, but sadly one that O'Connor didn't live to see completed. I knew in broad terms what had happened to forestall that, but was not looking forward to reaching that section of the book. The engineer's fate cast a shadow across everything that lay before it.

I looked out the lounge window, at empty paddocks and ever more eucalypts. A distinguishing characteristic of my journey to date had been the paucity of people outside the big cities. Everywhere I had ridden trains I had seen striking landscapes of mountains, plains, lakes, rivers – but seldom had they been peopled. My impression on the initial bus out to Normanton, of an Eden without humans, had been reinforced over and over. Even now as we approached Perth through farming country with its plentiful evidence of human activity – paddocks, sheep, wheat stubble, machinery, silos – I saw next to no-one. It put me in mind of the New Zealand movie *The Quiet Earth*, in which almost everyone vanishes from the world, leaving their artefacts behind. This natural discrepancy of numbers between city and country was widening as agricultural work was becoming increasingly automated. Presumably that would also further widen the comprehension gap between urban and rural lives, which seemed a gaping chasm already.

At Merredin we paused for our final driver change, next to a set of huge white silos and a marshalling yard scattered with hoppers waiting to transport grain to the big city.

Listening to the people chatting around me while I sat in the lounge car with my book, I concluded that this type of travel drew out what people had in common. Travel history, hobbies, past employment, personal tastes: people searched for what would interest others and forge connections. In a space such as this train, we were in a neutral zone and on our best behaviour, tentatively reaching out to each other. I liked it. It was civil, it was genteel, it was humans trying to bridge differences and make connections. It gave me hope.

We passed above the Avon River on our way into Perth, its water low after the end of summer. I remarked to Anna that I'd be happy to reach our destination. I'd vowed to take things as they came on this journey, but there was something about the Adelaide–Perth run, with its minimal stops and empty desert, that made me yearn on the last morning for crowded cityscapes and the ability to move laterally at will.

'Oh no,' she said, sipping a glass of port. 'I could stay here for days. The scenery is beautiful, and the drinks are free.'

Then the *Indian Pacific* pulled into East Perth Terminal, and I stood by the door, ready to dash over a pedestrian bridge to the suburban platforms for an imminent Fremantle train. In my haste I hoisted my backpack onto my shoulders without looking, and had a near miss with the passenger behind me.

'That almost collected you,' said a voice behind him. 'Lucky you're a dentist.'

####

Forty minutes later, on the train to Fremantle, I passed Victoria Street Station and the Indian Ocean filled the view through the right-hand windows as we ran close to the shore. Kitesurfers were active near the water's edge, and a cargo ship sat on the horizon atop bright silvery waves where the sun reflected off the ocean. It was the final day of March – exactly two weeks since I'd been swimming on the edge of the Pacific Ocean, at Lady Bay.

Fremantle to Robbs Jetty
On foot

It was finally April. I'd flown to Cairns on 1 March, a date that now seemed very distant. That was a quirk of travel: you paid so much attention to your surroundings that time seemed to stretch out and slow down. It was disconcerting to realise how little time had actually passed during a trip on which you were fully focused.

On my first day in Freo I had breakfast at Bread in Common, a restaurant inside a lofty brick building from 1898, a former chemical factory and maritime warehouse. That placed it very much in the era of C.Y. O'Connor, whose biography I was still working through. In the book I'd reached 1897, the year O'Connor was awarded the Companion of the Order of St Michael and St George. Fremantle Harbour had been completed to his design, and his water pipeline was under construction. It was a high point in his career, but he'd also made powerful enemies through his practice of using in-house workers rather than contracted labour. In the oligarchical society of colonial Western Australia, he was both a threat to vested interests and, as an outsider, an easy target.

The restaurant was dimly lit, but a number of Anglepoise lamps were arrayed along the back of the banquettes where I was seated. I twisted one around and kept reading.

After breakfast I walked to Fremantle Station. Built in 1907, it was easily the most attractive suburban station in Perth. It was faced in sandstone from Donnybrook, the south-western town where I'd gone to primary school, and on each side of the arched entrance were sculptures of swans. They were currently painted white, which seemed odd as the black swan was the emblem of Western Australia. The station building was established after O'Connor's time, but it was connected to one of his fiercest struggles: his plan to move the original railway workshops from this site to Midland, the eastern suburb I'd passed through on the *Indian Pacific*. The move had been resisted tooth and nail by short-sighted local interests, so it was good to see that O'Connor had eventually had the last word and that something beautiful had come from that battle. As an entrance to Fremantle it was on point: a compact but harmonious example of colonial architecture – precisely what Freo did best, and which characterised its civic heart. But the station was also a symbol of the decline of the railways from their central role in public life. In the nineteenth century, multiple platforms here had been thronged with gold prospectors transferring from ships to trains to the goldfields. By the mid-twentieth century the station's passenger traffic had declined so much that the passenger line from Perth had closed in 1979.

I remembered that calamity well, as I'd been living in Perth as a boarder by then, at Christ Church Grammar School near the railway line in Claremont. It had been an ideological decision by a Liberal-led government at the height of the 'cars good, trains bad' era, and it didn't last long. Residents vocally resisted the change, aided by an outspoken mayor of inner-city Subiaco, and a few years later the elongated 'bendy buses' that had replaced the trains were removed and rail services reinstated. Since then Perth had become notably more railway-friendly, having added two entirely new commuter lines to the north and south. Say what you might about its high car usage, the city paid a lot more respect to its railway users than did Adelaide.

C.Y. O'Connor's contribution to Western Australia's railways was far greater than I'd initially realised, overshadowed by his famous work on the harbour and the pipeline. When he'd first been approached by the Western Australian premier of the day, John Forrest, he'd enquired by telegram what exactly he'd be responsible for. Forrest's telegrammed reply was concise: 'Railways, harbours, everything.'

O'Connor had arrived to find a colony with dodgy rolling stock running over lightweight rails, and made sweeping changes to bring the network up to speed. During his time as chief engineer, the line to southern Bunbury was opened. Passenger services still ran along it, and it would provide my final train journey later in the week.

His design for the port of Fremantle had also stood the test of time, still operating within the Swan River's mouth where the engineer had placed it. Its construction had been complex, requiring much reshaping of the natural contours of the river, especially through the use of explosives to blast away the rock bar that had lain across its mouth. The west end of Fremantle near the railway station and harbour had a wealth of grand old buildings, the former homes of shipping offices and other maritime businesses. A particularly fine example on a nearby corner was the domed Jebsens Building from 1890.

Walking toward the port I crossed the tracks near the station at ground level, and noticed we were back in narrow-gauge territory. There were dual-gauge rails here: narrow-gauge track for the local trains, and standard-gauge for freight trains serving industrial works to the south. (Some time after my visit the Western Australian government announced plans to extend the *Indian Pacific* along these, so it could end its continent-spanning journey by the ocean that gave the train half of its name.)

What I'd not known when I was growing up in Western Australia and hearing C.Y. O'Connor's name praised in the schoolroom – because we learned very little about Aboriginal culture in those days – was the distress caused to the Noongar people by the extensive reshaping of the mouth of the Swan River (Derbarl Yerrigan in their language). In local Indigenous belief, the limestone bar at its mouth was the tail of Yondok, a spirit crocodile defeated by the rainbow serpent Wagyl who created the river. It was also an important crossing point from north to south, and a barrier between fresh and salt water. Looking back, I wondered what other Indigenous stories I'd missed on my journey around the edge of Australia: both creation stories and accounts of events in the colonial past. The railways had only cut through that landscape for a century or so, while Aboriginal people had inhabited the land for sixty millennia or more. Modern Australia – the nation, not the continent – had a shifty way of hiding its Indigenous past. Massacres were often obscured, but so were local traditions and rites and land management practices – anything that might remind its troubled new overlords that the concept of terra nullius was no more than a convenient fiction.

Fremantle's new harbour opened in 1897, but it took three more years to persuade the mail ships from Britain to call at Fremantle rather than Albany on the south coast. Once that was accomplished, Fremantle's eclipse of Albany as a port was assured. And here the harbour was in front of me, largely with the same layout as O'Connor had designed. It was rare in an Australian city to be able to walk to docks and see a port in operation, but it was still possible here. That was part of Fremantle's enduring appeal, that somehow it had resisted its functions being split up and dispersed. It still had the feel of a medium-sized town, replete with harbour, commerce and industry: self-contained.

Victoria Quay, where I stood on the river's left bank, had largely been given over to public use. The large goods sheds along the quay had been designated by letters, and on my left was E Shed, nowadays housing markets, restaurants and bars. But shipping action was still happening at North Quay, at North Fremantle on the opposite side of the river. I could see a big rusty ship on that side being loaded with shipping containers, up to six high. There was something appealing in watching large-scale industry at work: the huge vessels, the enormous cranes, the stacks of containers along the far shore, looking like the toys of an unusually tidy giant. Where I stood, the rails once used by cranes were embedded in concrete. I saw a father and son fishing from the quay next to C Shed, and further west the *Rottnest Express* ferry was loading up with daytrippers to the Indian Ocean island. There was a tourist railway there, along an old military line up to Oliver Hill, but I didn't feel like revisiting Rotto today. My aim was instead to follow O'Connor's work and life, to add some real-life context to the biography I was reading. Or perhaps it was the other way around – to add literary context to the real-life spaces. Either way, there was something powerful about visiting places that you'd read about, travelling with a goal in mind. It magnified the significance of everything you saw.

Passing the ferry at O'Connor Landing, I noticed how relaxed the boarding passengers were. Fremantle's aura affected people that way; certainly it affected me. It always seemed to be full of bright but relaxed people, heading in a measured way toward something enjoyable. I wondered, as I always did at some point on my infrequent revisits, why I had left here twenty years before to move to Melbourne. But you couldn't question decisions like that entirely on the basis of the vibe of a place. Everything else had to fit: a satisfying job and a fulfilling relationship and a broader society I could live within.

I thought of that old hymn again:

> What though the spicy breezes
> Blow soft o'er Ceylon's isle;
> Though every prospect pleases,
> And only man is vile

Western Australia in 1998 hadn't been the place for me; it had seemed too reactionary and remote from the world, especially since I'd recently returned from teaching overseas in Egypt and Poland. It had changed a lot since then, but it was too late to lure me back now. Too much water had flowed through that harbour. Still, the ghosts of what might have been haunted me along Freo's narrow streets.

Behind the ferry landing, a 'Welcome to Fremantle' sign was showing its age, with white strips covering map items such as the former Fremantle Motor Museum, which had since moved on. One icon indicated the 'Cappuccino Strip', the nickname that had been given to South Terrace, Fremantle's main street, back in the 1980s when Italian espresso coffee had broken out into the mainstream. I vaguely remembered marching along South Terrace as part of a participatory theatre piece which celebrated Freo's new-found coffee culture, behind a jubilantly raised model of a giant coffee cup. It had been a piece fashioned by the local Deckchair Theatre company. The company had since closed, but that curious memory lived on.

I walked past B Shed to the Port Authority building. Opened in 1964, this eleven-storey modernist block was utterly out of keeping with Freo's low-rise colonial flavour, but it looked impressive. The circular signal station atop its roof, bristling with communication dishes, gave it a serious space-age look. In a small plaza in front of the building stood a statue of C.Y. O'Connor on a high obelisk-shaped plinth. Around its base were depictions of his achievements, including the harbour, the weir constructed for the pipeline, and a railway tunnel. The statue was posed with O'Connor gazing into the distance as if pondering the future, a partly unrolled plan in his hand. In unveiling it in 1912, Forrest had referred to its look as 'thinking in bronze.' In the centre of the plinth was the legend 'C.Y. O'Connor. A.D. 1843–1902.' That final date struck an ominous note, foreshadowing a tragedy I knew about, but hadn't yet reached in the biography.

I peered through the glass doors of the Port Authority building and could make out some details – parquet floors, a roof decorated with plaster squares, yellow tiling under the lip of the stairs. But it was Sunday and the offices were closed, so I moved on.

Past A Shed was the curved white form of the WA Maritime Museum, the decommissioned submarine HMAS *Ovens* a dark hulking form to one side. From the quayside there was a great view of the river mouth, tapering at each side to two moles which reached out into the ocean, guiding ships into the safety of the harbour. South Mole had a distinctive low green lighthouse, North Mole a red one. These artificial peninsulas had been constructed partly with the exploded rock extracted from the removal of the rocky bar in the 1890s.

Sitting on a rust-flecked capstan and looking out to sea, I felt relaxed. The sky was blue, a light breeze was blowing, and small boats were coming and going through the river mouth. I could hear behind me the low heavy thrum of the engines of the *K Phoenix* (registered in Monrovia) as it readied for its next shipping container run. In checking its details on my phone, I found that its most recent voyage had been across the breadth of the Indian Ocean, from Réunion Island. It had taken eleven days.

A path led past the submarine through port buildings that were now part of a TAFE college, to a spot overlooking Bathers Beach. This small shady cove had been home to an early whaling station, and then a boat-building yard for most of the twentieth century. Now its industrial uses had receded, and it was a popular swimming beach. Behind the beach were limestone cliffs, through which the whalers had cut a tunnel to High Street. It was still there, a dark atmospheric cave, but fenced off due to worries about the unstable cliff face. Above it was the Roundhouse. This was Western Australia's oldest colonial building, a small jail built two years after settlement began in 1829. It had only escaped a planned demolition in 1922 because the then harbourmaster had valued it as a windbreak for his own nearby house. It was another place of grim memory to Indigenous people, as it had housed many of their men in transit to the jail on Rottnest Island (Wadjemup) – a popular tourist destination nowadays, but for many years a place of lost hope for Aboriginal prisoners separated from their families and country. At night, relatives of the incarcerated men would gather outside the Roundhouse's walls to speak to their loved ones within. Unlike the larger Fremantle Prison, the Roundhouse had not been constructed by convicts. Western Australia had started out convict-free, and it was only in

1850, well after the other colonies had stopped the practice, that the colony accepted convicts from Britain to address a labour shortage. The transportation of convicts to Western Australia continued until 1868. Based on this fact, I had once deduced that the convicts aboard the doomed ship in the Sherlock Holmes short story 'The Adventure of the *Gloria Scott*' had been bound for Fremantle. That was still an obscure source of satisfaction.

'Avery, stop and listen to Nonna! Put your shoes back on.'

A small boy was making a break for freedom as I paused by another interpretive sign. This part of Freo was awash with signage erected in different eras, conveying subtly different understandings and emphases. The one I was looking at named this path as the Manjaree Trail, and included details of the system of six seasons used by the local Noongar people. I almost passed by the WA Shipwrecks Museum, but I wandered in out of interest in the architecture of the heritage commissariat building in which it was housed. I was glad I had. One of the star exhibits was the remnants of the Dutch ship *Batavia*, which had been wrecked on a reef off the Western Australian coast in 1629. With the Dutch East Indies (now Indonesia) lying to the north, there had been many Dutch wrecks and the occasional visit by a Dutch explorer to that area; at school we had learned of Dutch names such as Hartog and de Vlamingh. But the *Batavia* had been something else altogether, a ship whose wreck ushered in a tale of terror that reads like a script for a thriller movie. It made *Mutiny on the Bounty* seem a picnic in comparison.

In 1629 the *Batavia* was wrecked on a reef in the Houtman Abrolhos archipelago west of modern-day Geraldton. After the near 300 survivors were transferred to nearby islands, commander Francisco Pelsaert and several of the ship's crew left on a hazardous voyage in a longboat to Java, in search of help. This was the cue for Jeronimus Cornelisz, a bankrupt apothecary and accused heretic, to strike. Arranging to move a group of soldiers to another island in search of fresh water, he took control of the remaining weapons and supplies and began a reign of terror.

His followers in mutiny spent the next two months summarily murdering over a hundred men, women and children in order to prolong their supplies and consolidate their power. However, the isolated soldiers had survived, as had Pelsaert and his longboat crew. When Pelsaert returned in command of a rescue ship, there was a race between the mutineers and the soldiers to board it first. The soldiers succeeded, and the mutineers were defeated in the ensuing battle. Pelsaert dispensed summary justice on the islands following the failure of the mutiny. Cornelisz and his closest allies were hanged, while two minor offenders were exiled to the Western Australian mainland and never heard from again. Others were clapped in irons to be transported to Java for trial. Of the original 341 passengers and crew, only 116 finally made it to the port of Batavia (now Jakarta).

A section of the *Batavia*'s hull had remained intact over the centuries and had been relocated to Fremantle, the water in its planks replaced with a water-soluble wax to stop them drying out. In the dim light it seemed as though it was floating above the floor, the ghost of a ship representing the ghosts of its victims. In a case by a wall was a skeleton recovered from the islands, a victim of the terror with a sabre wound to its skull.

At Fishing Boat Harbour further south, I paused at a statue of Bon Scott. The AC/DC frontman had emigrated to Australia with his family from Scotland and spent his school years in Fremantle. I'd joined a Bon Scott tour of the area once, which had ended at his grave in Fremantle Cemetery. The statue was diminutive, but then so was Scott. Next to the statue was a prominent ghost station, Esplanade. Though trains had originally continued south through this area, by the late twentieth century all passenger services terminated at Fremantle Station. When the America's Cup yachting races were held in Fremantle, however, this and two other stations had been built and opened for just four months from late 1986. This stretch of track had been served by a steam train and special suburban trains, and had closed after the event. The station was still here, though, between the broad green park known as The Esplanade and the popular restaurants of the Fishing Boat Harbour. It would be demolished five months later, along with the other long-dormant stations further south, but the line could one day provide an ideal route for a light rail service, I thought, once freight trains no longer needed it.

The stretch of shore south of Fishing Boat Harbour was littered with capstan-shaped signs marking the locations of teams in that America's Cup competition. It would be hard to overstate the key role that event played in the resurrection of the port city. When I'd visited Freo during my high-school years before the big yacht race, it had been run-down, dirty and unloved. The staging of the America's Cup provided the commercial impetus for beautiful old colonial buildings to be restored, and for restaurants and cultural venues to open within them. Freo had always had great bones, but they'd been overlooked until then.

I had a drink in South Fremantle at the South Beach Hotel, a pub I remembered well from my time living in Freo. A streetwalker had once propositioned me outside its doors, then sworn at me when I turned her down. It had changed since then, and was now full of wholesome family groups having Sunday lunch, but the old timber bar was still there with holes where the original taps had stood. The diners and drinkers were watching the West Coast Eagles play the Western Bulldogs at Aussie Rules football on the pub's TV screens. Wherever the game was, it was too hot to be thinking about football. I ordered a beer and sat on a couch, working my way through the O'Connor biography. I was nearing the end of the chief engineer's life.

From South Beach Fish and Chips I bought lunch. The tendrils of gentrification had reached even here: in addition to the celeb-obsessed *Woman's Day*, its magazine selection included copies of *Frankie*, *Dumbo Feather* and *Peppermint* ('Style, sustainability, substance'). I took my fish and chips to South Beach, lying on the lawn behind the sands, and finished the book. What I read surprised me, as it didn't tally with the account of his death that I'd thought I knew, that everyone thought they knew, that everyone related to me whenever I mentioned his name.

I looked about me. South Beach was the Platonic ideal of an Australian suburban beach. In front of the car park was a row of Norfolk pines, anchoring the broad grassy area where people picnicked and played ball games. Beyond low dunes was a stretch of white sand, meeting the blue-green water of the Indian Ocean. A breeze had blown up, and the ocean was ruffled by low white-capped waves. On the horizon, where the sunlight made the ocean appear a bright shining silver, sailboats and the low profile of Rottnest Island were silhouetted. It was perfection on a Sunday afternoon, and I again felt the pull of Freo, and a puzzlement that I had ever left. But life is more complicated than charming surrounds. It was along this route that C.Y. O'Connor had ridden his horse on the morning of 10 March 1902, under far too much stress to pay attention to its beauty. I had been putting this off, resisting its call, but now I felt I had to walk to where his journey had ended.

I followed the walking and cycle path south from the end of the public reserve, and immediately encountered a sign reading, 'Snakes live here. If you see a snake, do not approach it.' I didn't really need that instruction. I hated snakes. I used to encounter them at random on the farm as a kid, and I wasn't keen on walking along a path through bushland littered with them. But the street route would be much longer, so I strode briskly along, eyes darting back and forth to the vegetation on each side. Past North Coogee Dog Beach with its children's playground, the landscape suddenly became much wilder, with windswept native grass and twisted trees hugging high ragged dunes. To the south was the derelict South Fremantle Power Station, awaiting rebirth as either a housing development or a cultural centre. The beach was a broad stretch of sand with curious layering just above the waterline: a row of white seashells, then a churned-up row of footprints, then another row of shells which appeared slightly pink. The wind had picked up and was blowing sharply from the south-west, pushing the waves at an angle upon the shore. Offshore I could see the low form of Carnac Island, known for its dense population of tiger snakes. The weather had now become dramatic, matching the terrain, reflecting what I'd imagined C.Y. O'Connor's mood was that day in 1902 as he rode along these sands.

The water had not yet started flowing through his partially constructed goldfields pipeline; the official opening was nearly a year in the future. However, O'Connor was under intense pressure from a media campaign against him, which had accused him of playing favourites and engaging in corruption. This had led to the establishment of a royal commission, which had just begun receiving testimony. O'Connor had taken these attacks personally, and his mental health had suffered. In the days before his death, he'd started behaving erratically and exhibiting the effects of the strain. On the morning of 10 March, his daughter Bridget had been ill and hadn't been able to accompany her father on their usual morning horseride. So O'Connor had stepped back inside his house, taken a revolver from a drawer in his son Roderick's room, and ridden off with it. When he arrived at Robb Jetty, which lay just ahead of me on my walk, he dismounted, stood in the shallow water, and shot himself. His spooked horse bolted into the dunes, leading a passer-by to discover his body.

Over a century later I found a stark scene at Robb Jetty, which was no longer an actual jetty but a collection of wave-washed pilings. A sign warned of a submerged wreck, and a rusting section of the SS *Wyola*, a former tugboat, stood in the sand. Ironically, the vanished jetty was a testament to O'Connor's vision of a protected harbour within the river, rather than a structure subject to the Indian Ocean's whims. A cheaper competing plan put forward at the time had been for a harbour stretching from the shore just south of this point. Among the waves, about twenty metres offshore, was a jutting metal object. It was hard to recognise it as a statue, especially with the sun hanging low in the western sky, but with concentration I could make out the shape of a man riding a horse, his head turned to the north. It was a memorial to O'Connor, placed at the location he'd died, created by local sculptor Tony Jones and erected in 1999. The beach was a moody place even now, with suburbia staring to encroach on the industrial zone behind what had been renamed C.Y. O'Connor Beach. It retained some of the wildness of the pre-1829 era, but I wasn't alone on its sands. As I stood scribbling notes, dog owners and their animals passed me in a regular stream, the dogs yelping, chasing balls and running into the surf.

The passers-by might not have noticed the statue, but they had all benefited from O'Connor's work. I had too, crossing the Nullarbor on a railway whose establishment had been made possible by the goldfields pipeline's supply of water for the steam trains of his day. The legend I had heard, which had been accepted as truth by many, was that O'Connor had killed himself after the pipeline was turned on and the water had initially failed to flow. This nonsense had made it a neat and easily understood tragedy, but also offered avoidance of the awkward fact that media and vested interests had hounded him to death. It made me ponder the use of social media, the way we all piled on perceived transgressors until they were broken, with no second chances allowed. And the engineer's fate made me think about my own life, how isolated I had sometimes felt in times of trouble, and how that isolation could force people to a terrible end like O'Connor's. It was disturbing to consider. I never wanted to go so far down that path that no other option would seem possible. I'd been lucky in life and love, but sometimes I'd felt alone in my troubles and had dimly glimpsed that awful place in which those with such troubles could end up. I wished we'd done better by O'Connor, could do better by each other. I looked out to sea and the engineer was still riding through the waves, his gaze ever fixed on Fremantle.

I walked on, heavy-hearted, then decided to go for a swim. I'd started my journey by the Norman River which led to the Gulf of Carpentaria, I'd swum in Sydney Harbour, and now I wanted to swim in the Indian Ocean. Immersion had always soothed me and this was the ocean of my childhood, a symbol of a simpler past. Though the wind was up, the water was clear, and the sand beneath it visible and clean. At first I let the waves wet me, then I ducked my head under an approaching wave and was engulfed.

Afterward, ascending the path from the beach was difficult. My hands were full of boots and a backpack, and I could barely make progress through the soft, shifting sand. If a snake attacked now, I'd be dead meat. My hat had been partly crushed under my boots as it had sat on the beach, a necessary measure to keep it from blowing away, and was now dusted with white sand. No matter how pensive I might feel, the Akubra was having the time of its life. The reserve behind the beach was a neat grassy rectangle with barbecues and picnic benches, its lawn fringed by trees. Two young men were kicking a ball around, until a golden labrador went for the ball and the game became more complicated. Life went on, just above the point where the chief engineer, isolated and despairing, had shot himself. The name of the park was C.Y. O'Connor Reserve.

Perth to Crawley
905 bus

I lay awake at 5.30 am on 3 April, at the Perth City YHA. I'd switched accommodation from the Fremantle Prison YHA, within the walls of the former convict-built jail, and now I was staying in an austere room within a former ambulance depot near Royal Perth Hospital, where coincidentally my mother had trained in nursing in the 1950s. My thoughts kept running over a 2015 news article I'd read the previous day, about a woman who had died from a snakebite on the path where I'd been walking in South Fremantle. This past misfortune had disturbed me, had reinforced the feeling that the walk had been a brush with fate. Intimations of mortality had been unnerving me. For a couple of years I'd developed a mild fear of flying – not a good attribute for a travel writer – after the disappearance of Malaysia Airlines flight 370 and some bumpy experiences on small aircraft.

The previous night I'd had dinner with my friends Dave and Kay at their house in Shenton Park, an inner-west suburb on the Fremantle train line. They had a beautiful house, cleverly designed with environmentally friendly features including recycled bricks (something Ian the brick collector would have appreciated). As we drank wine on the back deck, I'd spoken about some of my troubles of the past few years, including my worries about my freelance writing career heading south. In response, Kay had pointed out that we all had our own homes, were alive and healthy. That we were lucky.

She was right, and it was something I needed to hear. We were all the same age, as we'd entered university in the same year, and had a lot to show for the time since, achievements outnumbering setbacks. We *were* lucky. But still I was awake before dawn, thinking fitfully of random snakes and the sadnesses of recent years.

And Perth. I'd had a strained relationship with Perth when I lived there in the 1990s, and had fled east with the feeling that the city was too narrow-minded, too conservative, too satisfied with its suburban mentality. Whenever I returned, I felt uneasy, as if the city was going to reach out from the past and drag me back. I needed to give it a second chance, as I had Brisbane. I had planned to walk through the eastern part of the CBD, past historic squares and graveyards, to Heirisson Island in the Swan River where a statue of Yagan stood.

This member of the Noongar – the Aboriginal people who originally occupied the south-western corner of Australia – led armed resistance to British settlement in Perth's early days and was now regarded as a hero by the state's Indigenous people. After he was executed in 1833, his head was removed and ended up in the possession of a museum in Liverpool in north-western England, only to then be buried with other remains in a graveyard. It was only exhumed, repatriated and buried with honour in the Swan Valley in 2010. His statue was placed on Heirisson Island in 1984, and was twice vandalised and beheaded in the 1990s. In the following years, however, Yagan as a symbol became less controversial and more widely respected. A month before I arrived in Perth, Yagan Square, a new public space next to Perth Station, had opened with a stylised statue of the warrior at its centre. That was heartening.

I wanted to sight the original statue in its quiet riverside setting, reflect on the contested past, and look for signs of change in the city since I'd lived there. But on this hot Tuesday

I was exhausted: tired of travelling, tired of the heat, tired of the endless note-taking. Instead of a long walk east, I decided to head south through the city centre to the new riverside developments, to divine what Perth stood for beyond sunshine and endless suburbia.

Breakfast was at Toastface Grillah (symbol: a cartoon toasted sandwich holding a gun and a blingy necklace with an amulet fashioned as a slice of bread), in an alleyway behind Barrack Street. It reminded me of the grungy Melbourne cafes of the 90s, with its scuffed wooden benches and minimal decor. In part, those cafes were what had lured me away from Perth in the first place; a visit to Melbourne in 1991, at the height of the era of cafes filled with mismatched second-hand furniture, had excited my faux-bohemian sensibilities.

On Hay Street I paused at the Perth Town Hall, completed in 1870. It was a dainty-looking brick structure with a clock tower. Its compact size made it look like the town hall of a moderately prosperous country town, and underlined how small Perth had been for most of its existence. By 1891, the city's population was still less than 10,000, though about to be boosted by gold discoveries. Perth had remained a backwater of the British Empire and a remote Australian city until the 1960s, when Japan's hunger for iron ore for manufacturing rocketed it toward prosperity and enlargement. Architecturally, the 1960s and 70s were the worst time to become flush with funds. Much of the city's older commercial stock had been knocked down and built over, with some gems remaining but a nondescript corporate 'could be anywhere' look generally taking over the CBD. The Town Hall looked supernaturally clean and unembellished, its clock face gleaming as if new. Beneath, the undercroft which had once functioned as a market was empty and sterile. The building could have done with some scuffs and stains to reflect its near-150 years on this central corner, but Perth didn't do grime. There was no appreciation of the patina of age in this young city: another reflection of its apparent fear, lurking just beneath the surface, that things would get out of hand if not kept pre-emptively under control. I wondered where this obsession with neatness and respectability had come from. Perhaps it was a holdover from the relatively late period of convict arrivals. I had a theory that cities each had an enduring personality imprinted upon them in their formative years: Melbourne still had the optimism of the early wool-grazing and gold-rush era; Sydney retained a dash of the aggression of its convict origins. Because Perth had received convict arrivals so late in its history, I suspected it had inherited an obsession with maintaining law and order and appearing respectable. Having said that, there was a vaguely frontier vibe to the CBD. I was noticing a lot of sketchy people wandering around on a weekday morning, probably struggling with mental health issues and homelessness. As I crossed the lights into the Hay Street Mall, a woman in vivid pink was singing loudly to music only she could hear through her earbuds.

The pedestrian mall was lined with identikit modern shopfronts, but above them were beautiful facades with balconies and wrought iron and delicate Corinthian pillars. This was where Perth's old architecture had gone to hide. One Hay Street building hadn't changed at all since I'd lived here, and was just as bizarre now as then. London Court is a shopping arcade decorated in an over-the-top mock-Tudor style. According to the Heritage Perth website, it was constructed for 'shady' goldminer and financier Claude de Bernales in 1937.

As I was making notes outside the Court's florid entrance in the mall, with its elaborate clock face copied from the medieval Great Clock in Rouen, France, I heard a voice say, 'Are you still making notes?'

It was Derek, the building materials recycler from the *Indian Pacific*, with his wife, Sue. They'd been to Rottnest the previous day.

'I didn't think much of it,' said Derek of the island, 'but the animal lover here liked it,' he added, indicating Sue. She grinned. If you went to Rottnest, you were sure to see quokkas, the cute rat-tailed marsupials who'd become near-extinct on the mainland.

We all agreed it was quiet in the Perth CBD, compared to the centre of Melbourne or Sydney. 'If you stood here like this in Sydney you'd be bowled over,' Derek said. Then he and Sue headed into the Court.

I stayed in the mall till the clock above the entrance struck ten. Four model knights in red and white rotated around a model castle above the clock face, one knight tipping back with his lance when defeated.

Beneath the clock face was a saying:

No minute gone comes ever back again
Take heed and see ye nothing do in vain

As I was jotting this down, a young man in black passed beneath, shouting obscenities to the air. A few minutes later a man wearing headphones stopped behind me, singing loudly as he withdrew money from an ATM.

According to its heritage listing, the spaces above London Court's shops were originally apartments, which cast an entirely new light on this twee homage to an Elizabethan age that never existed in Australia. The proliferation of interwar flats in Melbourne had given rise to fears about what people might get up to when unsupervised by their families, and I suspected it had been the same here. Who knew what bacchanalian excesses a shady financier might have indulged in above these prim shopfronts?

The interior of London Court was bright and somewhat ludicrous. Above one entrance was a statue of Dick Whittington and his cat, at the other end Sir Walter Raleigh. The Elizabethan theme was preserved all the way through, including curling 'olde worlde' lettering on the shops' signs – even if the shops were selling something as incongruous as ugg boots, or Aboriginal art. A more exact example of cultural cringe, in the form of a longing for an idealised England, was hard to imagine. At its lower exit on St George's Terrace, Perth's main corporate strip, London Court was dwarfed by glass and steel office towers. The Terrace, one of the few wide streets in the CBD, had been largely rebuilt by mining money over the decades.

At the bottom of Sherwood Court, off The Esplanade, stood a graceful survivor of the era of architectural destruction: the Atlas Building, the 1931 offices of the Atlas Assurance Company. This was now the home of the Museum of Perth, a non-government institution that had evolved from an online concept to a bricks-and-mortar presence. 'By the 1980s only 6% of the Terrace's built fabric remained,' read a caption here, referring to the wholesale rebuild of St George's Terrace in the early days of mining prosperity. Inside its entrance I browsed a series of boards outlining the story of the city, from its stagnant growth until the 1890s gold rushes brought 't'othersiders' from the east. Apparently this influx had helped establish Aussie Rules as the local winter sport. I was intrigued to learn about the White City complex, which had been sited nearby between the wars and was popular for its carnivals run by the memorably named Ugly Men's Association. This downmarket fairground had offered rides during the day, then adult entertainments such as boxing, gambling and dancing by night. It was also a rare spot in Perth where black and white Australia mixed socially. It closed in 1929, after a bout of moral panic in the lead-up to the city's centenary celebrations. A temporary exhibition in the museum featured the World War I memorabilia of Reg Walters, a soldier who'd fought in the Middle East and left behind a wealth of photographs, postcards and illustrations, along with his wartime diary, in a satchel which had only recently been rediscovered. As Walters had been a sign-writer and painter before the war, he had created elaborate chalkboard art for entertainments staged for the troops. One of the performing groups he created promotions for was the Whiz-bangs, a troupe of wounded soldiers who travelled from camp to camp performing musical revues. I was tiring of World War I flashbacks, after years of their co-opting by nationalistic politicians, but this material told the story of the human side of the war, of the softer emotions and the ability of art to ease pain.

On the Swan River was Barrack Square, within the new Elizabeth Quay development. This zone of apartment blocks and commercial outlets had been carved out of a previously bland foreshore of open lawns, and configured around a new lagoon with an island. The apartments were still being built, and the precinct resembled Melbourne's Docklands, which was not a compliment, given that district's piecemeal development which had left it feeling corporate and soulless. Why did new civic spaces always need a major commercial component before they could be built?

Within Barrack Square was the Bell Tower, a modern glass campanile resembling a swan, which had been erected in 2000. I picked up a brochure, which explained that a local mining entrepreneur had learned that the bells of St Martins in the Fields in London were going to be melted down and recast because their condition had deteriorated over the centuries. So – I wasn't quite sure how or why – Western Australian mining companies had ended up donating metal for new bells in exchange for possession of the old ones. Supplemented by an additional six bells, they had ended up here. The question the brochure didn't answer was, why? What possible relevance could twelve medieval bells have to twenty-first-century Perth? The fact that Elizabeth Quay was named for the Queen deepened my feeling of dismay. How was this city ever going to define itself if it kept looking to the past for inspiration – and not its own past, but someone else's?

It was very hot now, and all the tiredness of the long journey from Far North Queensland seemed to settle upon me as I stood in the square by the river, by this ridiculous bell tower. I realised I could never be objective about Perth. I had spent my youth here feeling stifled and wanting to leave, and it was impossible to shrug off the unease I felt when I returned. Fremantle I could do – I loved it – but not Perth. So I stopped trying.

####

That evening I caught the number 905 bus to St George's College at the University of Western Australia. It was Perth's most attractive bus route, running along the shore of the Swan River beneath Kings Park, past the former Swan Brewery which now housed restaurants and apartments.

St George's was the residential college I'd lived at when studying at UWA in the 1980s. The oldest of the university's residences, it was modelled after Selwyn College at Cambridge and had opened in 1931. It was another example of Perth looking to the UK for inspiration, but had been in place long enough to have acquired a patina of its own.

Snapping a photo of its central tower flying the St George's flag in the light of the setting sun, framed by trees, I texted it to Narrelle with the caption, 'Childe Roland to the dark tower came'. This line was from an 1855 Robert Browning poem, itself borrowing a line from *King Lear*, which told the story of a medieval man undergoing hardships along the path of his gloomy quest. Wodehouse had used the line to comic effect when Bertie Wooster arrived at Totleigh Towers in my favourite of his novels, *The Code of the Woosters*. Comedy value aside, I did feel as though I was nearing the end of my quest. I had just one more train trip to undertake, and this tower to conquer before I did so.

I walked up the drive, then across the front lawn where my college friends and I had once played croquet with an old set of balls and mallets found in a cupboard under some stairs. Seen whole, it was a stunning building in the late sunshine, a harmonious red-brick edifice. Through the main gate, I stood by the central pond. It had a new fountain, a metal structure in the shape of intersecting swans. You couldn't escape the swan motif in Perth.

Ian Hardy, the warden, stepped out from the east wing to greet me. I'd agreed to have supper and a chat with whatever students were there during the study break week following Easter, but first Ian wanted to take me for a tour. I hadn't visited the college since a twenty-fifth anniversary dinner in 2007. We stepped into the chapel, a stand-alone building beyond the courtyard with a high ceiling lined with polished timber. A student was playing Beethoven on the piano, and so as not to interrupt him we crept quietly around, looking at the interior and conversing in undertones.

In my day the chapel had been neglected; though the college was connected to the Anglican Church, few of my crowd had been religious. In recent years, however, it had become a regular venue for music performances, which added to its use and lent it relevance in more secular times.

On the lawn outside the chapel we fell into conversation with two students, and were shortly joined by the young man who'd been playing Beethoven. They stood before us in the soft evening light, seeming so intelligent, calm, luminous, flawless, that I had a strange sense of being somewhere quite separate from the outside world, as if the turning off Mounts Bay Road had concealed a portal into Narnia. Had I really lived in this demi-paradise thirty-five years before? It seemed hard to credit, on one hand, but on the other it was eminently believable. Something about the calm confidence of this place had brushed off on that country kid quietly yearning to see more of the world.

Dinner was a self-serve affair in a room behind the main dining hall, the latter resembling its counterpart in Harry Potter's world with its lofty timber beams, long benches and portraits of wardens standing in for wizards. As we ate, I explained to the students what I had been up to ('I caught the train here from Townsville'), and gave them a sketch of the memorable people I'd met along the way: Ken the train driver; the young men I'd met at a Cairns hostel who spent days at sea killing crown-of-thorns starfish; Linda with her Bali dog refuge; Uncle Chicka talking about the Redfern railways; Mr Singh on the Melbourne sleeper; Rhys with his Rhodesia rail memories; Ian the brick collector. With them as examples, I advocated an item of advice often given to aspiring fiction writers: 'All stories are about people.' That could be applied to any writing, including non-fiction. What made anything interesting to read was how it engaged with its subject matter and its effect on humans.

Of course, I hadn't really learned anyone's stories on my travels, the encounters necessarily being so brief. I'd experienced vignettes of people's lives at best, mere snippets at worst. If there was a coherent story here at all, it was mine. But my narrative was threaded through with flashes of these others. That was the wonderful thing about train travel, it smoothly facilitated such chance encounters. It would be easy to dismiss such meetings as trivial, but I thought not. Stories are important to us all: they help us make sense of the world, give us confidence in our grasp on how other people tick. They are ultimately what makes society: its component atoms colliding with each other day in, day out. I'd engineered a journey that ensured these random collisions were taken note of, and stood out in my mind. But they were the stuff of everyday modern life.

The students – so young! – asked questions about my travels and my writing. Then we moved to the Junior Common Room, where I'd learned to play pool on a vast snooker table which had since been relocated. We sat in armchairs and traded ideas in an improvised version of a literary salon, with Ian tossing in questions and acting as host. One topic aired was the recent report showing a big drop in tourists visiting Western Australia. No-one was quite sure why it was happening, and I wondered about it too. There were plenty of attractive aspects to the state in terms of climate – its bright, startling sunlight, for one – and activities.

'But what's its story, its narrative?' asked Ian. I was unsure.

It wasn't that Western Australia didn't have attractions, but that Perth itself had an identity problem – exemplified in the bell tower that had so exasperated me. So much that was built here echoed something from somewhere else, and it was hard to point to anything that said, 'This is Perth'. The city had grown so rapidly from the 1960s onward, from one mining boom to another, with endless new suburbia, that a distinct local identity was hard to discern. Colonial-era Perth had been a fragile plant, and now that it had grown strong it was something altogether different. But what precisely was that?

At the bus stop on Mounts Bay Road I opened the gift I'd been given by Ian, a copy of *The Merry-Go-Round in the Sea* by Randolph Stow. I'd last read it at school. The novel told in part the story of a man from Geraldton, some 400 kilometres north of Perth, who was captured by the Japanese in World War II and forever changed by his experiences. The plot progressed from the eternal optimism of childhood to the complex trials of adulthood. As Ian had suggested, I opened the book to page 289.

> The red-brick Norman fortress of
> the college was green under Virginia
> creeper, and pink oleanders flowered
> around the tennis courts. Beyond the
> college was the wild bush of Kings
> Park, and in front of it, beyond the
> sloping lawns, the broad blue moody
> river.

I looked up, and saw that river. Behind me was the college with its bright young things, with their laughter and music and questions, living in their mock-castle, itself somehow removed from time, liminal, built on privilege, but a good thing nonetheless.

Perth to Bunbury
Australind

'There were soldiers who arrived in Brisbane without orders. Spent the whole war like that, got married, went home, all without orders.'

Bill was an American I'd got talking to as we waited on Platform 3 at Perth Station for the *Australind* train to Bunbury. He lived in Florida, near the Kennedy Space Center, but had deep Australian roots.

Bill's mother was a Scot who'd emigrated to Australia and then married an American soldier who'd come to Brisbane in World War II to serve with the US Army's Air Corps. His uncles had served in the Australian Army, and one had been at Tobruk.

'My grandfather was with the British forces at Gallipoli,' he added. 'I've still got his trench whistle from the Western Front too, where he was gassed. He had lots of operations after that, to keep the mucus from building up.'

Tall and white-haired with a Minnetonka fold-up leather hat, Bill had been to Australia in his youth, and had some hair-raising adventures. 'I was travelling up to Darwin with a guy I'd met hitchhiking. I was sleeping on top of the car at night for safety from creatures on the ground. He was inside the car but got bitten by a spider. I remember tearing up the highway with him gasping for breath. He survived but they had to keep him under observation for a few days, so I had a good look around Darwin.'

Bill's gripping tales kept me distracted from the fact that the *Australind* hadn't shown up yet. At one point a Transwa staff member had walked along the platform saying something about a technical fault involving an airbag (did trains use airbags?) and a resulting delay. This was the very last train of my trans-Australian journey, the final 184 kilometres which would conclude the trip, and I could sense a rail-replacement bus looming. If that contingency arose, I would wait instead for the evening train, or for the next train, whenever it ran. I hadn't come all the way from Townsville by rail to get on a damn bus at the end. But at 10 am, half an hour late, the train pulled into the platform and we were able to board.

For some reason, possibly its modest length but more likely its narrow-gauge wheels, the Australind was the only long-distance train that ran all the way to Perth Station; the others terminated at East Perth. It was a pity the *Indian Pacific* and the Kalgoorlie *Prospector* couldn't stage a grand arrival here in the city centre, instead of ending at an awkward location outside the CBD.

I was back on a government-run train, and this was order-obsessed Western Australia, so house rules had to be outlined and enforced. The *Australind* had always had an annoying boarding procedure, forcing passengers to line up and be ticked off a list, rather than boarding at leisure and waiting for the staff to come to us. We'd skipped the list rigmarole to save time because the train was late, but we'd still had to line up like schoolkids to board.

I'd drawn the short straw with my seat allocation, receiving a window seat with restricted leg room, thanks to a glass pane separating the cafe area from the seating in Car 1. I complained about this and the attendant said she'd see if I could be moved once we headed out. In the meantime I talked to my neighbouring passenger, a young woman heading home to Bunbury. She'd previously worked in Perth for a mining company, she said, but had switched to training as a primary school teacher. She was thinking twice about it, however, having just been through her first practice teaching session.

At Armadale I was moved to Car 2, where I was cautioned to stick to my new seat, and found myself sitting next to Mitchell. He was a fly-in fly-out worker who lived in Bunbury and regularly flew north to Onslow to work in the gas industry. It wasn't a bad life, he said; he'd have a week off at home and get some 'Dad time' with his children. 'If I lived onsite in Onslow instead, it'd be pretty basic.'

As we passed through Perth's south-eastern suburbs, the Darling Ranges followed us to the east. It was there that C.Y. O'Connor had dammed the Helena River by constructing Mundaring Weir, creating a reservoir which would feed the goldfields water pipeline. The body of water created by the weir was now named Lake C.Y. O'Connor. Past the city fringes the farming land was drier than I'd expected, neatly divided into paddocks. At one point we passed a block of gum trees neatly planted in equally spaced rows, a plantation for use as timber.

At Pinjarra, a sizeable town, I remembered we used to drive this way to Perth when I was a young child because the coastal road via Mandurah was not yet sealed. I had vivid snatches of memory from that period, particularly of the moment during each trip when we passed beneath a rail bridge around here. On this trip I was remembering possible markers of my interest in trains, and this was one of them. I'd been so young at the time that I hadn't realised in later years that we'd switched to the Mandurah route, and wondered where the rail bridge had got to.

We passed Yarloop, a town that had been devastated two years before by a bushfire that had torn through here on its way to the coast. Within seven minutes the fire had burnt down almost everything, from an old church to the pub. There weren't many signs of the damage now, but I could see new houses being built. It was a reminder that natural disasters didn't only happen in the north; as it happened, the week I was in Western Australia's south-west saw the fortieth anniversary of Cyclone Alby, which had hit the region with winds of up to 150 km/h in 1978. These had led both to the flooding of the coast and to raging bushfires strengthened by the winds.

On the *Australind* they made regular announcements about the 'buffet' rather than the cafe, an echo of the past and its buffet cars. I chatted to its staff about the upcoming timetable change whereby the train would make a later return to Perth at weekends. I assumed this was intended to encourage Perth people to take daytrips to the country, but one crew member thought it might be connected with the new Perth Stadium we'd passed earlier, clearing a window for more suburban services.

The *Australind* took its name from a visionary settlement scheme of 1841, when a coastal township was founded north of Bunbury in the belief it would become a thriving centre of exports from Australia to India (hence the name), particularly of horses for the British army. The settlement failed to thrive, and was eventually abandoned. By 1898 only thirty-three people lived in the area. In recent times it had grown as a satellite of Bunbury, and now had a population just under 15,000. Australind lay on the Leschenault Estuary, a long north–south body of water which connected to the Indian Ocean, the name of which was a hint at the presence of my old acquaintances from the Baudin expedition of 1800 to 1803 – in this case the expedition's botanist, Jean-Baptiste Leschenault de la Tour. The Frenchmen had mapped this south-west corner of Australia, and many of their place names survived. Bunbury's Casuarina Point had been named after one of Baudin's ships, as had Geographe Bay and Cape Naturaliste further south. Curiously, though the train was named after Australind, the train didn't stop there and the town had never even had a railway line.

When I had caught this train as a child it had been drawn by diesel locomotives, with creaking old carriages which might have dated from its launch in 1947. (I later found a 1970 pamphlet boasting that 'Fluorescent lighting was introduced to Australian railways on this train when it began running in November 1947.' Imagine!) I dimly remembered the atmosphere of catching the train from the station in the centre of Bunbury's commercial centre, with its old-fashioned railway restaurant. Since 1987 the train had been a set of three or four railcars, which had been built along similar lines to the XPT trains in New South Wales. Though motorists largely took the faster coastal road to Perth, the Australind still used an inland route from C.Y. O'Connor's time, intended to serve the agricultural towns along the way.

The train crossed the Brunswick River by a caravan park, then passed the landmark Peters Creameries building which served the local dairy industry. This town was still called Brunswick Junction, though the passenger train from here to the inland coalmining town of Collie was but a dim memory. Brunswick Junction was a prime example of a settlement created by the coming of the railways. It hadn't existed when the line had started operating in 1893, but it quickly grew into a busy farming town. A statue of a cow named Daisy now stood as testament.

Nearing the end of the journey, we curved around to the west, past paddocks and eucalypts, and industrial works at Picton. Near here was once the Mayfair Drive-in, which we'd visited as a family to see movies. It was our favourite of the two drive-ins in Bunbury, and as it was less central had seemed more secret. I still remembered the snack bar's sloppy joes, and the speakers that had hung on the windows of car doors.

Forty minutes late, we slid past postwar brick-and-tile houses, a cemetery and a machinery hire business to arrive at the 'new' Bunbury Station, which had opened in 1985. In another of those short-sighted land grabs which had truncated railway lines to less convenient termini (see Townsville), the original CBD station had been closed and the rails leading to it torn up. The line now ended in the city's south-eastern suburbs, nowhere near shops or other facilities, and passengers had to switch to taxis or buses to complete their journeys to anywhere useful. This had been generally recognised as a mistake for years, leading to numerous proposals to run the train around to a new station along existing track next to Koombana Bay. But I'd believe it when I saw it.

####

My rail journey was over. I'd boarded the *Gulflander* exactly four weeks earlier, which now seemed like months in the past. From north-eastern Australia to its south-western corner, I'd taken seven trains to cover 7,112 kilometres of track. From Townsville it had been an unbroken rail journey of 6,960 kilometres – and that didn't include the many kilometres ridden along suburban railways and tramways in Brisbane, Sydney, Melbourne, Adelaide and Perth.

As I stepped out onto the nondescript 1980s platform in the Bunbury 'burbs, about to look for my dad's car in the station car park, I paused for a moment to consider the end of my rail trek. How did I feel? Quietly satisfied, I concluded, happy to have done it and happy to be at the end of the task. I remembered my nervousness in rain-soaked Normanton a month before, intimidated by the quest ahead and worrying it would go off-track from the beginning. Then the sense of growing confidence from Townsville as the majesty of the railway reasserted itself against the weather, successive trains bearing me on, heading south, then west, then south again, in that effortlessly confident manner of a moving train when not delayed – on the move, on track, always forging a path into the future.

Now there was just one more city to explore, and it was one I knew well.

Bunbury to Dalyellup
843 bus

On a Friday morning I was standing in an ALDI supermarket, a handful of shoppers circling slowly around me beneath the fluoro lights, as if herding me toward the exact centre of the store.

This was where I had been born. Possibly somewhere above the aisle with the steam mops on one side and the meerkat garden figures on the other. For many years the St John of God Hospital had stood on this site, then the nurses and doctors had departed. Over the next two decades it had become a derelict building, then a vacant lot, and now it was a supermarket selling an odd assortment of groceries and household goods. I drifted through the aisles, idly wondering where the long-lost maternity ward had once hovered: above the vegetable slicers ('Professional Style') or the potted olive trees or the inflatable pool slides or the Easter Island head garden statues? Not that it was important. We'd all moved a long way in our orbits since then. And I preferred a supermarket to the vacant lot that had been here before, its emptiness speaking volumes about entropy and decay. I picked up a bottle of water for the sake of having something to buy, and was generously waved through by two women with shopping trolleys stacked high. I asked the young cashier how long the supermarket had been there.

'A year or so,' he said. 'Used to be a hospital here, a while back.'

'I was born here,' I said, gesturing vaguely toward the produce aisles.

'Oh, really?' he said, in the manner of someone commenting on the weather. 'That'll be ninety-nine cents.'

The young can be so cruel.

Outside I sat on a low wall and tried to phone my mother, Kath, in Perth, to ask if she remembered which end of the hospital the maternity ward had been in. But she wasn't answering.

Walking north along Spencer Street, I passed William Barrett & Sons, Funeral Directors, Est. 1897. This was the oldest part of the city, founded in 1836, just seven years after Perth. It had been named after Lieutenant Henry William St Pierre Bunbury, who'd established the township on the orders of Governor Stirling.

I hadn't lived here as a child, but it was a regional hub I'd spent a lot of time in. It was where our family had done its grocery shopping, and where I'd developed my love of comic books by fishing through the dog-eared issues on sale at a second-hand dealer's near the train station. I'd never liked Bunbury much. As a kid it had seemed to me that all its historic buildings had been torn down in favour of dowdy modern shops and houses. It had little of the historical allure of Albany, the south-coast port with its heritage buildings and former whaling station. That had seemed a gloomy, pessimistic time too, in Bunbury and inland Donnybrook, where I went to school. To a teenager with a budding interest in history and culture, Bunbury then was an impoverished place. Beyond the seeming lack of grand old buildings, there were no indoor cinemas (television had seen them off), not much variety in food (an Italian restaurant and a Chinese restaurant was as exotic as it got), and a pervading air of conformity. I wondered how much it had changed.

Inside the Bunbury Museum and Heritage Centre, established in late 2016, was a sign calling for 'MUSEUM MANNERS PLEASE'. It reminded me of the time Narrelle and I had visited the Petersen Automotive Museum in Los Angeles, and heard a teacher telling his young charges, 'Museum hands, museum voices', as they'd stepped through the entrance.

Among the exhibits, I could see immediately that things had moved on since my childhood. The region's Indigenous people had barely been acknowledged back then, but here was a section focusing on the Noongar people's relationship to the land and their fate under forced removal during colonial times, which had 'quashed Noongar language, society and culture.' There were also details of the Chief Protector of Aborigines of that time, and his role as dictator of Aboriginal lives, as powerfully depicted in the film *Rabbit-Proof Fence*. The displacement of Aboriginal people out of the area around Normanton had been brutal, and that part of Australia still felt like a far frontier, but white settlement had been just as damaging here in the green and pleasant south-west. At least local attitudes had shifted. In 2013 Wardandi Memorial Park had been established above the Indian Ocean on the city's west side, partly because it was a traditional burial site which could be used to lay to rest Aboriginal remains that had been held by the Western Australian Museum.

Elsewhere among the exhibits I was delighted to find a blown-up old photograph of the *Australind* train departing from the original Bunbury station. The photo showed a grimy diesel engine towing four white-and-green carriages out of a broad marshalling yard, with BP oil tanks on the hill beyond. Nowadays the marshalling yard was a bland shopping centre, the tanks were gone and the hill was dotted with expensive homes. *Sic transit gloria mundi*.

I left the museum and walked the CBD streets. It was interesting to note which historical figures were honoured in Bunbury. Former premier John Forrest, a local lad, was everywhere. But above Victoria Street was a banner featuring L.C. Freycinet, a navigator on Baudin's expedition, and there was a bust of Baudin himself on the Leschenault Inlet waterfront. With the passage of time, the French explorers had gone from being a threat to the British Empire to being an exotic ingredient in the early history of the settlement.

Rounding the corner of Prinsep Street, the old Bunbury railway station stretched out in front of me, reduced now to the indignity of acting as a bus station. It was a functional rather than attractive nineteenth-century structure of brick walls painted a pinkish-cream colour, with broad verandahs held up by timber posts. Through a locked door I could see the original ticket office, with its glass ticket window and low vinyl-covered seating. There was a plaque on the back wall, and by magnifying a photograph of it I discovered it marked the 150th anniversary of the first running of a railway from Darlington to Stockton in the UK, in 1825. There was something melancholy about this celebration of rail travel within a station which had closed a decade after the plaque was affixed. This building was so familiar, an echo from my youth. The station restaurant had gone, but there was a cheap-looking cafe in its place. On the station's eastern side was a view over the blue waters of Leschenault Inlet, which in my childhood had been hidden by the railyards. What a pity they hadn't found a way to combine both the station and the vista.

Everyone knew it had been a mistake to terminate the train line so far from the CBD, and everyone wanted to correct it somehow. Regardless of the possible solutions, the original station was still here, its structure imbued with the rattle and clatter of a century of trains. If O'Connor's statue thought in bronze, this building dreamed in brick, of a day when the railway would return. Its presence spread that dream to others, it seeped into public discourse, it unsettled people until they wanted to make it come true.

These unsettled dreams of the marooned station had made me melancholy, so I left and walked further north, past noodle bars and sushi joints and the Funkee Monkee Eatery and Bar, to Guppy Park, marked by an old arched sign with weathered metal lettering. When I was a kid, this tiny park had been the annual home of the Penny Arcade, a seasonal set-up. Under its canvas tents were wooden-framed arcade games. The one I remembered most strongly was a box into which I'd insert a coin, then flick a handle to send it flying along curved metal ramps. If it landed in a slot marked 'Win' rather than 'Lost', I won a packet of Beechies chewing gum. I'd loved that game. The park had been prettied up with circular stone walls and new benches, but had survived the upmarket rebuild of the surrounding area. There was just enough remaining to provoke memories and nostalgia.

On Casuarina Drive, a set of old silos had been turned into an apartment block. There were shops and restaurants scattered through this part of Bunbury, but it felt as if gentrification had faltered here – the district was dead on this Friday afternoon. I was the only pedestrian, and there were few passing cars.

At a big white anchor which marked the entrance to Bunbury Port, I veered right past new apartments and reached the Jetty Baths. Much had changed in Bunbury, but this beach was ringing bells. Though the timber jetty was gone, I recognised the long tapering point on one side, holding back the ocean, and the rocky breakwater on the other. This was now a harbour for recreational boats, but beyond was the working port as I remembered it, with big grimy silos and fuel tanks, and a cargo ship at the dock. Aside from a couple of kids fooling about at the water's edge, I was alone on the beach. A few late lunchers lingered at the restaurant overlooking the sand, but otherwise it was unpeopled. By the time I'd changed and entered the water, the children and their families had left, and I was alone in the harbour.

As a child I'd once stood on something sharp by the jetty here and cut my foot, but in the cloudy water we'd never discovered whether the sharp object was broken glass, a piece of metal or something living. Today the water was clear, with schools of tiny silver fish darting through it, and only a few grains of the mineral sands that had once blackened the shore.

I went out far enough to duck down to shoulder depth. The water flowed over my torso and shoulders, cooling me on this hot day. It was peaceful here, with little noise other than the cries of seagulls and the rumble of a distant motorboat. Water had featured so often on my journey. The monsoonal rain in Normanton, the floods cutting the railway to Townsville, the Coral Sea glimpsed from the air, the waters of Sydney Harbour, the Indian Ocean being blown onto South Beach. I ducked my head under the surface, immersed again, arrived at my destination at last, the thousands of kilometres of railway behind me.

Surfacing, I realised it was time to go home.

I sat with my father, John, on garden furniture in the backyard of his house in Dalyellup, one of the newest suburbs of Bunbury. That 'up' suffix was repeated throughout the south-west of Western Australia, and was evidence of an Aboriginal place name – in the Noongar language it signified 'place of', though the meanings attached to individual place names had been poorly recorded over the years. For example, the town of Boyanup near where I grew up had a name which meant 'place of quartz', but no-one I spoke to knew what Dalyellup meant. From my experience, it could stand for 'place of silence'. I'd never lived in full-blown suburbia in my life, instead inhabiting either the country or the inner city. Modern suburbs unnerved me, and Dalyellup was the epitome of a modern suburb. The houses were wonderful – brand new, loads of comfort – but the neighbourhood was dead silent and there was little sense of community. I'd often thought the basic problem with newer suburbs was the lack of corner shops where locals could meet one another. Instead there was one big impersonal shopping centre, too far away for most residents to walk to. The result was serenity, undisturbed by messy human interaction. I could see the appeal of having a peaceful haven one could return to after work, but these suburbs took the concept too far.

Within that suburban serenity, we sat beneath the blue sky – it was another stunning autumn day – and talked about the old days in Argyle, the inland fruit-growing district where I had grown up. Nowadays it was just a locality, but in those days it had been a proper town.

'There used to be a post office and general store on the highway, and a timber mill opposite,' Dad said. 'Then the mill burnt down around 1946 – there was a rumour the company had a habit of burning them down for insurance money when the timber started running out.

'Then the original post office and store burnt down too, so they moved the post office into the old mill office.'

The local school had vanished by the time I'd grown up in Argyle, so we were bused to Donnybrook for our studies. It and most other Argyle buildings had been demolished by then, leaving behind a pattern of trees that had been planted around the site.

The sole survivor of this purge was the elderly postmistress, Mrs Billinghurst, who eventually retired in 1976. I remembered strongly the aroma of old paper and glue that pervaded her post office, alone on the slope where a town had once stood. It was an aroma that I sometimes picked up when I visited the Melbourne GPO's sorting area on Bourke Street to pick up parcels, evocative of the lost postal past. To we kids, Mrs Billinghurst had seemed a strange old lady, dotty or perhaps a witch. Now my dad told me something astonishing that I'd never heard before.

'Earlier on in the century she'd been a nursemaid to Rudyard Kipling's children,' he said. 'She used to tell me a story about him sending a Rolls-Royce around to pick her up.'

I supposed it might have been true.

One other structure I remembered from my childhood was a small shed at the Argyle siding, where there had once been a station. I asked Dad what he remembered of the railways of his era.

'When the passenger trains came past, there were a lot of people waiting on the platform to catch the train to Bunbury or Donnybrook. My dad would be going up to town on the Saturday in our car, and he'd yell out "Room for one" or "Room for two" – whoever he had room in the car for.

'I remember being in Donnybrook as a kid on a Saturday, while Dad was in the pub and Mum was shopping. We'd go over to where the goods trains were shunting up and down. The drivers knew us, and they'd stop the engine so we could climb onto the footplate. We'd roar up and down on the old steam trains. That was great! You wouldn't do it now though.'

The past was clearly a different country when it came to occupational health and safety.

Dad shared my conviction that the Bunbury train should be extended to the tourism and wine-growing region around Margaret River. There had been passenger services there once, via a line that had run from Busselton all the way down to Flinders Bay near Augusta. It had been notoriously slow and uncomfortable as a passenger service, running along lightweight rails and up steep gradients.

'Your Uncle Peter used to take the train as a kid from Perth to Flinders Bay, to stay with his uncle. He said he had to take a meal with him, as it used to take twelve to fourteen hours to get down there. That served the Group Settlement Scheme down there.'

That scheme had been an assisted migration program after the World War I, co-funded by the federal and state governments along with the British government. It had aimed to open up farming land in the state's south-west corner, to reduce its dependence on imports. Settlers, usually untrained in agricultural work, were given a property and a subsidised loan for equipment. It had had mixed results, bedevilled by isolation, substandard equipment and a lack of proper training. About a third of settlers had left their properties by the mid-1920s, and the advent of the Depression finally put paid to the scheme. It had, however, helped establish a successful dairy industry in the area, as well as a number of towns. The area's glory days as a premium wine-producing region were but a glint in the future's eye at that time. It would take two academic papers on the subject by Dr John Gladstones, an agronomist at the University of Western Australia, to kickstart that industry in the 1960s.

My dad had left the farming life on his orchard when he was about the same age I was now. I asked why he had decided to leave.

'I'd still be there if I hadn't had to borrow money at twenty-five per cent in the 1990s,' he said. 'I had no hope of servicing that. I left in 1991. I could have sold one or two blocks, but it's all gone. There are houses there now, on big blocks.

'We used to produce twenty thousand cases of fruit per year. We'd been there, supplying the city markets, for a hundred years.'

Farming in those days involved a lot more physical labour than it does in the modern era, and my dad's back was bent over as a result.

'Heavy work, trying to do too much – stacking fruit, lifting cases, carrying irrigation pipes,' he said. 'It was a big, old orchard, not set up intensively. Nowadays they're smaller and the watering is all done by reticulation.

'The backpackers only came in as labour near the end of the time I was there, otherwise we had our own seasonal mob. But we treated them well. My mum would always run out with a plate of curried eggs; I'd never seen a plate of curried eggs go so quick. An old bloke called Reg used to make home-brew, he'd come out on the weekend with it. Good days.'

'Is it good to be retired?' I asked.

'I suppose it's good,' he said, but he was resisting being dragged back to the present.

'If you hadn't had those high interest rates to deal with, how long would you have worked? Till your sixties?'

'Until I cracked up, I suppose,' he said. 'That was the type of property it was.'

I was trying to glean some lessons from my dad's experiences, a hint of which direction I might take, but was struggling to draw a thread between the hard manual labour of my father's time and the mental labour of my life today.

'With the writing,' I said, 'I could keep doing it forever if my health was okay. But it would be nice to semi-retire at some point.'

'I think that'd be the way to go, if you had the money to do it.'

He made things sound simple. Maybe they were.

I think I'd been subconsciously hoping for a revelation at this end of my trip, a distillation of the knowledge and wisdom of all the people I'd talked to, via the reflective filter of travel. It hadn't happened – not exactly – but I'd gained glimpses of what might make me happy, either by embracing new challenges or learning to be happy with what I had. I needed, somehow, to meld these two approaches when I returned to Melbourne.

And there was one more thing I needed to do.

Epilogue
Cairns to Forsayth and return
Savannahlander

Eighteen months later I was back in Far North Queensland, aboard the *Savannahlander* at last. The Australian Society of Travel Writers' annual conference had been scheduled for October in Cairns, and it seemed an ideal opportunity to snare the one train that had eluded me on my first attempt. After the event ended, I joined the *Savannahlander* for its weekly four-day tour west through rainforest and savannah to the former mining town of Forsayth and back. Finally, after several false starts, I had actually caught a train from the platform at Cairns Station.

It was now the end of the dry season, and once the train had passed through the Kuranda Ranges above the tropical city this would become evident, the savannah dotted with parched gum trees and yellow grass. Up toward Kuranda Station, however, the rainforest was still thick and lush, exhibiting more shades of green than seemed likely. As Glenville Pike's book had promised, this railway was an almost absurd engineering triumph, with fifteen tunnels and numerous bridges just to get us beyond this first geographical hurdle.

'If it wasn't for tourists, this railway wouldn't be operating today,' said our driver, Anthony, as he sat at the controls in the front of the open-plan carriage, a railmotor which was propelled by its own engine rather than by a separate locomotive. And what a vehicle it was – a confection of postwar non–air-conditioned train travel with timber beams holding up a corrugated iron roof, and a gleaming curved steel nose that was a thing of beauty.

Past Kuranda the terrain morphed into thick woodland, preparatory to us passing through a corner of the Atherton Tablelands with their vast crops of mangoes, limes, avocados, bananas and other tropical fruits. This had not so long ago been wall-to-wall tobacco-growing country, but the recognition of that crop's health risks had put paid to that, and forced diversification.

On a food tour to the Tablelands with some colleagues a few days before, the guide had expressed nervousness about the trend among some Melbourne cafes of spurning the ever-popular 'avocado smash' for other more innovative dishes. Where Melbourne's hipsters go today, the nation goes tomorrow, seemed to be his point of view, though I didn't think he had much to worry about.

It was good to be on the *Savannahlander* at last, and back in Far North Queensland, where my epic rail journey had begun in such rain-drenched confusion the previous year. As we rattled along the first section of the journey west from Cairns (and the *Savannahlander* rattled a lot, though not as much as the *Gulflander*), I leant my arm on the window ledge and contemplated the foliage. I was far more relaxed now than on that earlier trip, and felt pleasingly immersed in nature. Last time had been hard; this time seemed easy.

Is this what fate meant me to do? Come back to where it began, square the circle? Or was that an illusion produced by rail travel, via that sense of smoothly sliding through the world, untouched by mundane troubles, always in the landscape but never of it? Rail travel as a metaphor for life, or at least life as we would like it to be: linear, uncluttered, ever-progressing.

Though of course trains get delayed, and cancelled, and there is always a terminus up ahead somewhere, inevitably approaching. Christopher Isherwood once wrote a passage that was one of the most despairing things I'd read, contemplating all the thousands of steps to be taken in the next decade of a character's life, and all the weary moments yet to be lived. Thank God I didn't feel like that about life, about this journey. I was still interested in what lay ahead along the line.

Stopping at Almaden, well into the savannah, we alighted into a different, bone-dry world. The town was absurdly outback, the station standing in an expanse of dry dusty ground with the remains of old shacks nearby. Only the Railway Hotel, a low-slung pub with the inevitable corrugated iron roof and two bikers drinking beer on its broad verandah, gave any sign of activity. If we had glimpsed two gunslingers gearing up for a high-noon showdown between the pub and the station, it wouldn't have seemed out of place.

The same thought had occurred to others, said Anthony. 'I once had a group of American tourists who got out here, did a double-take, and said, "Ya gotta be kiddin' me! This is a real place? You didn't set it up?"'

We had a lunch break on the second day at Mount Surprise, which I'd previously passed through by bus when I was slinking away from the savannah with my tail between my legs, beaten by the last of the wet season rains. After the meal at the Mount Surprise Store I glanced at my watch, saw we had fifteen minutes till the train resumed its journey, and had an idea. I walked the short distance to the BP service station to see if Pat, the owner, was there. She had been the one who'd first introduced me to the missing Hayden on my way out to Normanton, and I wondered if she'd heard anything new.

Pat was behind the counter, and remembered me. I asked about the elusive man, and she shook her head, conspiratorially drawing me over to one side of the counter while another staff member dealt with motorists coming in to pay for petrol.

'He never turned up,' she said. 'They found a shoe in a creek bed, then a wallet, but that only had thirty dollars in it, when he'd withdrawn eight thousand. So where's the rest?'

'Maybe he's left the country to start a new life?' I suggested.

Pat shook her head. 'Maybe he's still out there. Who knows?'

Fair enough. I was sorry for Hayden's family and friends, and for the man himself, but it seemed fitting that my return to the outback should end in much the same way my first journey had – with unresolved questions, and a sense of uncertainty hanging over the proceedings.

And, across the road, a train to catch.

Acknowledgements

This book was written on the traditional lands of the Wurundjeri people of the Kulin nation. I'd like to pay my respects to them and their elders, and to all First Nations people whose country I crossed in my long journey.

This epic rail adventure would not have been possible – or remotely affordable – without the generous support of many. The following organisations gave me free or discounted fares and accommodation in order to undertake my journey (listed in the order of travel). I highly commend their services to you.

- Trans North Bus & Coach, transnorthbus.com
- Albion Hotel, Normanton
- Queensland Rail Travel (*Gulflander* and *Spirit of Queensland*), queenslandrailtravel.com.au
- Cairns Central YHA, yha.com.au
- Novotel Cairns Oasis Resort, novotelcairnsresort.com.au
- Bally Hooley Rail Tours, Port Douglas, ballyhooleyrail.com.au
- Ibis Styles Brisbane Elizabeth Street, all.accor.com
- NSW TrainLink (XPT trains), transportnsw.info
- Sydney Railway Square YHA, yha.com.au
- Naturaliste Tours (French Island), naturalistetours.com.au
- Journey Beyond Rail Expeditions (*Overland* and *Indian Pacific*), journeybeyondrail.com.au
- South Australian Tourism Commission, southaustralia.com
- Fremantle Prison YHA, yha.com.au
- Perth City YHA, yha.com.au
- Transwa (*Australind*), transwa.wa.gov.au
- Cairns Kuranda Steam (*Savannahlander*), savannahlander.com.au

The *Gulflander* chapter expands on a travel article first published in *True Blue*, the inflight magazine of Regional Express Airlines (Rex), in December 2019.

There are also many individuals I must thank, above all Narrelle Harris. She provided encouragement and commiserations as I undertook the trip, and later proofread the manuscript more than once; it's hard to fully express my love and thanks to her for her help, and for putting up with all my doubts in the two years before the book found a publisher.

Thanks also to Anthony Dennis, national editor of Traveller, the travel arm of Fairfax Media (now part of Nine), and his team, for publishing many of my train travel articles over the years and thus feeding my passion for writing about rail.

Gratitude also goes to editor Mary Rennie at HarperCollins, the publisher of my fantasy thriller novel *Mind the Gap*. She gave early feedback on the manuscript which helped shape it into a more readable form.

Hugs to all the friends who met me on the way, thus making the journey a little less lonely, including: my old school friend James Beck and my colleague Dr Tiana Templeman in Brisbane; Richard Graham in Sydney; Jen ('Honoria Glossop') Scheppers in Adelaide; Celia Andrews and Jack Lewis in Fremantle; David and Kay Horn and their family in Perth; and all the gang I met up with at Whitehart Bar in Melbourne, including our good friends Craig and Julia Hilton. Not all those conversations made it into the book, but they were all helpful. Love also to family members I spent time with in Western Australia, including my parents, my brother Paul, and my nieces Caitlin and Faith.

Thanks also to all those people who I met on my path, who spoke to me about their lives and brightened my days. Where they weren't aware I was writing a book, I've changed their names to protect their privacy. I've also changed the name of the missing man in the outback, not wanting to intrude on his family's grief.

Finally, thanks to editor Armelle Davies, publisher Georgia Richter, and their team at Fremantle Press for taking a punt on this long and complex train travel tale and helping to tune it up, ready for its own timely departure.

The following materials have been reproduced with the permission of the publishers:

- Extracts on pp. 26 and 138 from *The Dig Tree: The Story of Burke and Wills* by Sarah Murgatroyd, published by The Text Publishing Company Australia.
- Extract on p. 64 from *Cocktail Time* by P.G. Wodehouse. Published by Arrow. Copyright © The Estate of P.G. Wodehouse. Reproduced by permission of the Estate c/o Rogers, Coleridge & White Ltd., 20 Powis Mews, London W11 1JN.
- Extract on p. 229 from *The Merry-Go-Round in the Sea* by Randolph Stow, published by Penguin Random House in 2009. © *The Merry-Go-Round in the Sea*. Reproduced by permission of Sheil Land Associates Ltd.
- Extract on p. 253 from *Affection* by Ian Townsend, published by HarperCollins.

Bibliography

A non-exhaustive list of useful works encountered in my research:

Affection, by Ian Townsend. Fourth Estate, 2007.

Along Parallel Lines: A History of the Railways of New South Wales, by John Gunn. Melbourne University Press, 1989.

A Century of New South Wales Tramcars, by N. Chinn and K. McCarthy. Vol. 1, South Pacific Electric Railway, 1962.

C.Y. O'Connor: His Life and Legacy, by A.G. Evans. University of Western Australia Press, 2001.

Cocktail Time, by P.G. Wodehouse. Penguin Random House, first published 1958.

Conquest of the Ranges, by Glenville Pike. Pinevale Publications, 1984.

The Dig Tree, by Sarah Murgatroyd. Text Publishing, 2009.

Exploring the Railways of Far North Queensland, by Brian Webber. Australian Railway Historical Society Queensland Division, 2004.

Following the Equator (published in the UK as *More Tramps Abroad*), by Mark Twain. American Publishing Company, 1897.

Juggernaut!: A Story of Sydney in the Wild Days of the Steam Trams, by David Burke. Kangaroo Press, 1997.

Lonely Rails in the Gulf Country: The Story of the Normanton–Croydon Railway and the Gulflander, by J.W. Knowles. Second edition, Australian Narrow Gauge Railway Museum Society, 1993.

The Management and Operation of the Melbourne Tramway System, by Graeme Leslie Turnbull. PhD thesis, RMIT University, 2004.

The Merry-Go-Round in the Sea, by Randolph Stow. Penguin Random House, first published 1965.

The Puffing Pioneers and Queensland's Railway Builders, by Viv Daddow. University of Queensland Press, 1975.

Road Through the Wilderness: The Story of the Transcontinental Railway, by David Burke. New South Wales University Press, 1991.

A Short History of the North Melbourne Tramways and Lighting Company Limited, by K.S. Kings. Tramway Publications, 2016.

The Union of the Railway Systems of New South Wales and Victoria: Celebration at Albury on the 14th June, 1883. Thomas Richard, Government Printer, 1883.

About the author

Tim Richards is a freelance travel writer based in Melbourne, Australia. His writing has appeared in numerous newspapers, magazines and websites, and in Lonely Planet's guidebooks. In 2014 his debut novel, *Mind the Gap*, a fast-paced fantasy thriller, was published as an ebook by HarperCollins. In 2017 he self-published *The Kick of Stalin's Cow*, a travel narrative exploring post-communist Poland. In 2021 Hardie Grant will publish *Ultimate Train Journeys: World*, Tim's exploration of the world's greatest rail trips.

You can see extracts from his published work on his website, iwriter.com.au, and he writes regularly about travel at his Patreon site, patreon.com/timrichards.